*Legal Norms
and Legal Science*

Legal Norms
and Legal Science

A CRITICAL STUDY OF KELSEN'S
PURE THEORY OF LAW

Ronald Moore

The University Press of Hawaii / Honolulu ☿

Manufactured in the United States of America

Library of Congress Cataloging in Publication Data

Moore, Ronald.
  Legal norms and legal science.

  Bibliography: p.
  Includes index.
    1. Law—Philosophy. 2. Kelsen, Hans, 1881–1973.
I. Title.
K339.M6   340.1   77–12392
ISBN 0–8248–0516–X

Contents

Preface

What is law? This simple but stubbornly perplexing question has been a focus of jurisprudential inquiry for centuries. No textbook, no course in legal theory fails to address it at the outset. No political scientist or social philosopher can altogether ignore it. No common citizen, however rude, however naïve, has failed to form some rough answer to it. And yet, in a fundamental sense, the question remains unanswered. To be sure, we have readily at our disposal a generally clear body of regulations to which we affix the title "law." This body provides a corpus of studies for law schools, a subject matter for legal practice, and a basis for juridical application. What we do not have, however, is a *definition* of law which embodies a rigorous analysis of legal normativity and systematic structure, a definition which makes clear the inventory of traits which are common and peculiar to laws, a definition which will serve as an indelible standard for deciding independently of culture, place, and time whether a thing is entitled to be called law. Hans Kelsen's Pure Theory of Law is a scheme of jurisprudence aimed at providing just such a definition of law.

Hans Kelsen was born of Viennese parents in Prague on

October 11, 1881. He died a naturalized American citizen in California on April 19, 1973. At the time of his death he had been the supremely dominant figure in the world of jurisprudence for half a century. His legacy to jurists and jurisprudents is immense. He taught at the leading institutions of four nations. He authored more than six hundred publications, some of which have been translated into two dozen languages. He wrote the Austrian Constitution of 1920, which was abolished during the Nazi period, and which has since been reactivated. In 1934, Roscoe Pound spoke of Kelsen as "unquestionably the leading jurist of his time." When Julius Stone reiterated the remark on the occasion of Kelsen's ninetieth birthday *Festschrift*, it was no less true.

Kelsen's work is the high-water mark of philosophic efforts to state the nature of law in precise but general terms. His Pure Theory of Law provides a distinctive method for apprehending legal norms and their interrelational structure, based on "formal-logical" analysis, or "logical formalism." This method is supposed to provide a scheme for the cognition of law which is more coherent, more comprehensive, and indeed more realistic than any previously advanced. Indeed, Kelsen claims that it supplies the basis for a system of knowledge that has been the unattained goal of most prior legal theories, namely, a *science of law*. The present study is chiefly concerned with this last claim.

It is only fair to admit at the outset that the Pure Theory of Law exhibits a conspicuous looseness, an almost haphazard development of its fundamental ideas. In part, this looseness is due to Kelsen's persistent parrying of incidental thrusts made by opposing and divergent theorists wherever they occur. But it is also a sign that the formal scientific project Kelsen announced early and frequently reemphasized did not remain fixed in his thinking. Even the fondest Kelsenite will admit that Kelsen's ambitious efforts have been programatic rather than comprehensive,

fragmentary rather than cohesive. Moreover, the protracted development of Pure Theory has been considerably
marred by frequent ambiguities, inconsistencies, and irri-
tating vaguenesses at key points. Indeed, it remains an
open question whether the project Kelsen forecast can be
realized within the framework of suppositions it accepts
and on the scale to which it aspired. The proof of Kelsen's
claim is simply not given in his own presentations of Pure
Theory; the parts of the project must be put together and
the gaps filled before it can be properly assessed. This task
Kelsen has left to his interpreters. To date no comprehensive explication, no "reconstruction," of Pure Theory has
appeared; nor does the present study presume to fill that
need. Yet, I do aim here at what I believe to be the essential
first step in the proper direction. I have selected for detailed examination Kelsen's account of the general science
of legal normativity. And within that area, I have trained
special attention upon what Kelsen has proposed as formal
"presentation." Kelsen conceives of the presentational role
of the legal scientist as revealing a species of *meaning*, specifically, the meaning of norms imbedded, in one way or
another, in law as it is made and applied by legislators and
jurists. I critically scrutinize this conception of meaning,
as well as a number of allied issues surrounding it. It has
been necessary to draw together disparate threads from
Kelsen's uneven presentation, elaborating what has sometimes been left in blueprint form, and selecting from various sayings what seems the clearest and most abiding representation of its formalistic intent. Doing this has made it
possible to exhibit the barebones logical-analytical program that stands behind Kelsen's claims for legal science.
In what follows I isolate and clarify the assumptions on
which this program draws; I test the consistency and coherence of its parts; and I draw some new conclusions
about the sort of legal science that it produces.

This study could not have attained its present form were

it not for the generous assistance and guidance of a number of people. I am particularly indebted to Martin Golding for his detailed comments on and criticisms of an earlier draft. I am also very grateful for several pages of commentary by the late Wolfgang Friedmann, received shortly before his tragic death. Part of the present chapter 2 appeared in a somewhat different form in *UCLA Law Review* vol. 20, no. 5 (1973). I am indebted to Professor Golding and to Irving Copi and Chung-Ying Cheng for suggestions that improved the quality of this section. An expanded version of part of chapter 4 has appeared in *Archiv für Rechts- und sozialphilosophie*, 59, no. 3 (1973). My wife, Nancyanne Moore, rendered invaluable assistance in proofreading the entire text, and suggesting numerous stylistic improvements. I am grateful to the University of Hawaii Intramural Research Office for making funds available for the preparation of the final manuscript, and to Linda Lum for her expert and untiring efforts in typing it.

Key to Reference Symbols
for Works of Hans Kelsen

EJRP   "Derogation." In *Essays in Jurisprudence in Honor of Roscoe Pound*, edited by Ralph Newman. Indianapolis: Bobbs-Merrill, 1962.

GTLS   *General Theory of Law and State*, translated by Anders Wedberg. New York: Russell and Russell, 1961.

HS   *Hauptprobleme der Staatsrechtslehre*. Tübingen: Mohr, 1923.

ILR   "On the Pure Theory of Law." *Israel Law Review* 1 (1966): 1–7.

LL   "Law and Logic." In *Philosophy and Christianity: Philosophical Essays Dedicated to Professor Dr. Hermann Dooyerwerd*. Amsterdam: North-Holland Publishing Co., 1965.

PGNR   *Die Philosophischen Grundlagen der Naturrechtslehre und des Rechts positivismus*. Berlin, Charlottenburg: Pan-verlag, R. Heise, 1928.

PTL   *Pure Theory of Law*, translated by Max Knight. 2d. ed. Berkeley: University of California Press, 1967.

RLi   "Recht und Logik." *Forum* 12 (October 1965): 421–425.

RLii   "Recht und Logik." *Forum* 12 (November 1965): 495–500.

RPS   "Professor Stone and the Pure Theory of Law." *Stan-ford Law Review* 17 (July 1965): 1128–1157.

WJ   *What is Justice?* Berkeley: University of California Press, 1960.

I

The Aim of Formalism in Pure Theory

INTRODUCTION

In the 1920s and 1930s, Kelsen laid the foundations of an elaborate legal theory which he has since developed expansively and with considerable faithfulness to its original construction. The announced goal of the program was to transform jurisprudence from "philosophic" (that is, metaphysical) enterprise to a science. The opening move in this undertaking, as Kelsen designed it, was for the jurisprude to expunge from his account of law every object that is not part of actual (that is, existing or historical) legal systems—systems which are understood to have been made, obeyed, and enforced wholly through specific human actions. Notably, considerations of the so-called natural order, the good, the just, the divinely ordained, were to be excluded from the theory of law conceived as science. Thus "purified," Kelsen maintained, jurisprudence need only examine what enters into the composition of observable systems of coercive rules. What legal science examines and what it understands on the basis of this examination are, however, quite different things. For, pure, theoretic science seeks to comprehend positive law through the ordered hypothetical relationships of norms that shape it; and these relationships are frequently not apparent among the surface features of legal systems. Pure Theory, therefore, fastens its investigations to the covert and the assumed, the uniform structural fabric of norms that is obscured by the diversity of devices embodying it.

Kelsen did not contend that ridding legal theory of metaphysical suppositions would of itself convert philosophical jurisprudence into science. Dephilosophizing legal theory was admitted to have only the modest effect of circumscribing a domain of inquiry for legal science. And what is done to make way for science does not in itself make science. To change legal philosophy into legal science, Kelsen advised, we must practice a kind of conceptual therapy on already dephilosophized subject matter. The therapy Kelsen devised was largely "formal" in character (in a sense soon to be discussed at length) and Kelsen accordingly referred to his enterprise as "formalistic," or "formal-logical" in nature.

Just as strong as Kelsen's concern to establish legal theory as a science was his wish to demonstrate the independence of this science from other sciences, particularly those of sociology and "the science of politics." The science of law, Kelsen argued, diverges from these on three counts:

(1) Legal science is a science of *norms*. It conceives its object as a specific form of "meaning-content," one in which it is declared that a certain human behavior or a certain social relation ought to be. Because the science of law which Kelsen depicts deals with legal norms as a species of "non-natural" object,[1] it sets itself off distinctively from the so-called "natural sciences":

> The reality . . . at which a science of law is directed, is not the reality of nature which constitutes the object of natural science. The specific reality of the law does not manifest itself in the actual behavior of the individuals who are subject to

the legal order. This behavior may or may not be in conformity with the order the existence of which is the reality in question. The legal order determines what the conduct of men ought to be. It is a system of norms, a normative order. The behavior of the individuals as it actually is, is determined by laws of nature according to the principle of causality. This is natural reality. As in so far as sociology deals with this reality as determined by causal laws, sociology is a branch of natural science. Legal reality, the specific existence of the law, manifests itself in a phenomenon which is mostly designated as the positiveness of law. The specific subject of legal science is positive, or real law in contradistinction to an ideal law, the goal of politics. (GTLS, xiv)

(2) Legal science is *anti-ideological*. In describing and comprehending norms, legal science is prohibited from *evaluating* them. To be sure, Kelsen makes room for a "scientific theory of value" to be used in conjunction with pure-theoretical analysis, but this theory confines itself to "objective values" that are posterior to norm-creation and strictly system-relative:

> The object of a scientific theory of value can only be norms enacted by human will and values constituted by these norms. If the value is constituted by an objectively valid norm, then the judgment that something real, an actual human behavior, is 'good' or 'bad,' expresses the idea that the behavior conforms with an objectively valid norm: that the behavior ought to be the way it is; or that it does not conform with the objectively valid norm: that the behavior ought not to be the way it is. Then the value as an 'ought' is placed in juxtaposition to the reality as the 'is'—value and reality belonging to two different spheres, just as the 'ought' and the 'is.' (PTL, 18–19)

In short, no judgments that norms are "good" or "bad," or that they "ought to be" or "ought not to be" are allowed to intrude upon pure-theoretical analysis from *without*. Nor are any transcendental ordering principles (such as "justice"), through which judgments proper to one or another particular moral, metaphysical, or political viewpoint might enter, allowed to intrude. By hermetically sealing itself from external valuations Pure Theory aims to provide the neutrality needed to certify that the normativity it explicates is, in fact, that of the subject order, and not some other. By being anti-ideological, Kelsen maintains, Pure Theory becomes universal. For, if ideological factors are what create the differences among particular legal systems, an analysis which frees itself from these factors will deal with only those factors that are common to all legal systems, the essential features of law.

(3) Legal science is methodologically *analytic* (or, as Kelsen sometimes puts it, "transcendental-logical"). Because the essential features it investigates are *a priori* and strictly "formal," Pure Theory is not constrained to consider empirical characteristics of particular positiv law systems. Kelsen conceives of legal science as being primarily a calculus of "schemes of interpretation" *(Deutungs-schemata)*:

> The external fact whose objective meaning is a legal or illegal act is always an event that can be perceived by the senses (because it occurs in time and space) and therefore, a natural phenomenon determined by causality. However, this event as such, as an element of nature, is not an object of legal cognition. What turns this event into a legal or illegal act is not its physical existence . . . but the objective meaning resulting from its interpretation. The specifically legal meaning of this act is derived from a 'norm' whose content refers to the act; this norm confers legal meaning to the act, so that it may be interpreted according to this norm. The norm functions as a scheme of interpretation. (PTL, 3–4)

Since these "schemes of interpretation" are not natural, yet serve as a "framework" for natural contents, their knowledge is held to be logically prior to the knowledge of contents. In Kelsen as in Kant, knowledge of possibility precedes knowledge of reality. Hence, Pure Theory employs a prioristic "critical theory of knowledge" to explicate the norm structure underlying actual legal systems. Kelsen speaks of this explication as "a structural analysis of positive law" (GTLS, xv), and claims that the analytical technique separates legal science from natural law philosophy on the one side and sociological jurisprudence on the other. The analytical technique, he says, is the key to the purity of the Pure Theory of Law.

This notion of "purity," at first referring only to the *method* of legal science, was soon applied by Kelsen in characterizing its *product*. From a "first draft"[2] which appeared in 1911 *(Hauptprobleme der Staatsrechtslehre)* and which was generously expanded upon in 1925 *(Allgemeine Staatslehre)*, there eventually emerged a system of results known as "Pure Theory." In his earliest works, Kelsen referred to the theory simply (and perhaps misleadingly) as "normative jurisprudence," in order to distinguish it from the "sociological jurisprudence" which was gaining ascendancy. But in *Reine Rechtslehre* (1934), Kelsen chose to emphasize the purity of his system rather than its normativity, and to insist that the purity pervaded the entirety of his analytic program, its ends as well as means.

Unhappily, Kelsen's various efforts to explain the peculiar "purity" of Pure Theory have been uneven and ill-coordinated. Sometimes, he stresses the descriptivity of the system; at other times he stresses the distinction it draws between effectiveness and validity; and at yet others he stresses its enforcement of the Humean-Kantian razor principle (the rigid segregation of "is" and "ought"). Usually, when Kelsen wishes only to make his point in broad terms (PTL, 1; WJ, 267; GTLS, xiv), he says that his theory is pure in that it excludes "foreign" (that is, extralegal) elements from the proper study of law. This has the uncontroversial and uninformative ring of tautology. Pure Theory is pure, it would seem, by being purely a theory of law, not some other thing. If this were the whole of the matter, it would be hard to see why Kelsen's theory would provoke heated controversy. But his several claims about Pure Theory's purity have, in fact, been far from uncontroversial. Critics generally (and perhaps wisely) have paid less attention to what Kelsen has said about the sense of the term "pure" than to what he says to back up the claim that Pure Theory is pure. Here, Kelsen places prime emphasis on the normativity of its object and objectivity (anti-ideological neutrality) of its procedure; that is, upon the first two features in virtue of which Kelsen declared his legal science to be distinctive from other sciences. These aspects of Pure Theory have been the source of interminable and undiminished dispute.

The obvious neo-Kantian tone in Kelsen's account of the normativity of legal rules inevitably suggests consanguinity with prevalent Continental views of jurisprudence. Accordingly, legal theorists who hold the Continental tradition in disfavor seek and find grounds for disagreement with much of what Kelsen says about normativity, particularly with his insistent use of "ought" in a descriptive sense. On the other hand, Kelsen's emphatic expulsion of justice and allied notions from the subject matter of legal science indicates a sharp departure from mainline neo-Kantianism. So critics who distrust the direction of Kelsen's movement toward "objectivity" (mainly the Continental thinkers) castigate his work as "antiseptic," "artificial," and "pointless," even "atheistic" and "immoral."

There is no point in adding to the plentiful criticisms already available on these scores. What cries out for attention, and what has not been the subject of any detailed study to date, is the *third* vector of pure-theoretical legal science's divergence from other sciences; namely, its avowed formalism. This, then, is the feature of Kelsen's jurisprudence that will serve as the centering notion for the analyses and criticisms that follow. Before beginning the work of explaining the assessment of Kelsen's peculiar brand of formalism, however, it may prove useful to sketch its interrelation with other moments of Kelsen's projected legal science.

NEO-KANTIANISM AND PURE THEORY

Kelsen's debt to Kant is universally, recognized but frequently misunderstood. Critics very often fail to demarcate the part of Kant's legal-moral philosophy which Kelsen retained from the part he disavowed. While incorporating into Pure Theory much of Kant's epistemological priorism,[3] Kelsen firmly rejected the natural law position Kant espoused in the *Metaphysik der Sitten*. In doing so, he believed himself to be bringing a wayward, uncritical doctrine back into line with strict Kantian orthodoxy. He charged that Kant, by embracing the metaphysical duality of Christian pietism, lost sight momentarily of transcendental method, and inadvertently fell back to a prereflective position antithetical to critical idealism. Kelsen proposed to retrieve the principles of Kantian jurisprudence from the transcendent by making them consistently formal and thoroughly scientific.

By 1923, when the second edition of *Hauptprobleme* appeared, Kelsen had openly fallen in with the Marburg School of neo-Kantianism. He declared: "I acquired the decisive epistemological viewpoint, from which alone it was possible to construct the concepts of State and Law, through Cohen's Kant-interpretation, especially through his *Ethic of Pure Will*. (HS, xvii; my translation) But by insisting on a scrupulously scientific view of law, Kelsen departed from the neo-Kantian legal philosophers dominant in that day, in particular R. Stammler and G. Del Vecchio.

In his *Theorie des Rechtswissenschaft* (1911) and *Lehrbuch der Rechtsphilosophie* (1923), Stammler had developed the view that law, as a species of *"verbindenes Wollen"* (the sum-total of rules, conceived as a will), is legitimated according to a universally valid idea of Right. *"Richtiges Recht,"* he argued, bears its own identifying mark: It shows itself to be in agreement with *"Reine Wollen,"* the will conditioned by the idea of justice in the harmonious community of rational ends. Del Vecchio, in *El Sentimento Giuridico* (3rd ed., 1908), *Formal Bases of Law* (1921), and *La Giustizia* (1951), had argued along somewhat similar lines for a notion of law derived from an *intuition of justice.* *"Giustizia,"* according to Del Vecchio, is ultimately identical with the ideal of autonomy postulated by human spirit. And because this ideal realized itself historically in the never-ending quest for a universal world order based on natural law, Del Vecchio concluded that the concept of law is *essentially* connected with a natural law metaphysics.

Kelsen's criticisms or the Stammler-Del Vecchio mode of neo-Kantianism appeared first in *Hauptprobleme.* His attack centered on Stammler's notion of "purpose" *(Zweck)*; Kelsen recognized in this notion a fraudulent nexus of moral and legal orders. He charged Stammler with employing "purpose" so as to introduce surreptitiously strains of natural teleology (atavistically hearkening to Cicero and Aristotle). The idea, allegedly, was to derive "ought," with normative weight, from observed social tendency (an empirical phenomenon, an "is"). But Kelsen pointed out that it is precisely in the province of legal theory that such a metaphysical ploy becomes pointless; for here we are forced at the outset to distinguish a norm's purpose (the aim of its creation) from its function (the operational, formal role which it fills). Kelsen observed that such views as Stammler's amount to outright denial of the possibility of a purely formal juristic construction,one which analyzes only the structure (logic) of normative relationships without regard to the ulterior aims which projected them. Kelsen held that such a program is not only possible, but indeed necessary if we are to display the essential nature of law untrammeled by teleological considerations. To defeat Stammler, then, it would be sufficient to produce such a system; and that is just how Kelsen proposed to do it.

Kelsen's general mode of attack was to demonstrate that a theory which uses justice and allied normative notions in its definition of "law" or its standard of legality illegitimately determines what law *is* (its "nature") on the basis of what *ought to be*. This is certainly a simple criticism; it comes down to an insistence that transcendent method (in Kant's sense) is inadequate for science, or conversely, that only transcendental-logical method is adequate. Now, assessment of what law ought to be surely has its place. But this, Kelsen insists, is not the place of *science* of law: For science necessarily begins with *Denaturierung* of its object (PGNR, 7); it consigns notions involving purpose and value (and this includes both Stammler's *verbindenes Wollen* and Del Vecchio's *Giustizia*) to legal philosophy, while saving the value-neutral array of legal-normative relations to itself. These two fields, legal philosophy and legal science, are, in Kelsen's eyes, absolutely independent. But in stressing this dichotomy Kelsen insisted that he was saying nothing new; he was only affirming for legal theory the ontological rift which Kant and all neo-Kantians already accepted:

> One may be misled into identifying the two phenomena, by defining the validity of law as its efficacy, by describing the law by "is" and not by "ought" statements. Attempts of this kind have very often been made and they have always failed. For, if the validity of law is identified with any natural fact, it

is impossible to comprehend the specific sense in which law is directed towards reality and thus stands over against reality. Only if law and natural reality, the system of legal norms and the actual behavior of men, the "ought" and the "is," are two different realms, may reality conform with or contradict law, can human behavior be characterized as legal or illegal. (GTLS, 120–121)

Among the "naturalistic" normative concepts, it is *justice* which comes in for Kelsen's strongest attacks. He speaks of justice as "an irrational ideal," and an object "not subject to rational cognition" (GTLS, 13). The outlook of pure-theoretical legal science is rational, Kelsen thinks, because it takes into account only objectively determinable acts as they are deployed in a positive order. It is concerned with the "is" of legal orders. If there should be two orders of norms which satisfy all the objective criteria of legality, but which differ in some point of value (perhaps in the way they satisfy the interests of subjects), it may be appropriate to establish that only one of the two is just. But such a determination, Kelsen insists, cannot be rational; it cannot be the product of legal science. Such a determination will be based on evaluation, subjective consideration, rather than the descriptive representation of norm-relations in the system. Only what is objective, what "is," can be an object of science. The question of whether a given norm is law must be cleanly separated from the question of whether it is a just law. To confuse the two, as natural lawyers have always done, is to hand over legal science to metaphysics, politics, or rational theology.

Justice is irrational. Does this mean that we are to abandon efforts to determine which of our laws are just and which unjust? When the poor, oppressed, and disenfranchised cry out for justice are they crying out for nothing? When scores of philosophers from Plato to Rawls try at length to define are they merely wasting words? Not at all.

Justice, in Kelsen's view, is by no means an empty notion. It is, however, strictly a value notion. And there are compelling reasons for taking up the question of a thing's value only after we have settled the question of what the thing is. Legal science, as Kelsen conceives it, is wholly devoted to specifying the "is" of law. If the question of what law ought to be is made part of this specification, the deliberately value-free science of law is undercut. Here Kelsen is contending with what we might call the "preemptive fallacy," a widespread tendency in philosophic circles. An excellent example is Cicero's dictum that unjust law is no law. Another is the view enjoined by some art critics that bad art cannot be counted as art. The intent behind such views as these is to make the reckoning of a thing's value a part of the thing itself. But, far from enhancing values, this form of preemption makes it impossible for us to hold a value as a reason for admiring or rejecting the valued object. Cicero is bound to deny that any law can be unjust, the preemptive critic to deny that any art is bad art. By holding the determination of legal "is" to be prior to the determining of legal justice, Kelsen believes we preserve the possibility of taking the unjustness of a law as reason for disobeying it. It may be quite important to recognize that what we have chosen to disobey is indeed a law, and is not made a nonlaw by our choosing to disobey it.

As Kelsen sees it, the intrusion of justice into consideration of the "is" of law is the mark of natural law philosophy. And because natural law philosophy essentially refers for its legitimation to higher and ulterior orders of being in building its ideology-laden metaphysics, it relinquishes its claim to the intersystematic objectivity required of science. To be pure, the science of law must account for the phenomenon of law in such a way that those features and only those features are exhibited that are elements or all actual systems of positive law—good or bad, here or there, then or now. Hence, the product of pure legal science cannot be of use in partisan ideological advocacy. Indeed, this is the measure of its strength; it stands above and immune to the struggles for power which ideologies generate.[4]

POSITIVISM AND PURE THEORY

Kelsen was quick to see that the "is"/"ought" distinction cuts two ways at once: While legal science is a study of what law *is*, and not of what it *ought* to be, law itself, the object of that science, is a phenomenon whose nature it is to be exclusively "ought," and not "is." Consequently, although Pure Theory is science, it cannot be a *causal* science; for whatever is essentially normative cannot be comprehended as a system bounded by causal relationships. Expressions of this Kantian view are to be found in all of Kelsen's works (see, for example, PGNR, 8, 9; GTLS, 46; HS, 11–19; PTL, 76–81). The subject is discussed at length in "Causality and Imputation" (WJ, 324, 349). In accepting this view, Kelsen found himself distinctly at odds with even those Continental critics of natural law who had, like himself, opted for the empirical approach to jurisprudence.

SOCIOLOGICAL JURISPRUDENCE AND PURE THEORY

The chief scientistic activity in European legal philosophy at the time of Pure Theory's creation was spent in the direction of sociology. Its main forces were R. von Ihering and E. Ehrlich. Ihering is commonly acknowledged as the father of the school which has since come to be known as "sociological jurisprudence." His works, of which the most widely read are *Scherz und Ernst in der Jurisprudenz* (1885) and *Der Zweck im Recht* (1883), combine keen satire of empty neo-Kantian conceptualizations with substantive remarks on the nature of law emphasizing its coercive element. "Law," he said, "is the sum of the conditions of social life in the widest sense of the term, as secured by the power of the state through the means of external compulsions."[5] Ihering further argued that law's place in the state is determined by the convergence of particular interests for mutual projects. Ihering's approach claims for itself "scientific" status in part because of the vector-sum technique it recommends for analysis of this interest-pattern, and in part because of the hedonistic calculus (a straightforward Benthamite design) it recommends for its appraisal.

Ehrlich, whose principal thought appeared in *Grundlegung der Soziologie des Rechts* (1913), advanced the view that law is but one among many orderings of human behavior, different from the others only in style, not in kind. The legal order, he observed, is devised as a means of coercion; nevertheless, people adhere to the order generally unmotivated by fear of consequences. Thus, he reasoned, it is not enough to consider the coerciveness of the legal order in determining its nature; one must consider its "wider behavioral effects." If law is conceived, not as rules of juristic decision-making, but simply as a system of rules men live by, it becomes a sociological object like other sociological objects, subject to the same techniques of study and analysis. The social scientist, then, simply observes conduct (and infers the underlying motives) in the social milieu; he need not concern himself with formal-logical ingredients of legal theories. According to Ehrlich, law exhibits itself inevitably and fully in the *"Tatsachen des Rechts;"* once these facts are recorded, the sociological jurisprudent's work is practically finished. All that remains is organization of data and inductive interpretation. This Baconian view, with a shift of emphasis from society-at-large to the judicial chambers, became a prime motive-force in the development of American "Legal Realism."

Kelsen's opposition to sociological jurisprudence was, once again, first voiced in *Hauptprobleme der Staatsrechtslehre*. It is, however, a distinct counterpoise to his criticism of neo-Kantian naturalism. Where he found fault with Stammler et al. for compounding law and the moral "ought," he found with Ihering, Jellinek, Laband, and company for failing to recognize the normative content law enjoys on its *own*. He deplored the sociological juris-prudents' reliance on a reverse kind of teleology; they had adopted the neo-Kantian account of purpose to a strictly causal account of law. Kelsen argued that however law evidences itself in orderly social operations (its "effective-ness"), *these* cannot of themselves provide the reason for its validity. A science which aims at comprehending what law *is* cannot settle for mere description of its material ef-fects. Sociology, he says, can only be "metajuristic"; it is constrained to consider acts. Legal science, on the other hand, must consider the norms which condition these acts by imbuing them with juristic meaning. Put differently: The sociologists' interest-calculus comprehends only "sub-jective law." But legal validity arises only when subjective and objective orders converge. And the principle govern-ing this convergence transcends the empirical-social plane; it is a formal-logical principle. PGNR begins with a cri-tique of the sociological approach; GTLS ends with the same critique softened somewhat. In the former work, Kelsen insists that sociology cannot comprehend the object of law, and dooms the effort to make the study of law a science to failure. In the latter, he is more generous. Here Kelsen wants to allow sociology its domain and wish it well; he wants only to maintain that "normative jurispru-dence" (even the name is holdover from the early work) should be allowed its own integrity as science, and its own transcendental-logically defined domain. The two, he thinks, are compatible, perhaps complementary.

Kelsen agreed with Ihering and other sociological juris-prudes that law is an essentially coercive order. But he in-sisted against them that the nature of legal coercion is not to be understood by the historical-sociological *("natur-*

geschichtliche") method. Legal coercion, Kelsen contended, is *internal* to law. Its force is not that of a psychological threat, but rather that of attaching, within the formal structure of the norm system, a prescriptive reaction to the description of an action. The details of this specifically "internal" form of coercion will be discussed at length in a later chapter. Here it will suffice to say that Kelsen's opposition to the method of sociological jurisprudence is founded on his view that only a structural analysis of norm relations is capable of exhibiting what is in this sense formally intrinsic.

Kelsen singled out Ehrlich for special criticism at the beginning of *General Theory of Law and State.* Here he directly charged Ehrlich with misrepresenting the nature of legal coercion. Ehrlich had argued that the inattention of the law-governed citizen to law's coercive intent excuses the legal scientist from centering his attention on this factor, and promotes more general social-scientific projects. But Kelsen rejoins:

> The doctrine that coercion is an essential element of law does not refer to the actual behavior of the individuals subjected to the legal order, but to the legal order itself, to the fact that the legal order provides sanctions and that by this very fact and only by this fact, that is, by this specific social technique, is it distinguished from other sciences. (GTLS, 25)

Discussion of motives, Kelsen concludes, is a matter for psychology or (in the case of sin and the threat of divine reprisal) for the sociology of religion. Unless the formal sanction-delict relation is taken into consideration, Kelsen insists, no hope remains for distinguishing the *legal* order from other, similar social orders. And it is just this lack of definition that Ehrlich fell prey to:

> The result of Ehrlich's attempt to emancipate the definition of law from the element of coercion is the definition: the law is an ordering of human behavior. But this is a definition of

society, not of law. . . . Even if we limit the concept of order or organization to relatively centralized orders which institute special organs for the creation and application of the order, the law is not sufficiently determined by the concept of order. (GTLS, 28)

ANALYTICAL JURISPRUDENCE AND PURE THEORY

From what has already been said, it will be apparent that, even in its earlier development, Kelsen's legal theory bore a striking resemblance to that of J. Austin. Yet, surprisingly enough, there is no mention of Austin or of his "analytical jurisprudence" in Kelsen's early works. He began to mention the view by name only after the first editions of *Reine Rechtslehre* and *Allgemeine Staatslehre* had been published. Kelsen's first protracted discussion of Austin appeared in 1941. By the time of *Allgemeine Staatslehre*'s second edition and first English translation (1945), Kelsen had clearly recognized the extent of his agreement with Austin. He was willing to say then that in the respects of orientation and aim, "there is no essential difference between analytical jurisprudence and the pure theory of law" (GTLS, xv).

All the same however, Kelsen did not wish simply to *identify* Pure Theory with Austin's system. In revising *Allgemeine Staatslehre*, Kelsen specifically introduced a number of passages whose role was to point up differences between the views. In respect of these differences, Kelsen held that Pure Theory was an improvement over Austin's analytical jurisprudence. The differences arise, Kelsen explained, because Pure Theory carries out Austin's methods more rigorously and more consistently than Austin and his followers had been able to do.

Several dissimilarities between Kelsen's and Austin's accounts of positive law deserve special notice. The most important *formal* difference between their theories concerns the modality of the conditional relation in legal norms:

Kelsen held that the sanction (necessarily) *ought* to follow the delict; whereas Austin allowed that it *probably* would follow, albeit the chance of its *not* following would be slight. Austin's formulation permitted him to regard normative relations as strictly analogous to causal relations; Kelsen's formulation prevented this contruction. Kelsen's divergence from Austin on this score caused him to develop the theory of the "imputational connective," an allegedly unique sort of "if-then" connective which was to be the keystone of the pure-theoretical logistic.

Austin's jurisprudence is frequently termed the "Sovereign Command" theory, because it identifies law with commands issued and enforced by political superiors over political inferiors. Kelsen concurred with Austin in regarding the command as the major constituent of certain kinds of legal norms (and certainly the most important kinds), but he differed sharply with him on the *nature* of legal commands: He insisted that: (1) Not all commands are (legally) *binding*; and that what determines a command's binding force is something external to the command itself and its issuance. The chief factor in this determination is the question of whether already valid norms in a system authorize the commanding individual to issue such a command. (2) If laws are to be construed as commands, they must be "de-psychologized" commands, commands that do not entail the existence of a "will" in the psychological sense. It will not do to regard the fear felt by a legal subject as a *cause* (in whatever sense) of the subject's legal obligation.[6]

There is much in Kelsen that is directly counter-Austinian. There is also much that coheres perfectly with Austin's program of jurisprudence. On the whole, Kelsen's attitude toward Austin seems to be one of uneasy compromise. Austin's theory turns on the notion of command; Kelsen accepts Austin's key "primary/secondary" distinction between commands, but adds to it a clarificatory analysis

(GTLS, 63), whose conclusion is that the secondary (or as Kelsen prefers to call it "sanctioning") norm is the genuine norm, and that the "primary" norm is ultimately "epiphenomenal." This typifies Kelsen's approach to Austin; it is one of approval mingled with distrust of specifics. Evidence of Kelsen's specific dissatisfactions with Austin are to be found throughout GTLS. Notable among them are the following: Kelsen was displeased because Austin (like most other jurisprudents) distinguishes rather than identifies, legal and physical persons. Kelsen takes it that the identification follows with necessity from positivist premises that are consistent. He regards as inflated Austin's estimate of the importance of the notion of "duty" for positive law analysis; and he thinks Austin's attempt to explicate the notion is unsuccessful. Finally, he regards Austin's affirmation of *ignoratia juris nocet* on the basis of administrative practicality as entirely implausible.

On the other hand, many features of Kelsen's and Austin's work place them together against a host of various foes. Both explain (at least some) legal norms as commands; both insist on their essential generality. That both accept the "primary/secondary" distinction indicates mutual recognition of the differing "deontic directions" within the norm. Their respective notions of responsibility, duty, right, and the like, are similar both in spirit and in enunciation. Above all, they are firm allies in defense of the "is"/"ought" dichotomy against the forces of naturalism. On balance, it appears that Kelsen considers Austin's analytical jurisprudence to be a right-minded positivistic system spoiled by a too-broad construction of its fundamental terms, and by a slavish adherence to psychological rather than philosophical (that is, formal-logical) aspects of legal phenomena.

"FORMALISM" AND PURE THEORY

"Formalism" is a term that has established currency both in jurisprudence and in philosophy. In both arenas, the term has acquired ambiguous reference through unsystematic and uncritical employment; it has also attached a broad range of emotive meaning. It is possible, however, to find rough strains of a "primary sense" for both philosophic and legalistic usage; and when this is done it becomes apparent that: (1) there is a stronger kinship between some sorts of legalistic formalism and philosophical formalism than has generally been realized, and (2) Pure Theory incorporates formalism of *both* species.

"FORMALISM" IN JURISPRUDENCE

Kelsen follows a lengthy tradition among Continental legal theorists in laying special stress on "formal" as against "material" aspects of law and the study of law. Continental jurisprudents had throughout the nineteenth century and into the early twentieth conspired to elevate logic (by which they meant *syllogism*) to the status of *méthode par excellence* for philosophy of law. Even Savigny, famed for his insistence on the nonuniversality of a law's application and on its historical evolution and social renovation, allowed that the backbone of his theoretical enterprise was a "juristic mathematics of concepts," organized along syllogistic lines.[7] Formalistic emphasis on the role of logic in jurisprudence has been sustained in Continental circles by the recent work of U. Klug[8] and K. Engisch,[9] among others. Common to the various "formalists" were beliefs that (roughly stated): (1) Legislators make laws with the joint aim of (a) logical consistency in respect to constitutional rules and (b) deductive utility as major premises for juristic application; (2) Jurists apply law by subsuming specific cases (events, actions, persons, and so on) under the principles provided by legislators (thereby completing syllogisms); and (3) Jurisprudence itself is in some sense a logical discipline (the minimal sense being that jurisprudes are obliged to make their accounts of legal systems coherent through adherence to rules of logic).

Kelsen insisted (and entirely correctly) that *his* employment of logical technique in the formal understanding of law marked a radical departure from earlier modes of legal formalism.[10] For, Kelsen maintained that not only are the operations of the legislator and jurist in making and applying law and those of the legal scientist in analyzing it bound by the constraints of logical form; but, much more emphatically, *law itself*, as it is revealed by the analytical procedures of the legal scientist is and must be a *formal object*, an object whose unity (completeness, consistency, and so forth) is like that of a logical system. This last tenet sharply divides Kelsen from earlier formalists by excluding absolutely the "social character" which ameliorated the rigidity of logical constraints on their views and allowed them to take into account historical and "evolutionary" considerations. Logic, Kelsen thinks, takes as its object normative orders which are unaffected by whatever social activity they condition. For, as he puts it (in a somewhat Husserlian way), "the acts of human thought, which are regulated by the norms of this order, do not refer to other human beings; one does not think 'toward' another man in the way one acts toward another man" (PTL, 24).

To the extent, then, that logic plays a role in shaping the legal-scientific presentation of legal norms it will be through the regulation of *Denkakten*, and not *Willensakten* (nor *Akten simpliciter*). But what is this role to be? On this crucial question Keslen repeatedly vacillates. When he speaks of the norm order in the "nomostatic" connection, Kelsen hints that member norms are deducible from other norms (or at least from the *Grundnorm*) by strictly logical means. When he takes the "nomodynamic" perspective, however, he generally denies the possibility of this kind of inference. It is clear, in any case, that Kelsen thinks of logic as playing some organizational role in Pure Theory. And it is clear that Kelsen regards the "logical unity" of his constructional system as a safeguard against the incursion of alien elements. For whether these be ideological or causal factors, to the extent that the system is "controlled" by logical mechanism, it will obviously be different to and therefore, unaffected by them all. To some extent, then, logical formalism is employed in Pure Theory as a purifying tool; it links legal-scientific analysis to *form*, and drives out much of what was formerly thought a matter of vital *content*.

This position, of course, openly invites the charges of "priorism," "hollowness," analytic detachment from living legal institutions, and the like. And hosts of critics have been quick to accept the invitation. C. K. Allen spoke for the majority of Anglo-American sceptics when he observed:

> It is perfectly true that law, considered only as a body of rules or a scheme of logic, is, and must be, a *system of concepts*, and can only be apprehended as such. But if, having disengaged our concepts and having arranged them in a *Deutungsschema* of flawless logical pattern, we stop at this point, what a barren task we have engaged upon! . . . If all legal norms could be deduced, one from another, with the same mechanical certainty as stone can be placed on stone in an accurately designed building, half our legal problems would be solved and the judge, far from being "creative," would be a mere slot machine.[11]

Kelsen was criticized no less vehemently by those German writers who had awakened to the dangers of Kantian priorism: W. Jöckel, writing in 1930, roundly condemned Kelsen for what he called *"verachtung des Stoffes,"* contempt for matter;[12] and he was joined in this appraisal by numerous others on the Continent. Perhaps the most vicious attacks came from the Roman Catholic jurisprudents, who had, after all, a vested interest in the natural law legal theory that Kelsen so strenuously attacked, and that seemed to them so plainly to exceed Pure Theory in human relevance.[13]

To be sure, this form of criticism, hostility to what is

currently called "logicism" (after Holmes) or simply "the abuse of logic" (after Stone), was abroad long before Kelsen began his work on Pure Theory. F. Gény, the preeminent legal "practicalist," popularized the same complaint as early as 1899.[14] Gény's view that the a priori scaffolding of conceptions and constructions is valueless apart from the material considerations of legal operation has become the standard line of attack against Kelsen's formalism. But the preponderance of this sort of criticism only demonstrates the blindness of Kelsen's critics to his true aim. It is, as Kelsen puts it, a bit like criticizing the geometer for his disaffection from content (HS, 93), or like reproaching the economic theorist for his apparent disdain for groceries, pocket-change, and what-not, which concepts quantify, but abstract from. Kelsen dismisses this attack as naïve and mistaken because it turns on the issue of impracticality. The Pure Theory of Law *is* practical, but its usefulness does not consist in untangling the web of any particular legal system to find specific legal facts. Its use is general. And from its general perspective, the contents of legal norms are by no means irrelevant, nor are independent criticisms (even ethical criticisms) inappropriate.

Kelsen's conception of "formalism" (in the legal sense) is, in fact, simply not strong enough to lay itself open to the kinds of dangers its critics allege. Pure Theory does not give us a plan for deducing from the *corpus juris* judicial decisions that "we can apply to the real facts of life." The logic in Kelsen's program applies only to an underlying framework of norms which, he says, makes intelligible ("comprehensible") the law which is embodied in particular legal systems. It does not tell us how those systems work, nor how the laws in them are to be applied. Primarily, Kelsen uses the term "formal" (in the *legal* context) to indicate the *generality* of Pure Theory, its attention to universal traits of law, rather than to incidental traits of particular legal systems.

As a general theory of law the Pure Theory must disregard the contents of the legal norms insofar as they differ in time and space. In this sense the Pure Theory of Law has—and by its very nature must have—a formalistic character. This does not mean—as is sometimes misunderstood—that the Pure Theory of Law considers the contents of the legal norms as irrelevant. It means only that the concepts defined by the theory must hold what is common to all positive legal orders, not what separates them from each other. "Formalism" can be no objection to a general theory of law, although, as a matter of fact, it is frequently brought forward against the Pure Theory of Law. (ILR, 4)

Few if any of Kelsen's Continental critics mean to attack the *generality* which Pure Theory claims for itself here. The notion of a legal science which applies to all actual legal systems indiscriminately is a presumption which they (in contradistinction to many Anglo-American jurisprudes) for the most part countenance. Widespread European acquiescence to the plausibility of a general theory of law may be attributed to the clinging predominance of essentialism in Continental juridical thinking—a general willingness to accept as reasonable a project that seeks to understand law by uncovering a *meaning* or *nature* which lies coiled in the heart of all that is legal. It is moreover a popular belief among European thinkers (though again by no means as popular in English-speaking lands) that the universalistic approach to a subject of cognition is of *practical* as well as theoretical value. Kelsen decidely plays to this taste.

Lauterpacht, the first commentator to bring the Pure Theory of Law to the attention of the wider audience of English-speaking jurisprudence, spoke admiringly of Kelsen's technique as "grasping things notionally," and as "comprehending juridical realities." Such a technique, he believed, is a nearly ideal prophylactic against ideology and partisanship in legal science. Kelsen, he reported, "is impatient of the cry that jurisprudence must serve the needs of life. The needs of life, he says, can also be served by helping to comprehend objectively the nature of things, including the nature of the State and of the law."[15]

Formalism in the legal sense, then, is an indispensable part of Pure Theory. Its role is wholly conditioned by the aim Pure Theory sets itself—to understand what is common to laws in general by disclosing the nature of law as an item among the natures of things. The bases of the common understanding it seeks are a conviction that whatever is properly legal has a determinate and specifiable essence, a conviction that this essence can be made comprehensible through a certain kind of "structural analysis," and a conviction that analysis will conduce to the objectivity and value-neutrality without which no legal theory can claim to be a science.

CONFUSIONS REGARDING THE SCOPE, INTEREST, AND MEANING OF "FORMAL" IN KELSEN'S WRITINGS

To what extent, however, is Kelsen's work "formalistic" in the *philosophical* sense? Here, the case is not quite so aboveboard. Before addressing this question directly, it is necessary to dispel a number of confusions which have attended Kelsen's claims that law is a "formal" system, and that its science is "formal-logical" in methodology. Over the years, Kelsen's writings have exhibited three sorts of glaring uncertainties in this area. These have to do with: (1) the range of objects which he supposes to be logically structured (hence, requiring formal-logical treatment); (2) the range of persons who are supposed to be occupied with the kind of formal analysis Pure Theory provides; and (3) the ranges of meaning which are allowed "logical," "formal," and correlative terms in Kelsen's accounts on these issues.

The first problem is easily enough dispensed with. It is sometimes said to be unclear whether Kelsen thinks legal norms themselves are imbued with logical (formal) structure, or whether it is only their *arrangement* in legal systems which exhibits this structure. After some early equivocation, Kelsen has come to a more-or-less settled position on the question. From *General Theory* onward, Kelsen makes it clear that he wishes us to consider *both* legal norms and their systems—insofar as they are comprehended by the legal scientist—as logically structured phenomena. This is supposed to hold whatever the nature of laws and legal systems may be in situ. Kelsen has very little to say, in fact, about the formal and informal qualities of law *prior* to the application of the pure-theoretical scientist's structural analysis. In the ordinary manifestation of legal objects, logical form (both at the level of norm and of the system) is *disguised*; and it is for this reason, Kelsen thinks, that one might be inclined to doubt its actuality. The role of the pure theorist, of course, is to expose the logic beneath its disguise. And once this exposure has been achieved, the "true character" of legal norms and their orders—the logic which pervades and unifies them— becomes unquestionable (GTLS, xv, 46–47; PT, 70–75; WJ, 325, 360–368). It is perhaps worth noting that Kelsen's remarks in this direction are quite similar in tone and spirit to the claims of constructional analysis made by Russell in "On Denoting," *Introduction to Mathematical Philosophy*, *Principia Mathematica*, and elsewhere, and by Wittgenstein in *Tractatus Logico-Philosophicus*.

It would be wrong, however, to assume, as antiformalist critics are wont to do, that because Kelsen wishes to maintain that systems of legal norms are logically ordered he must construe the formal program of legal science according to the strict model of the logical syllogism. Typical of Kelsen's attackers on this count is C. Boasson. Boasson claims that Pure Theory is built on a deductive-syllogistic model, the syllogistic idea having come from Sigwart and the motive of deductivity (along with much pure-theoretical terminology) from Fichte.[16] Although Kelsen freely admits that the possibility of a rigorously syllogistic logic of legal norms appealed to him in earlier years, he has recently been most emphatic in denial of this possibility. In one of his latest articles, Kelsen has taken special pains to rebut Boasson's charges. He denies that syllogistic in Sigwart's sense is involved in Pure Theory's treatment of the "basic norm," and denies having *read* the work of Fichte from which Boasson alleges much of Pure Theory's aim and language came. Kelsen is especially anxious to correct the mistaken impression (of Boasson, among others) that it is the specific function of the "basic norm" to make the rest of Pure Theory (in which it takes an admittedly supervenient position) strictly deductive. This impression, he says, simply "comes out of thin air." He insists that the doctrine of "basic norm" has absolutely nothing to do with the question of the inductivity or deductivity of legal science.[17] And he insists with equal vehemence that Pure Theory does not foster deductive "logification" in juridical application. But that Pure Theory does not verge into deductive syllogistic at either extremity (the theoretic ceiling of "basic norm" or the practical floor of material application) does not mean that logic plays no role in the ample space between. In denying the syllogistic nature of juridical reasoning, Kelsen repeatedly stresses a "constitutive" element which, although it does complicate the picture considerably, does not obviate the need for conceptual machinery to organize the norms once constituted. As we shall see, there is in this notion of "constitution" more than a seed of the "logification" which threatens to make Pure Theory into the sort of "Rechtslogik" Kelsen abjures.

The second confusion is also readily dispelled. It is often unclear from what Kelsen says whether he thinks lawyers and judges as well as legal scientists are or ought to be concerned with the kind of analysis Pure Theory involves. Particularly in his early writing (for example, PGNR, 12), Kelsen often suggested that lawyers and judges would have occasion to employ Pure Theory in their professional dealings. Recently, however, Kelsen has attempted to correct this impression. The confusion arose, he supposes (beginning in GTLS), because he formerly had not been sufficiently careful in distinguishing legal norms themselves from propositions about them made by legal scientists, theorists, judges, lawyers, and others. He *now* restricts the domain of "structural analysis" to a species of propositions *about* norms; namely, "rules of law." Practitioners of law, whose dealings are more usually with norms in their "raw form," need not concern themselves with those complicated displays which the pure-theorist must stage to organize "rules," comprehend their interrelation, and explicate their internal workings. But it should be emphasized that Kelsen does *not* deny the relevance of the *outcomes* of pure-theoretical labors to everyday juristic practice. No sooner would he deny that the pure-mathematician's labors may prove useful to the applied mathematician and the engineer. Admitting that few legal practitioners will find it useful to invoke Pure Theory in their everyday labors does not mean denying that the object Pure Theory seeks to understand is the same object which is applied—though perhaps imperfectly understood—by lawyer and judge. Assuredly, one can work with a thing, and work well, without fully understanding it. But just as assuredly, analytical understanding is often a means of informing a thing's function.

It is the third confusion—that of the indeterminacy of the terms "formal" and "logical" in Pure Theory—which is the gravest. Kelsen has, upon various occasions, characterized his enterprise as "logical," "logico-juristic," "formal-logical," and "transcendental-logical."[18] And although he has repeatedly insisted that these designations point to a significant advance Pure Theory makes over previous theories, Kelsen has nowhere paused to fix the exact sense of "logical" he intends for these contexts.

Otto Bondy, who contends that Kelsen and his followers

"successfully determined the role modern logic is called upon to play in legal theory,"[19] throws some valuable light on the subject. He argues, *contra* certain Anglo-American critics of "logicism," that the Pure Theory of Law is a direct continuation of an extremely important development that owes its inception to Leibniz and Bolzano, a view according to which logic as *mathesis universalis* is equally well applied in every area of science. In more recent times, F. Kaufmann and F. Schreier made the effort to apply it to "normative jurisprudence." But, Bondy believes, it remained for Kelsen to direct logic *qua mathesis universalis* to a threefold purpose in the law field: (1) the determination of a methodology for the discipline of legal science; (2) the clarification of the object of that discipline; and (3) the determination of the means of verifying the propositions that result from the application of the discipline.[20] The main weight of Kelsen's Pure Theory, Bondy says, is applied to the first of these tasks. Here, the role of logic is "to make explicit those essential rules which the intuition of a genius would more or less unconsciously apply."[21] This is admittedly a queer way of putting it; but it is, after a fashion, something that Pure Theory does attempt to do. Kelsen does believe that the technique of "representation" he provides can make explicit legal meaning which, once exposed, will have the certainty of self-evidence. But, illuminating though they are, Bondy's comments do not reach very far. Logical methodology is not the same thing as analysis of a logical object. And when, pursuant to Bondy's second "purpose," Kelsen analyzes the legal norm-hierarchy itself, he strongly suggests that the logical ordering at issue in some sense belongs to the order itself, rather than to the method of investigation.

Bondy moreover leaves unanswered the crucial question: In what sense is Kelsen's employment of logic "formal?" On this issue, we find Kelsen's own statements ambiguous, rather than vague. G. Bergmann and L. Zerby[22] have distinguished three meanings with which the term "formal" appears in Kelsen's writings: (1) "formal" as free from admixture with foreign elements (what I have elsewhere called "purity"); (2) "formal" in roughly the same sense as Kant's categories are said to be formal; and (3) "formal" in the comparatively loose sense in which social events become legally relevant only insofar as they are subsumed under criteria which appear in legal rules. It is true, as Bergmann and Zerby allege, that Kelsen uses the term "formal" (or its variants "formal-logical," and others) in all of these ways, and from time to time compounds the uses, to the great confusion of his readers. But Bergmann and Zerby are conspicuously unsympathetic interpreters of Pure Theory. They train attention on these three meanings because they suit the purpose of casting Kelsen's work into disrepute. This perjorative bias has caused them to overlook a *fourth* and far more telling use running throughout Kelsen's writings; namely, (4) "formal" as "structural," in somewhat the same sense in which the term is used by the Vienna Circle positivists. There are, in fact, substantial grounds for attributing to this last sense a leading status in Kelsen's thought. And it is this sense which makes Pure Theory *philosophically* formalistic.

"FORMALISM" IN PHILOSOPHY

When Kelsen uses "formal" to characterize the attention Pure Theory pays to the *structure* of norms and norm-systems (the fourth sense mentioned above), he enters an arena in which a number of contemporary philosophers have been busily engaged. To understand the connection of Kelsen's "structural formalism" with recent philosophic activity it is useful to consider the historical circumstances out of which the pure-theoretical venture arose. Kelsen's early work was done, by and large, in Vienna. During the time that Kelsen's own "Vienna School" of legal positivism was forming, the celebrated Vienna Circle

of philosophers was in full swing. These "logical positivists" (as they were to call themselves) centered about M.
Schlick; among the principal early members were Hahn,
Neurath, Waismann, Feigl, Menger, Gödel, and Frank. R.
Carnap, the chief systems-builder, served as a semiofficial
spokesman for the group. The entire Circle was very greatly influenced, though largely indirectly, by the thought of
L. Wittgenstein. Given Kelsen's widely attested syncretic
facility, it might naturally be assumed that he might seek
to incorporate in his legal theory the advances which these
philosophers achieved. Such an effort was, after all, entirely in order: Kelsen meant Pure Theory to be a method of
treating the subjects of law and legal inquiry in a distinctively *scientific* way. And the latest, most exacting tools of
scientific explanation at hand were in the possession of
Carnap, Neurath, and company.

Surprisingly, however, Kelsen never explicitly indicates
to his readers that he is familiar with the work of the
"logical positivists," let alone that this work has had any
effect upon the program of the Pure Theory. Even in those
writings in which Kelsen contrasts doctrines from philosophy of science with doctrines from philosophy of law (for
example, "Causality and Retribution," WJ, 303–323;
"Causality and Imputation," WJ, 324–349), he does not
mention the Vienna Circle or its views. When Kelsen discusses the notion of "construction" *(Einstellung)*, it is
sometimes (for example, HS, xvii) with reference to Cohen
and the Marburg school, but *never* with reference to the
positivists. Nor has the possibility of such a connection
been discussed at any length by philosophers associated
with the latter group.[23] There is really no point in pursuing
the historical questions of contact and influence here; all
the available evidence seems to be inconclusive. Whatever
historical links there may be between Kelsen and the Vienna Circle, we may be sure they are extremely thin. Yet
there are important affinities between their doctrines and

outlooks, affinities which make a brief comparative examination profitable. The important question for our purposes is not how Kelsen's theory came to resemble those of the logical positivists, but what it gains from the consanguinity, whatever its origin.

There are indeed quite a number of points at which Pure Theory and logical positivism share perspectives. In a recent study, W. Ebenstein singles out ethical emotivism and general antimetaphysical perspective as areas of their "deep affinity."[24] If, however, our interest lies in discerning those common features that contribute most directly to the two views being counted as "formalism," then two other points will appear to indicate the deepest affinity: First, a notion which Kelsen seems to share most obviously with Carnap, the idea of "rational reconstruction"; and second, a notion he seems to share more directly with Wittgenstein, the "representative" view of "logical form."

Kelsen comes closest, it seems, to identifying the methodology of pure-theoretical analysis with positivistic "rational reconstruction" in *Die Philosophischen Grundlagen der Naturrechtslehre und des Rechtspositivismus* (perhaps even the title of this work hints at the author's predilection). Here, while discussing the "irrational idea" of justice, he refers to the therapeutic enterprise of legal science as "rationalization" and as "logical reduction." He speaks of the "logification" *(Logisierung)* of notions formerly conceived of as estranged from logic, a process which is directed by a "logical ideal" connected with the unity of an order (PGNR, 69). And he indicates that the larger purpose of pure-theoretical analysis conceived along these lines is the returning to *logos* of a host of jurisprudential conceptions that have been estranged from it (though he does not include justice among these conceptions).

In PGNR as well as in later works there appear a number of terms which also appear as significant technical terms in Carnap's works ("*Stufe,*" "structural analysis," "basic element," "basic relation," "unanalysable units," and so forth). However, Kelsen's employment of these terms is somewhat idiosyncratic and skewed by attention to normativity, an interest wholly apart from the program of the *Aufbau*. It is in the broader methodological patterns that the resemblances of Kelsen's system to Carnap's become significant. Pure-theoretic method, like Carnapian "rational reconstruction," requires as a first step the derivation of a "basis" through conversion of propositions from one "raw" form to a less "direct" form; the conversion closely parallels Carnap's transformations from "material" to "formal" form. Pure Theory then arranges the derived "second-order" propositions in a hierarchy; the ordering of this hierarchy is achieved, as with Carnap, through "ascension forms." Finally, Kelsen, like Carnap, supposes that the outcome of his systematic analysis is the exhibition of a formerly-hidden "true form" or "nature" which belongs somehow to the data which it originally absorbed.

Indeed, it is not difficult to see in Kelsen's often repeated declarations on the "unity of law" an effort at convergence with the positivist's highest goal—unity of science. Nor, when he explains the "constitutive character" of legal science (for example, PTL, 72), is it hard to perceive echoes of Carnap's "constructional" view of natural science. It is especially noteworthy that Kelsen continually stresses the epistemological character of legal-scientific constitutivity. For he has occasionally indicated (PGNR, ch. 2) that legal positivism (at least *his* form of it) is distinguished from its naturalistic forbears specifically by its adherence to a "transcendental" viewpoint, one in which relativistic and especially *logical* considerations are foremost. And it is precisely when Carnap locates his construction-theory in the domain of *Erkenntnis* that he characterizes its properties as "formal-logical";[25] this, of course, is *just* the term Kelsen employs in the corresponding connection.

No doubt much of the similarity between Carnapian and Kelsenite notions of reconstruction is due to shared philosophical grounding. After all, both Carnap and Kelsen find the roots of their respective methodologies in Kant and the neo-Kantians. They share the nostalgic inclination which, according to Bergmann, makes scientism and formalism converge; namely, a yearning for old-fashioned critical philosophy. Indeed, Bergmann suggests, it is really *that* and not some "new order" that the positivists are after: "What the reconstructionists hope to reconstruct in the new style is the old metaphysics."[26] But even if this view is correct, we are left with the questions: What is significantly new in the "new style" of rational reconstruction as Kelsen applies it? And, what impact does the importation of constructionist strategy have generally in the program of Pure Theory?

Hints of answers to these questions—but little more than hints—began to appear in critical articles as early as in 1944. It was in that year that F. E. Oppenheim published a Carnapian-style "logical analysis of law," employing several of the same analytical distinctions that Kelsen had used in *Reine Rechtslehre* ("static/dynamic," "valid/effective," "basic/derived rules," and so on).[27] Oppenheim did not, however, discuss the connection of his scheme of analysis with Pure Theory. In fact, he expressly said that his own discussion of legal norm-hierarchies is a "purely logical one" having nothing at all to do with Kelsen's "Stufenbau."[28] Yet, A. Wedberg, writing in 1951, cites the Oppenheim article as an interesting exposition of the same "rational reconstruction" that he developed, a system of analysis for legal rules that purports to be faithful in its main lines to Kelsen's pure-theoretical technique.[29] Wedberg argues that rational reconstruction (which he takes to be synonymous with "logical analysis") is one species—a legitimate, important and properly "external" species—of what Kelsen had previously called "legal interpretation." Although Wedberg's own elaboration of legal-scientific rational reconstruction diverges at points from Kelsen's, Wedberg indicates the differences with scrupulous care. Thus, Wedberg's readers obtain (mainly in a series of explanatory footnotes) a running account of what, according to Wedberg, Kelsen's rational reconstruction of the structure of legal norms *would have been*, had Kelsen's employment of Carnap's methodology been more aboveboard. Oppenheim and Wedberg say little, however, to explain the novel significance of the analyses they provide. And, as might be expected, given the positivistic tone of their articles, they draw no metaphysical conclusions. At the most, these reconstructionists claim for their analyses an improved clarity and rigor of presentation, a faithfulness to their object, a sense of leaving things as they truly are.

Far more illuminating, and more emphatic in its affirmation of an affinity between Carnapian and Kelsenite reconstructionism is M. Golding's definitve study, "Kelsen and the Concept of 'Legal System' " (1961). Like Wedberg, Golding trains critical attention on Kelsen's notion of "representation"; he cites several passages from the *General Theory of Law and State* in which "representation" plays a key role, and concludes from them that this term is simply Kelsen's word for the positivist's "rational reconstruction." Golding indicates the central importance of the constructional approach within Pure Theory as follows:

> The underlying motif of Kelsen's "pure theory of law" and the relation of his legal positivism to logical positivism is the application of the notion of rational reconstruction to legal systems, or normative orders. Just as a body of knowledge or a scientific concept often needs reconstructing, so also do le-

gal systems require rational reconstruction.[30] Given a legal system, the material produced by the law-making authority of a community, the function of jurisprudence, or the science of law, is to construct the "representation" of that material.[31]

Centrally important in Golding's account is the recognition that Pure Theory's position on the nature of "legal system is essentially *radical*. Golding sees that Kelsen's legal scientist is supposed to "represent" the legal order in a way which differs substantially from that in which the legislator presents it or that in which lawyers and judges apply it. It is only through the process of "representation" that "legal system" emerges: Assumptions hidden in the order of norms are exposed; the hierarchical structure of the order appears; the "proper" formulation of the member norms are made explicit. Hence, Golding observes, the product the legal scientist produces is not a mere re-presentation (one-to-one reproduction), but an *ampliative* reconstruction. Both with respect to the form of the individual norms of the order and the structure of the order itself, the reformulation effected by Pure Theory is "ideal"; it is, according to Kelsen, a *superior* expression from the standpoint of legal cognition. The standard objection to jurisprudential reformulations of legal orders is that they are, however clever and informative, only reproductions, and hence practically removed from the "genuine article" which does the *work* of law. But, according to Golding's interpretation of Kelsen, Pure Theory undercuts this objection in a novel way. It argues that it is the "legal system" the legal scientist discovers (or perhaps devises) and not the "raw stuff" that is the "genuine article."

> The reconstruction differs from the original materials not only in the manner of formulating legal norms, but also in that the reconstruction contains more than is to be directly found in these materials. This is so in that the reconstruction contains those norms which are *assumed* by officials. . . . The no-

tion of "legal system" is actually a presupposition of the jurisprudent. It is he who systematizes the law . . . ; and this he
might do in a way which the officials . . . never thought or
dreamt of. The key to the understanding of the concept of
"legal system" is the idea of rational reconstruction. The systematic character of a given legal order is a construction of
the jurisprudent and not necessarily the fabrication of individuals who have been delegated lawmaking power.[32]

It is certainly true that Kelsen regards Pure Theory as
representationally "constitutive" (that is, ampliative) in
the manner Golding suggests. The question of whether
Kelsen's peculiar "ideal" formalization of legal-normative
orders is, in fact, a conscious extension of the project of rational reconstruction invented by logical positivists thus
becomes philosophically muted. The crucial question now
becomes: Given the similarities of overall attitude and approach attested to by Wedberg, Golding, et al., to what extent is Kelsen's description of pure-theoretical science as
"formal" individualistic, and to what extent does it only
mirror the sense of "formal" already current in positivistic
formalism?

It is Kelsen's conviction that by a specific radical technique structural properties of the legal order that display a
relational pattern not evident in their matrix systems can
be brought to light. The presentation of this hidden structure is the whole work of Pure Theory. Both Carnap and
Wittgenstein link "formal" and "structural" in an analogous fashion. Carnap identifies the totality of a relation's
formal properties with its "structure,"[33] and he describes
the central motif of the *Aufbau* as: "the thesis that science
deals only with the descriptions of structural properties of
objects." Carnap maintains that the only sensible scientific
statements are ostensive definitions and definite descriptions. He shows that definite descriptions may be structural, even *purely* structural, and concludes that every scien-

tific statement can in principle be transformed into a structure statement. Since the tools for reducing definite descriptions are already at hand, thanks to Russell, Carnap believes that the way is now open for "objective science." "Objectivity" in the scientific sense, says Carnap, means intersubjective validity purchased through construction of a standpoint different from and epistemologically superior to particular experiential standpoints. And the possibility of "objective science"

> lies in the fact that, even though the material of the individual streams of experience is completely different, or rather altogether incomparable, since a comparison of two sensations or two feelings of different subjects, as far as their immediately given qualities are concerned, is absurd, certain *structural properties* are analogous for all streams of experience. Now, if a science is to be objective, then it must restrict itself to statements about such structural properties, and, as we have seen earlier, it can restrict itself to statements about structures, since all objects of knowledge are not content, but form, and since they can be represented as structural entities.[34]

Changing the focus from *general* science to *legal* science, and changing the perspective on sensation to one on normativity, one finds in this remark a very clear statement of the "presentational" program in Kelsen's Pure Theory of Law.[35]

Wittgenstein is quite direct in the way he links "formal" and "structural." He says that the structure of a state of affairs *(Sachverhalt)* is the determinate way in which its objects are connected (2.032), and that form is "the possibility of structure" (2.033).[36] This notion of form *simpliciter* is contrasted almost immediately, however, to that of "pictorial form." In this way, Wittgenstein lays the foundation for the celebrated "picture theory of meaning." When, as Wittgenstein puts it, we picture facts to ourselves, we picture them in "logical space," that is, we picture them in a matrix of possibly existing or nonexisting states of affairs (2.1–2.12). "Pictorial form" is the way in which elements of a situation or of a picture of that situation are mutually related; it is the structural commonality which makes a picture a picture of its subject (2.15–2.151).

Now, it is Wittgenstein's fundamental conviction in the *Tractatus* that language cannot picture reality in an arbitrary manner; *something* must legitimate the representational function of the proposed symbol. "Pictorial form" fills the bill, Wittgenstein tells us (2.1514–2.17), because it is precisely what the picture has in common with reality. The same form, as it appears in reality, is called "logical form" (2.18). The *Tractatus* attempts to provide a logically perfect (that is, strictly truth-functional) way of representing the way (descriptive) language of *any* sort can say (or, equally important, *fail* to say) things about the world. Wittgenstein believes that whatever language can say it can say clearly ("Author's Preface," p. 3). But he makes it plain from the outset that not all (descriptive) propositions are clear as they stand; indeed, it seems more likely that he thinks that *none* are (3.251).

Kelsen, likewise, finds the norm-bearing expressions which are employed in juristic practice and in legislation to be typically, or perhaps inevitably, unclear. He thinks that Pure Theory provides the appropriate program to right this. So, it is not hard to see in Kelsen's scheme of "representation" just the same sort of therapeutic device for normative language that Wittgenstein thinks the *Tractatus* provides for descriptive language. The "formal" structuring in Kelsen's program comes in with the legal scientist's constitutive rendering of "rules of law," correspondent to legal *norms in situ*. These "rules of law" are ordered by within their *Deutungschemata* in much the same way Tractarian "states of affairs" are ordered in "logical space." Both Wittgenstein and Kelsen seem greatly concerned with devising a language of "clear" expression through which the sense of some other language can be precisely stated. Neither writer takes this "other language" (in Wittgenstein's case "ordinary" fact-language; in Kelsen's, the language of legal practice) to be other than a *real* language. But, both writers insist equally vehemently that propositions in that language can become what they are *meant* to be only through the logical reformation provided in second-order languages.

What exactly Wittgenstein thinks would count as "clear" expression and what changes would have to be made in what we say to make expression "clear" are matters of extremely heated controversy among interpreters. Certain features of the Tractarian account, however, have been regularly identified as guideposts on the matter: Wittgenstein holds that what a proposition *says* and what it *shows* are radically different (4.121, 4.1212, and others). In saying that such-and-such (a state of affairs) is the case, a statement will at the same time *show* how the world is (4.022)—specifically that the world is such that this linguistic formula can be *about* it. What Wittgenstein says about this twofold process sounds a good deal like what Kelsen has to say about the relation between "rules of law" and "legal norms." Wittgenstein says that the statemental operation "constructs a world with the help of logical scaffolding" (4.023) such that one can see (clearly) through the construction how things must be in the world if the proposition is to be true. This construction does not, of course, show that the proposition *is* true; but it circumscribes, as it were, the conditions of its potential for being true. This account parallels Kelsen's portrait of legal-construction language: What is "constituted" by legal science is the legal object-as-a-meaningful-whole; in this epistemological construction, "logical scaffolding" is inevitable (and can always be made explicit). The conclusion of the constructional process is that normative validity (what, in a deontic system, corresponds to truth in the

Tractatus and the *Aufbau*) *will* follow, given certain system-dependent conditions.

This raises the question of whether what is shown by a proposition can be said at all—by *other* propositions, say. Wittgenstein has been widely misunderstood on this point. He holds that although propositions state facts, they are *themselves* facts as well (2.141, 3.14). As facts, they are part of the world; they help make up "what is the case" (1.0, 2.063). Hence, their logical form can be shown (though not said) by appropriate metalinguistic expressions. Indeed, the *Tractatus* itself consists mainly of this latter sort of proposition. At this point—where Wittgenstein is after the "structural properties" of fact-language generally—the *Tractatus* becomes extremely difficult. Wittgenstein wages his battles on this question in a dense and baffling network of tightly woven allied notions: "formal properties," "structural properties," "logical form," "pictorial form," "form of representation," and others. At the end of much infighting, however, he emerges with two remarkable trophies—a picture of the general form of propositions (6), and a general rule for transitions between propositions (6.01).

Wittgenstein does not—as some have guessed—think of this twofold result as providing Archimedean leverage for turning out all true material statements (any more than Kelsen thought of the "basic norm" as entailing all valid norms of a legal system). What he does claim is that whatever rightly represents facts (among them statemental facts) must, often despite surface appearances, be of a determinate "structure" or "form," and that if other propositions are to be connected inferentially to this, they must be generated according to a rule that also has a determinate "structure" or "form." It is no exaggeration to say that Kelsen's Pure Theory is—on this score at least—an effort to do for legal value-language just what the *Tractatus* did (or tried to do) for fact-language. Kelsen's enterprise aims at "representation" *("Darstellung")*, and projects this aim in a strikingly similar manner. It is Kelsen's idea that this "representation" *clarifies*, and does this primarily by showing the "structure" normative propositions in law must have if they are to be valid. He searches for a rule entirely like the rule of *Tractatus* 6.002–6.01, one which will set the way in which norms must stand in relation to other norms to be norms. Kelsen continually stresses the difference between what juridical language *says* and what it *shows* (indeed, he makes this distinction the means of dividing the operations and language of legal science from those of juridical practice). The similarity here reaches many levels of the two writers' thinking; even the terminological similarities are impressive. Perhaps the most suggestive element of convergence, however, is to be found in an easily-overlooked parallel: Where Wittgenstein says that correct logical pictures are occasioned in the coincidence of pictorial form and logical form (2.181), Kelsen tells us that legal normativity is occasioned in the coincidence of objective validity and subjective validity (PTL, 47). Kelsen goes on to say that subjective meaning (validity) may be regarded as legally irrelevant in the case of an act in accordance with the "basic norm" (PTL, 51–52); this corresponds to Wittgenstein's preoccupation in the body of the *Tractatus* with the form of propositions, rather than the form of "the world."

Kelsen allows that "form" is indeed something that cannot be depicted in *the language of legal practice*; but he insists that it can be depicted within a language that *describes* that language (and at the same time "constitutes" its object). This second language, Kelsen thinks, is very like what Carnap calls the "language of science." Its essence is rules, and rules divided into much the same kinds Carnap specifies (that is, "formation" rules and "transformation" rules). The propositions of legal science are supposed to present the law in a complete and rigorous manner; indeed, they must show us the nature of legal norms more *clearly* than their original formulation and their applications do. Even so, these propositions, inasmuch as they *are* propositions, and hence true or false, omit the very element that makes legal normativity functional; namely, imperative force. Thus, "rules of law" are at once "ontologically" richer and poorer than the norms they represent: Their strength lies in their capacity for making the *sense* of norms clear; their incapacity (itself more a strength than a weakness) is their inability to convey legal normativity.

The discussion so far has underscored the similarities between Kelsen's use of "formal" and the uses of this and related terms by Carnap and Wittgenstein. Roughly the same language-patterns may be observed in other positivists. Yet there remains a crucial discrepancy: Though values (norms) and facts ("the world") are alike in the having of structure and tacit formal interrelations, the structures they *have* are radically different. The insight Russell, then Wittgenstein, and ultimately all the positivists developed springs from attention to logic. It is that the very possibility of descriptive fact-language resides in the potential for isomorphism in logically-formed propositions and the facts they picture. But the extensionalism that came out of this insight excluded norm-language (and this was perhaps the most notorious aspect of the positivist program) precisely because norms, which cannot be true-and-false, resist logification. What was left for Kelsen to discover, then, was that the general position of positivistic formalism could be retained for the analysis of norms if a fundamental change were made in interpretation of the logical composition of norms. Kelsen says that reformulation of the normative connective was what was needed, but he lacked the logician's sense for the details of the reformulation. It thus remained for von Wright, Ross, and others to rediscover the break Kelsen detected, and drive into it the wedge of deontic logic.

II
Kelsen's "General Theory of Norms"

INTRODUCTION

In the present chapter, I am concerned with only the broadest features of Kelsen's theory of norms. The claims to be scrutinized are those which Pure Theory makes about legal-norms-in-general, their relation to science, to logic, to truth, to legal systems. The objects to be examined are the features of norms and their presentation which purportedly unite all legal systems. Those are the elements by which the pure-theoretic scientist is supposed to consider diverse legal phenomena in such a way as to find in them "logical unity." Although the essential generality of these concerns will prevent the discussion from making contact with particulars (the hard data of statutes, rules, and authorizations), it will not prevent our seeing how Kelsen's theory of norms gets back to them. A theory for which it was impossible to show this means of access would be of no interest.

Here I follow Kelsen's theoretical progress from an analysis of the nature of law itself to an analysis of the structure in which Pure Theory presents law (a structure which must be erected, Kelsen holds, if the meaning in law is to be discovered). The two chapters which follow this

one build upon the foundation laid here. There, the analysis passes from the general to the specific. The aim will
be to identify the three "logics" within the general theory
of norms, and to proceed along similar lines of criticism in
assessing and explicating them. At the completion of this
critical examination of Kelsen's theory of norms, it will be
possible to weigh the adequacy of the system as a whole to
the establishment of claims Kelsen makes for it as a foundation for legal science.

THE NATURE OF LAW

Pure Theory, we have seen, lays claim to being "positive
law philosophy" or "legal positivism" chiefly on account
of the rigor it advocates in separation of the factual "is"
and the normative "ought." It is manifestly apparent,
however, that Kelsen sometimes straddles the line he has
so carefully drawn between fact and norm. He does this
particularly frequently in connection with one key term. It
is the centering term for Kelsen's explicative enterprise,
the term "law."

When Kelsen was accused recently of having failed to
provide a definition of law in any of his major works,[1] he
replied with alacrity and no small amount of annoyance.
It is true, he admitted, that no one-sentence analysis of the
concept is to be found in his works; but, in fact, whole sections (for example, RR, part II; PTL, sec. 6) of his main
works are given over to the definition of law (RPS, 1130).
Kelsen may, indeed, have defined law somewhat too often.
For, among all his various explications of the concept
there seems to run a fundamental ambivalence: On the one
hand, Kelsen wants to identify law as a social phenomenon, one among others, but differentiated from the rest by
its specific mode of coercion (PTL, 30–37, GTLS, 3–4,
18–19, WJ, 231–256, 274–276). On the other, he wants to
equate law with a norm or system of norms (PTL, 47, 65,
GTLS, 50, WJ, 209–216, 267). Accordingly, it is neces-

sary to distinguish two senses in which the term "law" appears in Pure Theory. I shall refer to these simply as (a) the factual sense, and (b) the normative sense. It will be a major part of the work of the following section to explain the distinction between these senses. It should be made clear at the outset, however, that Kelsen shows no sign of being disquieted by the apparent equivocation involved in his use of "law." On the contrary, it is quite evidently part of his polemical message on the nature of law that this duality of usage is demanded by the subject itself.

When he has in mind the factual sense, Kelsen adamantly insists that law is an essentially *empirical* phenomenon. It is, he says, a specific social technique, a technique which consists in the organization of force, inducing by coercive means those who are subject to it to obey a system of rules of behavior. To determine that this technique is in effect it is sufficient to ascertain whether social force is *in fact* organized in the supposed way; that is, whether the requisite rules and machinery for their execution *exist*. These determinations, Kelsen suggests, are matters of straightforward empirical observation. Thus, where Kelsen says, for example, at the outset of *General Theory of Law and State*, that "law is an order of human behavior," he is talking about an order which, like the order of customs, or that of etiquette, or that of gaming, is the way it is as a matter of *fact*.

Frequently, however, Kelsen emphatically identifies "law" with "norm" or "normative order"; and the point of this would seem to be to cast law out of the realm of fact altogether. It is important to point out that when Kelsen uses the term "order" in conjunction with "norm" or "normative" he is using it in a *special* sense. An "order" in these contexts is something independent of, and hence not discoverable from, empirical fact. Indeed, this sort of order does not even come into *being* prior (and the priority here is *logical* priority) to the implementation of pure-theoretic construction: "the multitude of general and individual legal norms, created by the legal organs, becomes a unitary system, a legal 'order', through the science of law" (PTL, 72). Laws in the normative sense, then, have nothing at all to do with what *is* the case, but only with what ought to be done *if* something should be the case. The point here is a strictly Kantian one: Whatever is normative is not spatio-temporal; whatever is outside of space and time cannot be accounted for in causal science. Causal science is our only means of empirical explanation; therefore, the legal-normative order—or any normative order for that matter—is not subject to empirical investigation. This is not to say that it is impossible to determine in any case whether a given norm exists. To determine whether a law qua norm exists, it is necessary and sufficient to ascertain whether that norm is valid in the system under consideration. And this determination is not a matter of mere observation, but of rational reconstruction. It may be suggested that although the existence of a given norm in its order may be a normative matter, the position of that norm relative to other norms, and hence, the meaning of that norm, might be determined by factual, rather than normative features of the legal system. Kelsen specifically rules out this possibility; he repeatedly insists that the reason for the validity of a norm is always and can only be the validity of another norm (GTLS, 111; WJ, 219; PTL, 193). In this way law in the normative sense is purportedly sealed against the intrusion of factual considerations.

It would seem that this leaves us with an absolute irreconcilability between Kelsen's two senses of "law." Throughout his writings Kelsen remains steadfastly committed to the nonreducibility of norm-creating fact. Nor will he allow that the existence of a norm may be understood through the behavior pattern of a society (its punishments, rewards, and so forth) (WJ, 217–218). How can Kelsen preserve his implicit conviction that law is both fact and norm without abandoning the rigid positivist "is"/"ought" division? How is it that Kelsen manages to keep this conflict from coming to the surface? The easy answer here (though not the final one) is that the two senses of "law" are, for the most part, put to work in different contexts.

The factual sense of "law" receives stress wherever Kelsen contrasts the *object* of legal science to that of natural law theory (for example, GTLS, xv; WJ, 235–238). Generally, when Kelsen employs the predicate "positive" in conjunction with "law" it is clear that he has the factual sense in mind. Kelsen deliberately contrasts what positive law *is* to what various theorists (particularly the "metaphysicians," or "philosophers") have made of it; he insists that law is not "self-evident," not necessary, but "arbitrary," "relative," and "real." Law, he says, is something apart from what theories of law are; it is the object of those theories, but the theories may be unsuccessful in "capturing" their object. As an antidote to theoretic inaccuracy, Kelsen proposes that legal science employ a form of cognition concerned only with "objectively determinable acts."

> Such a cognition can grasp only a positive order evidence by objectively determinable acts. This order is the positive law. Only this can be an object of science; only this is the object of a pure theory of law, which is a science, not metaphysics of the law. It presents the law as it is. . . . It seeks the real and possible, not the correct law. It is in this sense a radically realistic and empirical theory. (GTLS, 13)

Nowhere in this formula does Kelsen suggest that the concern of legal science is with an "ought." Though there is room for disagreement between Kelsen and others as to what law is "real," it remains clear that the object identified as law here is purportedly "real fact," and that its science must be, as Kelsen claims, both realistic and empirical.

Kelsen also appears to have in mind the factual sense of "law" when he, in striking contrast to Austin (GTLS, xvi; WJ, 280–283), identifies the state with its laws. In this connection, the state is regarded as a *thing* against which sanctions may be imposed and to which delicts may be imputed. Kelsen speaks of the state as a "juristic person," corresponding on the macroscopic scale to the legal individual, the agent, who is accused, tried, punished, and so forth. To the extent, then, that the agent is empirical (causally efficacious, scientifically observable, and the like) the state, and hence law, is empirical. But, the picture here is far from clear. For, when Kelsen says "juristic person" he apparently does not mean merely the flesh-and-blood individual, but a *term* in a legal relation. And the status of that term ("ought" or "is") is obscure.

The normative sense of "law," on the other hand, is employed by Kelsen mainly in those contexts where the formal structure of norm-hierarchies is at issue. When Kelsen is working directly with the theory of norms, he generally uses "law" and "norm" interchangeably, often appositively. This facile equation is not, however, a casual or inadvertent one. Its effect is to underscore the prescriptivity of legal orders. And it is one of Kelsen's chief interests to show prescriptivity to be law's *principium individuationis*. Kelsen would like his readers to think that Pure Theory has performed a distinctive achievement in exposing to jurists and philosophers what they have hitherto disguised or left disguised—the normative essence of law. This sense of essentialistic discovery is most evident in PGNR, but it is also discernable in Kelsen's later writings (WJ, 359–363, GTLS, 44, 162–163, PTL, 75–76).

Yet it is patently counter to Kelsen's positivistic interest to equate the essence of law with the essence of norm *simpliciter*. Frequently, but perhaps too casually, Kelsen points out that the "ought" essential to law is a *species* of normativity, a species not to be assimilated in its analysis to the more familiar species—the ethical, political, and social. It would be poor strategy in arguing for the specialty of legal norms simply to point out some varieties of such norms and bluntly *declare* that these norms are known to employ a unique sort of "ought"-value. This strategy is sometimes imputed to Kelsen, but it is not the stand he characteristically takes on the matter. Admittedly, the question of ethical-normative assessment of a legal order (that is, as to its justice) is an issue Kelsen does not address in the context of Pure Theory, and such an assessment might prove elemental in establishing a connection between moral and legal norms. But, as Kelsen correctly points out, legal science as he has construed it has as its task description of structural properties and "formal" interrelationships, *not* evaluation (PTL, 68).

The question then becomes one of whether value-neutral description may discover a structural difference between the forms of legal and moral norms. And to this question Kelsen has an unequivocally affirmative answer:

> The legal norm has a more complicated structure than the moral norm. The legal norm does not, like the moral norm, refer to the behavior of one individual only, but to the behavior of two individuals at least: the individual who commits or may commit the delict, the delinquent, and the individual who ought to execute the sanction. If the sanction is directed against another individual than the immediate delinquent, the legal norm refers to three individuals. (GTLS, 58)

This difference in number of addressed parties is, if Kelsen is right, a crucial formal difference between the species of legal and moral norms. But, what of the other species— those of etiquette, politics, protocol, games, and so on? Though Kelsen gives no exhaustive answer to this question, his intent is clear: Proper "structural analysis" will demonstrate that the internal (logical) form of legal norms is unique. Ultimately, this is because "imputation" in the legal order turns out to produce an entirely distinctive sort of ought-connection. But discussion of this point must be deferred until more general features of Kelsen's thinking about norms have been put in place.

An obvious disadvantage of equating law with a unique species of structurally identified norms is that it excludes much of what ordinary usage dictates as proper to the notion. Undeniably, common sentiment is closer to identifying law with fact (or some set of facts) than with norm, and not at all close to identifying it with the hidden complex phenomenon Kelsen supposes. It is one thing to suggest that "norm" is a necessary component in the meaning of law, and quite another to insist that it is its necessary and sufficient condition. If all aspects of legal orders apart from normative aspects are not part of law, then all of what Kelsen describes when he depicts law in the *factual* sense is strictly speaking extralegal, and patently irrelevant to whatever is to count as a serious theory of *law*. The brunt of Kelsen's "structural analysis" goes towards showing that the "logical innards" of legal norms as well as their hierarchical organization are quite different from what practitioners of law and prior theorists supposed them to be. But this means that these men must never have quite correctly recognized what it was with which they were dealing. It means that *all* of their talk about the law had to be mistaken. It means that they were not practitioners of *law* or theorists of *law* at all. These are paradoxical conclusions which do not fall easily to Kelsen's vigorous protestations.

Recently, Kelsen has grown more aware of this line of objection to the normative arm of his discussion of the nature of law. In the second edition of *Pure Theory* (the first English edition), he prefaces his remarks about the suspect norm-law equation with references to various words for "law" in different languages. He then observes:

> Our task will be to examine whether the social phenomena described by these words have common characteristics by

which they may be distinguished from similar phenomena, and whether these characteristics are significant enough to serve as elements for a concept of social-scientific cognition. The result of such an investigation could conceivably be that the word "law" and its equivalents in other languages designates so many different objects that they cannot be comprehended in one concept. However, this is not so. Because, when we compare the objects that have been designated by the word "law" by different peoples at different times, we see that all these objects turn out to be *orders of human behavior.* As "order" is a system of norms whose unity is constituted by the fact that they all have the same reason for their validity; and the reason for the validity of a normative order is a basic norm—as we shall see—from which the validity of all norms of the order is derived. (PTL, 31)[2]

This statement suggests that Kelsen may intend the factual "law" to specify a *denotation* (extension, reference) for the object whose *connotation* (meaning, sense) is "norm." This interpretation is perhaps supported by Kelsen's occasional distinction between defining a concept and defining its "object matter," or "object." But, as the citation shows, if the sense-reference distinction was in Kelsen's mind, it was that distinction at a far remove from the standard Fregean model. Instead of supposing *en base* that the references of "law" share a common univocal sense (that being precisely what qualifies them as instances for the same term), Kelsen conceives it as possible (though not the case) that referential diversity might prevent there *being* such a sense.[3] Kelsen makes a somewhat heavy-handed epistemological (or perhaps psychological) move to void this possibility: He declares that upon comparing the several references "we see" that there is one connotation underlying them all, this sense being tied to "norm" through the intermediary of "order." There is, of course, an obvious *petitio* in the appeal to what can only be a sort of "intuitive grasp" to legitimate the purported synonymy. But beyond this lies a subtler and graver problem: Although Kelsen presents the analysis in such a way as to suggest that the inventory of uses is undertaken prior to and in preparation for the operation of "social-scientific cognition," this clearly cannot be the case. For, in order for the scientific use-pollster to identify as "orders of behavior" in the relevant sense all the objects that ordinary usage designates "law," he quite clearly must know *antecedently* that order is systematically bound to "basic norm," indeed, that its unity is constituted by this "basic norm." And this recognition patently depends on prior acceptance of the peculiar mode of theoretic "cognition" provided in pure-theoretic construction. I have already noted, in reference to the "constitutive" character Kelsen attributes to legal-scientific cognition, that the very notion of "legal order" is supposed to be posterior to, and not antecedent to pure-theoretic construction (see PTL, 72). Now, if the unitary character of the legal order appears only *through* the operations of legal science, it clearly cannot be cited to identify the subject matter of that science. The circularity involved in this argument is compressed in the following passage:

> A single norm is a valid legal norm, if it corresponds to the concept of "law" and is part of a legal order; and it *is* part of a legal order if its validity is based on the basic norm of that order. (PTL, 31)

In this context if the normative sense of "law" were exclusively accepted, it would be enough to say "A single norm is a valid norm, if it corresponds to the concept of 'law' "; all the rest would be redundant. If, on the other hand, the normative sense should be taken to yield only connotation, the remainder of the citation would not be redundant, but either tautologous or materially inadequate: It is tautologous if "basic" in "basic norm" remains unanalyzed, or is analyzed into "highest in the norm-hierarchy," where "highest" remains a norm-bound notion.

Surely, in either case, there is no definitional gain; for this interpretation will only explain "normativity" and "validity" by reference to the *more* normative, and the *more* valid. It is materially inadequate, however, if "basic norm" is taken as ultimately referring to non-normative elements of legal systems. This is a fundamental condition of Kelsen's approach: Facts may *condition* norms; but they cannot determine them. And since what is at stake is the *criterion* by which a single norm may be judged to be valid, a conditioning relation is manifestly too weak.

The "easy answer" to problems posed by Kelsen's fact-norm dualism was supposed to be that the two opposing senses of "law" apply in different contexts. But it is now apparent that, at least in many passages (some of them undeniably crucial to Kelsen's overall program), the two senses converge or overlap. Worse still, Kelsen is, from time to time, guilty of playing off one sense against the other to gain special advantage. An excellent example of this dodge is to be found in his treatment of the anomalous situation which results when one and the same action is commanded by one norm of a given legal order, while forbidden by another (for example, PTL, 25f.). While many theorists might find these two norms contradictory and hence incompatible, Kelsen is forced by the manner in which he analyzes single norms generally to declare that they *can* be covalid, even if not jointly "satisfiable."[4] In the manner of "description" to which Pure Theory is committed, both have the value "valid." And assuming accuracy of presentation, one expects that in the legal order itself (that is, what the description presents) the two norms are also covalid. But we are surprised to find that Kelsen allows that this need not be the case. The two opposing norms in situ

> express two conflicting political tendencies, a teleological conflict. The situation is possible but politically unsatisfac-

tory. Therefore legal orders usually contain rules according to which one of the two norms is invalid or may be invalidated. (PTL, 25–26)

This passage is remarkable in that it openly countenances the intrusion of teleological (as opposed to logical, or "transcendental-logical") and political (that is, "ideological") factors into the makeup of "legal order." This can only mean that the *factual* sense holds sway here *in a contest with* the normative sense. Factual "law" appears here to include, by dint of fact (indeed *political* fact) supernormative "rules" which have the extraordinary capacity to invalidate that which would have been valid were the legal order identical with the constructional system of norms. The problem would not arise, of course, if, instead of "legal order" Kelsen had said "political forces," "ideological pressures," or the like, setting these off against the strictly scientific sense of "law." But to do this would have called into question the identification of law and state, which Kelsen makes fundamental on other grounds. Worse still, it would not have permitted "invalidation" in the requisite sense, as the validity of norms in the legal order is allegedly independent of such extranormative forces. Here then, facticity is played off against normativity for double effect—both to "correct" Pure Theory against the record of actual juridical practice, and to overcome its discomforting helplessness in the face of norm-conflicts.

The "easy answer," then, is not the correct answer. If, however, some final resolution to the problems of Kelsen's fact-norm dualism is to be found, it must emerge from the details of the pure-theoretical norm-logics themselves. If the rift which appears here is to be sealed, it will be only through Kelsen's treatment of features of legal norms and norm-systems which are peculiar to them, features whose anomalous station in the field of norms invites, or even requires, the admittedly awkward accounting which Kelsen provides. Before we approach the detailed analyses of Pure Theory a considerable amount of conceptual terrain must be surveyed. From the present vantage, however, we may glimpse part of Kelsen's solution. And this will lead us into the subject of the next section.

In "The Pure Theory of Law and Analytic Jurisprudence," Kelsen says that when the legal-scientific theorist regards law, he regards it as "a system of valid norms" and no more than that. Accordingly, we expect Kelsen to apply the *normative* sense of "law" throughout the article with customary positivistic rigor. But he makes it clear at once that the normativity which the system regarded by legal science enjoys is a *factually conditioned* validity. For one thing,

> (scientific) jurisprudence regards a legal norm as valid only if it belongs to a legal order that is by and large efficacious; that is, if the individuals whose conduct is regulated by the legal order in the main actually do conduct themselves as they should according to the legal order. (WJ, 268)

"Efficacy" (elsewhere "effectiveness") is plainly a straight-forward matter of empirical fact, for Kelsen specifically contrasts it with *validity*, which is the condition of assertability peculiar to *Sollen*. Moreover, legal science is said to be forced, in order to comprehend the norms of legal systems adequately, to take into account *some* facts which enter into the *content* of legal norms. The "validity/efficacy" and "content/form" distinctions will be examined later at some length. Here, however, I would like to draw attention to the *way* in which these distinctions are used to support a yet more fundamental pure-theoretical distinction, namely, that between the role of the jurisprude in *regarding* law and his role in *presenting* it.

When, as in the above-cited passages, Pure Theory is pictured as merely *regarding* law, it stands apart from it as science to subject matter. Accordingly, institutional peculiarities, effectiveness, and other contextually relative empirical considerations are relevant. When, however, Pure Theory is pictured as engaging in *Darstellung*, (presentation, representation), these considerations are dismissed. As a presentational science Pure Theory is pure in that it purportedly seals itself off from *Sein*, articulating only a network of strictly normative interrelations. These seemed straightforward and simple enough when we first heard of them. But now, after the appearance of "factual conditioning," the supervenience of effectiveness, and so on, the picture is considerably clouded. If the object that Pure Theory regards is admitted to be the sort of object in which factual elements have at least some shaping influence ("conditioning" effect, or whatever), we may well ask how its *presentation* can remain faithful to that object while rigorously eschewing facts.

Kelsen's answer to this—which must be put together from a variety of sources—is of a strikingly linguistic turn. The legal norm, he repeatedly insists (for example, PTL, 10), is not an act of will, but the meaning of an act of will. Specifically, it is the meaning of an act of will directed at a well-defined piece of human behavior (ILR, 1). In "presenting" legal norms as integral parts of a valid system of norms, however, legal science *describes* the ought-character of their meaning by means of is-expressions. And *these* expressions, the "constitutive" statements of the jurisprudent's rational reconstruction, appear in the form of assertions of fact (PTL, 71). The distinction between legal norms and the statements by which legal science represents them is something close to the core of the fact-norm duality in Pure Theory. Law as it occurs in the world of social experience (that is, the world of command and coercion, legislation, and promulgation) is what it is; Kelsen simply does not occupy himself with characterizing *that* phenomenon. In fact, it does not appear to matter much to him whether this thing is spoken of as fact, norm, or admixture. What *is* important, however, is that the phenomenon is recognized as a *meaningful* one: In it is imbedded a specific, determinate meaning. Pure Theory's task is to carry this meaning over into words and sentences, forming propositions. Now there is no denying that the resultant semantic phenomena are in many ways unlike the original social phenomena; but one common feature unites them, namely, the meaning they share.

There is nothing so very odd about this, prima facie. Propositions are, after all, perfectly natural (perhaps *the* natural) vehicles for meaning. And there is no denying that the law itself *means* something; that is, when a law is valid, something is *meant*. So there seems no overwhelming objection to saying that Pure Theory may regard the law in such a way as to allow its meaning to be cast into propositions.[5] One might quarrel with Kelsen's conviction that this meaning is (or is always) "that men *ought* to behave in a certain way," but it is reasonable, or at least not *obviously* incorrect, to suppose that the propositions Pure Theory describes will themselves be nonfactual. This allows that there may be an enormous difference between the law in situ and the semantic construction legal science makes from it. But seen in this light, Kelsen's original proposal that law is *both* fact and norm is intelligible. It is, at least in part, a claim that the program of presentation he has devised is not only feasible, but successful; that is, that it *does* carry over into the language of normative expression what was *meant* in factual existence.

THE PRESENTATION OF LAW IN PURE THEORY

Having glanced at the rather complex portrait Kelsen gives of law as an object for legal science, we may now pass on to examine the relationship which Kelsen maintains must exist between legal science and its object if that science is to achieve success. Judging from the relative emphasis with which he enunciates them, it appears that Kel-

sen's chief theses touching this matter are the following:
(1) *The propositions which comprise legal science* (called
Rechtsregein, "rules of law") *present* (or present) *the law*;
(2) *Rules of law are purely descriptive.*[6]

These theses have been the focus of a great amount of
misunderstanding over the aim of Kelsen's work. The
general trend among critics has been to construe the sense
of "descriptivity" to which they lead so narrowly as to
cause the presentational enterprise to appear trivial and
pedantic. If, it is argued, legal science represents law by
describing it in the way a witness might describe an accident or in the way a photographer or "representational"
painter might describe a subject, it is ultimately superfluous. Secondhand accounts are fine where the thing itself is
ephemeral, or past, or momentary; but where the thing
itself is at hand, publicly accessible, and of high practical
importance in its distinctive original form, such recapitu-
lations are of questionable value. To these critics, Kelsen's
creation of "rules of law" is a species of mimesis: It takes
us to a third remove from legal facts, and threatens to sub-
vert our interest from more immanent concerns.

The discussion above, however, has made it abundantly
clear that by "represent" Kelsen means something quite
different from the strictly correlative "mirroring" this line
of criticism assumes. Kelsen has, in fact, made an emphatic rejoinder on the point:

> The norm constituted by the legislator (prescribing execution
> against a person who does not fulfill a marriage promise and
> does not compensate for the damage) and the statement for-
> mulated by the science of law and describing this norm (that
> execution ought to be carried out against a person who does
> not fulfill his marriage promise and does not compensate for
> the damage caused)—these expressions are logically different.
> It is therefore convenient to differentiate them terminological-
> ly as "legal norm" and "rule of law." It follows from what
> has been said that the rules of law formulated by the science
> of law are not simply repetitions of the legal norms created by

the legal authority. The objection that rules of law are super-fluous is not so obviously unfounded, however, as the view that a natural science is superfluous beside nature, for nature does not manifest itself in spoken and written words, as the law does. The view that a rule of law formulated by the sci-ence of law is superfluous beside the legal norm created by the legislator can be met only by pointing out that such a view would amount to the opinion that a scientific presentation of a criminal law is superfluous beside this criminal law, that the science of law is superfluous beside the law. (PTL, 73–74)

Although this passage skirts the "mimetic" criticism nice-ly enough by pointing to a telling *logical* difference be-tween representational and repetitive description, in doing so it raises a number of challenging questions.

First, Kelsen has conceded to his critics what was not called for. He admits that the superfluity critique of the science of law enjoys a certain plausibility which the same critique does not enjoy with respect to natural science. He suggests that it does not because of any inherent weakness in the pure-theoretic account of law, but merely because of the likeness between what comprises legal science and what constitutes its object. Legal science, as Kelsen depicts it, relates words to words, rather than words to things; and this, he says, is enough to make it seem superfluous. But this response makes very little sense. Pointing out that a certain science and its subject matter are both verbal does not go far toward explaining what it is about the use legal science makes of its words that seems repetitive. Obvious-ly, there are many "sciences" (etymology, lexicography, linguistics) which use words in various ways to say things about other words; and none of these is superfluous in the sense that Kelsen's critics think Pure Theory to be. Kelsen's distinction between word-word and word-thing sciences misses the point his critics have in mind; they claim that legal science on the Kelsenite model is superfluous not be-cause it is verbal, but because it is *redundant*.

Turning again to Kelsen's examples (cited in the immediately previous paragraph), and anticipating the method of analysis to be exhibited and discussed later, we may record the following formulae, for a "legal norm" and its correspondent "rule of law":

(L-1) If x promises marriage to y and neither fulfills this promise nor pays the consequent damage, then a specific sanction S is to be imposed against x.

(L*-1) "If x promises marriage to y and neither fulfills this promise nor pays the consequent damage, then a specific sanction S is to be imposed against x" is valid (or "is law," or "is German law" and so forth).[7]

The difference, as Kelsen puts it between L-1 and L*-1 is just that L-1 prescribes a certain execution S, and L*-1 describes this prescription by affirming that S ought to be executed. L-1, as it stands, is only a piece of instruction; L*-1 says that this particular piece of instruction has "credit" as law.

One point needs clarification here: Let us say that the Iowa legislature votes a measure whose language is as follows: "Uncompensated breach of marriage contract is punishable by 10 years in prison or a fine of $5,000, or both." The question now arises (a question for the jurisprudent) whether this expression *itself* becomes law, or whether something else, related to it, becomes law (that is, its *meaning*, the intent of the legislators, what the courts will decide in respect to it, and so forth). In one sense, of course, this expression becomes "what the law says" on the matter of breach-of-marriage contract. But is there an important difference at work here between what the law says and what it *is?* Taking Kelsen's point of view, the question becomes: Is the statutory expression itself a legal norm, or does it only *embody* a norm? The corresponding metalegal question is: Does the legal scientist who provides the relevant "rule of law" simply describe (or redescribe) the statement "Uncompensated breach of marriage contract . . . ," or does he rather find in that statement a valid norm (perhaps of a different form) which he then describes (perhaps with L*-1)? Kelsen gives us no help on this score, for he seems to speak both ways. The ensuing discussion mitigates the difficulty somewhat by stressing the "constitutive" role of "description"; this will mean that a distinction will ultimately be drawn between what the legislators meant and what the statement (if indeed it is one) they made means. It will be shown that the legal scientist's role in the matter is that of unpacking the *real* meaning (which Kelsen supposes to be frequently disguised) in *whatever* particular formulation the legislators might have chosen.

According to Kelsen's critics, however, there is little room for L*-1 to say anything which L-1 has not already said; at best it can perhaps metalinguistically point to features that must have been in L-1, but implicitly. There seems to be absolutely no room for what Kelsen calls "constitutive" amplification. It is this apparent feature of rules of law that the superfluity-critics have attacked rather than anything to do with their verbal character. They want to say: Just as, according to the standard positivist analysis of "true," " 'p' is true" is only another way of saying "p," tells us no more than "p" does, has the same supporting evidential conditions, and so forth, what is expressed in "L*-1" can always be reduced without significant loss to "L-1." If it is true that L*-1 says only "L-1" it is unlikely that Pure Theory can provide the sort of explanatory force which distinguishes valuable science from copywork.

But of course this line of criticism overlooks a key feature of L*-expression. It is admittedly easy to overlook, for it is tacitly assumed in most of Kelsen's discussions of the relationship between rules of law and their correlative norms. This feature comes up for attention in other contexts generally, often when Kelsen is trying to expose the internal logic of norms themselves. Briefly, it is that L*-expressions either recast L-expressions in a specific and determinate form, or, as in the above case, certify that these L-expressions *may* be so recast. Any of a number of forms of expression could have been employed to "constitute" the norm L-1; these forms are as various as the modes of speech or writing which legal authorities might choose to use in making a given law. We all recognize that the language of several formulations might differ while all of these formulations, if passed upon, would make the "same law." I have, as a matter of fact, stated L-1 in a way no legislator would be likely to employ in drafting a statute; but it is important to see that (with due specification of the sanction S) even this form of words *could* be used in making law. The same is true of a potentially endless list of variants:

> (L-1a) No one in this state is permitted to promise to marry a party and subsequently willingly *not* marry that party without either paying a compensation or suffering [sanction S].
>
> (L-1b) The penalty for breach of marriage promise is [sanction S]. A promisor who has paid due compensation will be excused from penalty.
>
> (L-1c) Payment of due compensation is required in the case of broken marriage pact in this state; if such a compensation is not rendered within [a certain number of] days of the prospective marriage date the delinquent party will receive [sanction S].
>
> (And so on)

The instructive feature of legal-scientific representation is that—once it is cast in its expanded, fully explicit form—there is but *one* rule of law for all these expressions. There is a "basic form" for the rules of law which correspond to the "independent" type of legal norm. Here, the claim is that though the language by which one refers to rules of law might be various, all differences may always be eliminated by ulterior reference to the "expanded, fully explicit" rule in its "basic form." It makes no difference at this point whether we say that each L-1, L-1a, L-1b, and so on, *is* a norm, or that *in* each of them a norm (possibly identical in all cases) may be discovered. For, if there is but one norm for all the expressions, it is, according to Pure Theory, only discernable and specifiable *after* the rule of law to which it corresponds has been exactly formulated. The norm, after all, is a specific *meaning*; and this meaning becomes clear only *through* the presentational operation by which the legal scientist obtains the rule of law. This is *not* to say that the norm in question is unreal or disfunctional prior to this point. Rather, just as the manipulation and application of arithmetic preceded the achievement of number theory, which established its meaning, norms may be put to work before their nature is *known*. It is undeniable that number theory has strengthened arithmetic, not only cognitively, but by providing a foundation for new extentions of mathematics. It is Kelsen's hope that Pure Theory's presentation of legal norms will do the same for law.

The charge of redundance fails, however, not so much because there is *one* form for L*-1, L*-1a, L*-1b, and so on, but because in this particular form, the rule of law says something about the norm or norms involved which they (at least some of the formulations, and potentially all of them) do not say about themselves. In the series of statements L-1, L-1a, . . . L-1z there need not be an explicit occurence of "ought," the normative operator. In the expressions which comprise legal statutes, occurrences of the term "ought" are, in fact, extremely rare. In L*-1, on the other hand, the "ought" is made explicit; it *must* occur. To say "L-1 is valid" is to say "If the condition (legal antecedent) described in L-1 holds for x, then the sanction S is obligatory for x." This connection between delict and sanction is, Kelsen proposes, an essential part of what is *meant* in a legal norm, and thus an implicit part of what is meant in any of the expressions by which legislators and judges constitute norms. However variously it is indicated in legal normative statements, legal science will identify and enunciate the connection as "ought." Since, on this view, the "ought" *is* part of the meaning of a legal norm, and since *this* part of its meaning might not appear prior to its expression by the legal scientist, the true legal order (that is, the validity of its norms) may properly be said to be something produced at the hands of Pure Theory, rather than courts and legislatures.

The same observation, of course, is true of the specification of sanctions and delicts, and of the characterization of the ought-connection itself. In sum: the rule of law has the role of disclosing (or insisting on the disclosability of) formal features that are part of the meaning of norms, but which are frequently missing in the expressions by which they are made. It is Kelsen's distinctive twist to insist that the characteristics which legal science discovers in norms are not accidental features (features of legal politics, or of the standard pattern of norm-employment *tout court*), but rather "logical" features, and that their appropriate analysis is not merely close inspection, but *logical* construction.

Typically, when countering the standard "superfluity-critique" of his system of legal science, Kelsen simply points to the fact that this view amounts to the claim that legal science is superfluous beside law (PTL, 74). Effective as this rebuttal may be among some circles of Continental jurisprudes, it clearly carries no weight among many other legal theorists. The prospect of ruling superfluous and hence defunct the "rationalistic" project of *Rechtswissenschaft* is hardly one from which the Scandinavian and American Realists, for instance, would shrink. So, when Kelsen points out that the superfluity of rules of law, if proved, would entail the superfluity of legal science itself, we may assume that these theorists happily accept the inference, argue for the truth of the antecedent, and applaud both downfalls. But, when Kelsen speaks of a "logical difference" between norm-expressions and the statements legal science makes out of them, he makes the kind of claim which has force outside the coteries of *Rechtswissenschaftler.*

The core of this logical difference is a straightforward distinction of modality: Simply put, rules of law are *alethic* ("assertoric"), necessarily either true or false, while norms of law are *deontic* ("prescriptive"), necessarily neither true nor false in use. Conversely, norms are necessarily either valid or invalid, while rules of law are necessarily neither valid nor invalid.[8] A remarkable percentage of his interpreters fail to appreciate the impact of this thesis upon Kelsen's account of a descriptive legal science. Kelsen's nagging insistence that rules of law are purely descriptive—or more emphatically that they are "valuefree descriptions" (PTL, 79) is *not* a claim that they are photocopies of a certain degree of definition, and *not* a claim that they are images of normative expressions in which the norm-making elements have been eliminated or neutralized. These prevalent misconstructions fail to catch the force of *contrast* Kelsen intends to gain in using "describe." Pure Theory does not set "descriptive" off against "subjective," or against "inaccurate," or even against "evaluative." Kelsen uses "descriptive" to strike a contrast with "*pre*scriptive," underlining the distinctive way in which conditions apart from truth-conditions enter into the meaning and "verifiability"[9] of legal norms.

There is very likely no exhaustive way of specifying which among all legal expressions are prescriptive. The usual tactic is to pin prescriptivity to the presence of certain words—"ought," "right," "should," and the like. But, clearly, a great many sentences which include no such terms *can* function prescriptively. To take a familiar example, "The door is shut!" may be used in such a way that no question is left that a prescription is being made in uttering it (This is Kelsen's example at PTL, 6). It may, in fact, be the *same* prescription that is present in the standard-form normative expression "You ought to shut the door." Thus it becomes clear that no term or set of terms is to be regarded as *essential* to the making of prescriptions. The clearest recourse in the face of these conditions is to define "prescription" according to the *function* of prescriptive expressions. This is exactly what R. M. Hare, G. H. von Wright, and other leading exponents of what has come to be called "prescriptivism" in ethics have sought to do. Obviously, the chief functional difference between prescriptions and descriptions is that the former aim at guiding or directing conduct in a way the latter do not. Unfortunately, prescriptivists have not been wholly successful in stating just *how* prescriptions work in bringing together moral (or legal) words and moral (or legal) deeds.

If a theory of prescriptions is to be of use to the analysis of legal norms, two aspects of prescriptive use must be clarified: (1) The effect of the "performative force"[10] of these expressions upon legal institutions and metalegal constructions, and (2) The effect of their conduct-guiding function upon both the inner constitution of norms in a legal system and the logic of interrelations among norms. The first of these concerns is particularly telling. For Kelsen does not want to display systems of legal norms as mere *series* of commands, permissions, authorizations, and the like; he wants that which legal science presents to constitute a *Stufenbau*, an ordered hierarchy. To *some* extent (the question of degree is one which Kelsen has never fully answered) the familiar rules of formal logic ("Rules of Inference," "Law of Contradiction," and so forth) play an important role in the organization of the *Stufenbau*. But, whatever the extent, the presence of logical principles causes a problem for legal science; for the laws of logic operate only where expressions take truth values, while expressions that are used performatively are—by all accounts—neither true nor false.

Even though it meant a radical departure from established lines of Continental jurisprudential thinking, Kelsen committed Pure Theory to the view that their performative use permanently barred legal norms qua prescriptions from having truth values.[11] This, in fact, is the reason that Pure Theory is inevitably *indirect* in its presentation of norms. Once the nature of their use is discovered to prevent norms from being organized by logical rules, the *only* way a "unified" system can be made for them is by creating a parallel system of straightforwardly constative (that is, assertoric, true-or-false) expressions, ordering *these* logically, and showing that the connections between the two sets of expressions are such that the same order must hold for both. Thus, Kelsen is forced to do the real work of logical structuring in the domain of rules of law, rather than that of norms themselves. Since legal norms, being prescriptions (that is, commands, permissions, authorizations), can be neither true nor false, the question arises: How can logical principles, especially the Principles of the Exclusion of Contradiction and the Rules of Inference, be applied to the relation between legal norms if these principles are applicable only to assertions that can be true or false? The answer is:

> Logical principles are applicable, indirectly, to legal norms to the extent that they are applicable to the rules of law which describe the legal norms and which can be true or false. Two legal norms are contradictory and can therefore not both be valid at the same time, if the two rules of law that describe them are contradictory; and one legal norm may be deduced from another if the rules of law that describe them can form a logical syllogism. (PTL, 74)

This is, by all odds, an intriguing move. The rationale of reconstruction, of course, is to show what legal norms and norm-systems really are (allowing that their essential natures may be disguised in the form in which they are ordinarily displayed). But it now appears that in order to reconstruct norms, one must construct a different, and completely *non*normative, order of expressions, and then use *its* structure to present the purportedly *real* structure of the norms themselves. Obviously, the chief problem here will be that of keeping within a given rule of law correct information about whatever it was in the corresponding norm that made the latter normative, while "presenting" this information in a rigorously nonnormative way, so as to provide for the organizational use of logical rules. Unhappily, Kelsen skirts this problem, for the most part, rather than coping with it. Whenever he comes to it, he appears to be working on two flanks at once: When he wishes to demonstrate the constativity of rules of law, he stresses their *descriptivity*; when he wishes to assure critics that nothing essential has been lost from the original norm, he stresses their *presentational function*. But Kelsen does little to coordinate the two prongs of this offense. In fact, what he does say seems to leave him open to the charge that Pure Theory has made whatever gains it claims only at the expense of raising a dilemma: Either presentation and descriptivity are incompatible functions, or rules of law are not, as he claims them to be, theoretically informative in their own right.

Kelsen's thinking in this area is invariably guided by the correspondence model of truth-confirmation. That is to say, Kelsen believes that we can determine with certainty whether, for example, "German law is created by voice-vote in the *Bundesrat*" is a true assertion (a well-founded judgment) because we have standard, universally-accepted methods of checking on the relevant experiental evidence. And we can, he says, determine whether "German murderers ought to be punished by decapitation" can be asserted in a true rule of law in a *somewhat* analogous fashion. The temptation here is to say that rules of law are known to be true just because the corresponding norms they describe are known to be valid. But this, as it turns out, will not quite do. For one thing—as we have already seen—it is not on the prior recognition of normative validity that such judgments can be made, since the validity of legal normative orders itself first appears at the end of rule-presentation. Therefore, the solution of this problem, like that of the superfluity-critique, will perforce be an *indirect* one.

This brings us to the second requirement for clarifying prescriptive use, that having to do with the effect of legal prescriptions on the inner constitution of norms and norm systems. Because rules of law have a form in which they say something about norms which is not apparent in the norms themselves, it is to be expected that the kind of cognition which goes into knowing that a rule of law is assertable is different from the kind of cognition involved in prescribing the corresponding norm. But what in addition to all that is apparent in the norm must be known regarding the rule of law to justify its assertion? The answer proposed at PTL, 79 and elsewhere is, roughly put, that to know legal norm L-n is just to know that something is obligatory, while to know the corresponding rule L*-n is to know that *because* something is obligatory a determinate relation holds between given elements of a reconstructed formal order. Here, Kelsen is suggesting that to say "T*-n is true" is not only to say "T-n," but to add that the validity of T-n can be checked (perhaps by him who asserts T*-n) on account of its position in a theoretic system—part of the evidence being that this system is ordered in a certain way, unified, supervened by a "basic norm," adequated to the standards of "legal-scientific cognition," and so on. This is not to say, as some have intimated, that Kelsen gives over at this point to a "coherence theory," as will be shown shortly. Kelsen calls this determinate relation a "functional connection"; this is to say that it holds because of functions assigned to specific elements in the "structure" of the rule and of the rule-system. And he says that the proper consideration of such relations should be "structural analysis," as announced in the Preface to the *General Theory*.

Remembering what was said in chapter 1 about "structural analysis," it becomes apparent that what happens to legal-scientific cognition in the process of providing rules of law is the invocation of an order of *meaning* not apparent in, but implicit in, norms *in situ*, and the imposition, from out of the logic of *that* order, of standards of form, relevancy, and support for the norms themselves. Kelsen, it must be said, is only too willing to shunt the entire question of the nature of this order into the murky area of "legal-scientific cognition." He is more concerned with the problem of producing such an order than with the equally challenging question of showing why the particular order he produces is the right one. But, although what Kelsen actually says on this score is often confused and misleading, what he *wants* to say (that is, what squares with the program he actually works out) is fundamentally simple: Just as rules of law are found to differ from norms by virtue of making explicit features in their inner logic which are not apparent from the expressions in which they are made and applied, so the representational order they compose differs from the original system of norms by virtue of exposing the systematic nature it *really* has, and which would be seen immediately by an omniscient jurist. The difference, then, is one of logical explicitness; the constant factor is *meaning*. Here, the personality of the legal scientist is not an issue, since what he *means* in asserting the construction (alternatively, in expressing a constitutive judgment) can only be something that is *presupposed* in the system of norms it represents. Again, the jurists and legislators who originally made the norm-order may not have at the same time *meant* its systematic character; but the logical structure pure-theoretical analysis reveals is nevertheless part of the *meaning* of the norm-order they created. This suggests just the sort of criterion Kelsen needs for the adequacy of a norm's presentation: When, and only when, a given norm has been cast into a form that exposes the "functional connection" between the essential parts giving it normative meaning (which parts may be disguised or only assumed in its formulation as law) the position open to its corresponding rule of law will become evident. And once this locus is identified, the norm itself may be said to be valid. Norm L-n is valid, therefore, only if rule L*-n has found a determinate place within its order.

THE "INTERPRETATION" OF LAW IN PURE THEORY

Kelsen sometimes brings the notions of "norm" and "rule of law" together in an abrupt and puzzling way. "The rule of law," he allows, "says: If A is, B ought to be. The rule of law is a norm (in the descriptive sense of that term)" (GTLS, 46). This comes as a surprising turn; Kelsen's lengthy defense of the norm/fact distinction has left us unprepared for any suggestion that norms can have a *descriptive* sense. Indeed, norms seem in Kelsen's account to be the very *type* of things that are devoid of descriptive content. This would appear to be a minimum condition for their prescriptivity. But the remark cited from GTLS is by no means an isolated instance of this peculiar claim. Kelsen says much the same thing in PTL and in corresponding passages in other expositions of his theory of norms.

Kelsen not only countenances the "descriptive 'ought' "; he makes it a centrally important part of his program of jurisprudence. On the face of it this notion seems to undercut the strict value/fact dichotomy on which Kelsen bases the Pure Theory of Law. Kelsen does not hesitate to say that law is a system of norms, and that a norm is to be regarded as a legal norm only as part of such a system. He says moreover that legal norms, which are the "meanings of acts of will," mean the existence of "oughts" if they mean anything. And he straightforwardly declares that the "oughts" in legal norms fill the function of prescribing conduct. He specifically denigrates the project of sociological jurisprudence by charging that no study of what *is* can ever be adequate to the task of comprehending these "oughts." What, then, is the point of crossing this current of thought to insist that some legal "oughts" are descriptive? Nowhere does Kelsen provide a clearcut answer to this question. And in the absence of an answer, his critics have been quick to charge him with self-contradiction and obfuscation.[12] Kelsen's response to the critics has been simply to reaffirm his commitment to the stand he has taken. His most recent affirmation is exemplary.

> It is important to note that the term "ought" may be used not only in a *pre*scriptive sense—as in a norm—but also in a *de*scriptive sense—as in an assertion about a norm. The science of law describing, e.g. the legal norm concerning murder does not say: "if a man commits murder, he *will* be punished," but: "if a man commits murder, he *ought* to be punished." In this statement the term "ought" has a descriptive sense. (ILR, 3)

Such a statement makes it easy to see why the "descriptive 'ought' " has remained one of the most controversial and least understood features of Kelsen's Pure Theory. If the "ought" which appears in the legal scientist's description of a norm is in fact descriptive, is it really an "ought"? And if it does retain "ought"-force in such a context, can it really be said to be descriptive? Have we not found ourselves once more among round squares?

Predictably, Kelsen's admirers have sought to reinterpret this view in order to save Pure Theory from such untoward consequences. Golding suggests[13] that Kelsen has allowed his observation that "ought" occurs in two distinct sorts of legal expression to lead him to the mistaken conclusion that there are two distinct sorts of legal "ought." Kelsen, he thinks, falls prey to this error because of his inattention to a distinction to which modern-day philosophers of language have attached great importance, namely, the distinction between *using* and *mentioning* terms and expressions. To illustrate: "Just" is first *used* then *mentioned* in the statement "No one knows which acts are just because no one knows what 'just' means." Similarly, a norm-authority who says "All hijackers must be executed" *uses* an expression which the jurisprudent *mentions* when he says " 'All hijackers must be executed' is part of the law of State S." Golding thinks that Kelsen is misled by the fact that the word "ought" appears in both norms and the descriptive statements of legal science ("rules of law"). The word *appears* in both sorts of expression; but it is not *used* in both, Golding observes. "Rules of law" are descriptive precisely in that they mention the "oughts" norms use. What appears in a "rule of law," then, is never an actively occurring (that is, prescriptive) "ought," but always the *name* of an "ought" whose use is being mentioned.

If Golding's interpretation were right, the double-vision which caused Kelsen to inflate the notion of "mention" into a puzzling dogma would easily be remedied. Kelsen could escape his critics simply by speaking of descriptions *of* "ought" wherever he had formerly spoken of "descriptive oughts." One would expect that he would gratefully embrace this distinction, bury the superfluous "ought," and get on with the detailed business of norm analysis. Surprisingly, however, when this course[14] was proposed to him by H. L. A. Hart, Kelsen rejected it.

> Kelsen would have none of it. He insisted that the statements of the normative science of law representing the law of a given system were not paraphrases at all: he said they were

not "second order" statements about the law in which words were mentioned, not used. He stood by his terminology of rules and ought-statements "in a descriptive sense" and he urged me to read the works of the 19th century logician Lotze who also spoke of a descriptive sense of "ought."[15]

Reflecting on this (though avowedly not reading Lotze), Hart saw that Kelsen must have meant more by his use of "descriptive ought" than could be corrected in invoking the use/mention distinction.

> Since our debate . . . I have come to think that he was perhaps right, and that that distinction is too crude to characterize precisely the relationship between the statements of the normative science of law as Kelsen conceives of them and the law of the systems which they represent.[16]

To show what he now thinks Kelsen had in mind, Hart invents a story in which an interpreter (the analog of Kelsen's *Rechtswissenschaftler*) has the job of representing orders from a prison commandant (the legal authority) to prisoners of war under his command (legal agents). In this story the interpreter says things which represent faithfully both *what* the commandant has said, and *that* what was said was said as orders. It would be wrong, Hart argues, to speak of this anomalous form of communication as being a mere descriptive *mention* of directive language. Instead, he claims, it is an unusual *use* of that kind of language. Since it would be just as wrong to speak of the "descriptive ought" as a mere mention of directive language, Hart concludes that Kelsen was wise to respect the special character of its use by rejecting the proferred use/mention interpretation.

There are, however, a number of serious defects in Hart's explicative parable. In what follows, I shall argue that these defects are good grounds for rejecting the "constructive interpreter" account of Kelsen's scheme for representing legal norms. To replace it, I shall sketch an ac-

count of the "descriptive ought" which avoids the pitfalls
that were fatal to Hart's account, and which at the same
time casts some light on a number of other key elements in
Kelsen's general formalistic project.

Hart's commandant shouts *"Stehen Sie auf!"* The interpreter shouts "Stand up!" In doing so he reproduces
enough of the illocutionary aspects of the command-issu-
ance (mien, gesture) to insure that those who are being
ordered will understand that the original was an order.
This pattern of expressions is Hart's way of capturing an
all-important feature of Kelsen's notion of legal science:
However much the theorist who descriptively represents
law may do to explicate the nature of its norms as norms,
he is without authority with respect to them; the commands, permissions, and authorizations which become
clear *through* him are not *his* commands, permissions, and
authorizations. Yet clearly the interpreter does not do his
job merely by mentioning the commandant's orders and
giving the English equivalents. Despite his own lack of authority, he too must use, and not merely mention, the expression which was originally used authoritatively by the
commandant. For this special use for the imperative mood
the title "order in the descriptive sense" seems appropriate.

So far, however, Hart's picture leaves out a vital feature
of pure-theoretic norm-representation. The expressions of
the interpreter and of the commandant obviously stand in
a straightforward one-to-one copying relation. Kelsen,
however, has firmly insisted (PTL, 72–75) that the legal
scientist's descriptive representations of norms are not
mere "repetitions." Rather, they are, as I have noted
above, "rational reconstructions": With respect both to
the form of the individual norms of the legal order and to
the structure of the order itself, the reformulations effected
by Pure Theory are "ideal." They are, according to Kelsen, devices for expressing legal meaning more clearly

than the norms themselves express it. Hart's way around this discrepancy is this:

> Suppose the commandant to be a somewhat stupid man and very much afraid of fire. Whenever he sees anything inflammable lying around he orders the prisoners to pick it up. Day in and day out he stomps around the camp shouting in German "Pick up that box," "Pick up that paper," "Pick up that bundle of straw." The interpreter dutifully barks out the English equivalents and then one day a man of superior intelligence adds on his own motion "and pick up all inflammable material." The commandant on being told what he has said says "Good: I couldn't think of the right words. What a fine interpreter you are. In fact you do more than interpret my orders: You do what Professor Golding says the normative science of law does for the law of a particular system: You rationally reconstruct my orders."

So as Hart sees it, the pure-theoretical legal scientist uses normative language in a way which is both descriptive (that is, an adequate translation) and informative. He does this by stating not what some norm-authority *said*, but what he had *intended* to say, and by doing this in such a way that he retains the sense of the original's status as a norm, yet at the same time improves on its clarity, coherence, and consistency. Hart admits that although he does not especially like Kelsen's peculiar way of putting things, the idea behind the "descriptive ought" is apparently not pervious to criticisms which once appeared sufficient.

Hart's allegory is colorful and engaging. It goes further toward clearing up the mystery of Kelsen's double-ought than any previous accounts. It is, however, demonstrably misleading in a number of crucial respects. First, it seems to misplace the criteria of correctness for the interpreter's reconstructed presentations of the commandant's orders. Evidently, the interpreter aims only at "saying in the right words" what was, after all, only the commandant's implicit intent. So it appears that the success of his effort is measured against the commandant's satisfaction; he has done his job well if the commandant says "That's exactly what I would have said!" That he has done "more than interpret" here means only that he finds a cumulative term for all the specifically-referring terms his superior had used: and this category word is something the appropriateness of which the commandant himself can readily judge. But is this the case with the normative legal science? Does success in pure-theoretic presentation consist in saying something in a more succinct or compendious fashion that the legal authority would recognize as "what I meant all along"? Evidently not.

Kelsen makes a special point of sharply separating the modes of performance of legal authorities ("norm organs") and legal scientists. In issuing norms, legislators and judges express "acts of will"; they command, permit, or authorize specific kinds of behavior. What legislators and judges don't do, and what the legal scientist *must* do, is comprehend the created norm and its parent norm-structure as a "meaningful whole." Hart's story makes it appear that the legal scientist discovers and enunciates something that was already *there* (namely, the correct meaning of the norm); but this inverts the order Kelsen describes. According to Kelsen, the legal order, the basis of the individual norm's meaning, emerges for the first time through the legal scientist's act of comprehension. It is, Kelsen thinks, in the logically arranged structure of rules of law themselves (and not in the intentions of lawmakers) that the standards of their appropriateness, and hence of the validity of their corresponding norms, lie. Indeed, it is for this reason that rules of law, by exposing contradictions, are capable of exercising a correcting influence over norm-expressions. Clearly, the power of *correction* is something to which Hart's interpreter does not aspire. In Hart's story, the interpreter succeeds if he says exactly what the commandant meant. But to represent law in the way Kelsen wants is to provide a systematic formulation of normative relations which does show what is *objectively* meant by what the legal authority says, but which may not, and generally does not, show what he *subjectively* means when he says it.

A second problem arising from Hart's handling of the interpreter's utterances is that it is difficult to discern why these utterances are not to be thought of as "orders." They do, after all, have the effect that orders are supposed to have. It is clear that if the commandant were speaking through a translating *machine* (even one which could find shorter, cumulative ways of putting what he was saying) rather than through an interpreter what would come out of the machine would still be orders. Assuming that the prisoners were accustomed to thinking that the machine "spoke for" the commandant, even the gestures, inflection, and so forth, which accompanied his original speech would be inessential to the understanding of the orders as orders. However, if the interpreter's utterances are construed as orders and not just interpretations of orders, Hart's illustration is wasted. For what comes out of legal-scientific representation *cannot* be norms. On this point Kelsen is clear beyond question.

A third objection is directly related to the second. Whatever status the interpreter's utterances are said to have, it is clear that they are neither true nor false. Prescriptions by their very nature are valid or invalid, but neither true nor false. And clearly it is essential to the success of the interpreter's utterances that they appropriate enough of the force of the original commands that they retain their prescriptivity. But it is a distinctive and indelible feature of Kelsen's program of legal reconstruction that rules of law have *no* prescriptive force. This feature is, again, connected with the "constitutive" capacity which Kelsen attributes to legal science: The chief means which the legal scientist has for reconstructing a normative order is the corrective application of logical rules, for example, the Principle of the Exclusion of Contradiction, and the familiar canons of inference. These rules, however, are usually understood to apply only to assertions that are either true or false. And, as we have seen, Kelsen's point in preserving a purely descriptive character for the "oughts" in "rules of law" is to facilitate the application of logical rules to norms *through* them.

Finally, Hart's characterization of the relationship between the utterances of the interpreter and the norm-giving *authority* behind them clearly misses Kelsen's notion of legal scientific representation. The prison-camp story makes norm-authority appear to rest entirely in the intent (the command, the "sovereign decree") of the commandant. In this respect, Hart has come closer to portraying Austin's brand of positivism than Kelsen's. Pure Theory does not "depsychologize" the commands (and other norms) it presents merely by replacing expressions of will with expressions of legal "ought." It does not refer the coercive force of legal norms to the superior might of whoever happens to be in a position to make commands. Rather, the binding force of a command *qua norm* is traceable only to the order of norms in which its meaning is given in relation to the meanings of other legal norms. The singular norm, in short, draws its strength and its meaning from the "unity," the coherence of the system (of norms) itself. In criticizing Austin, Kelsen says:

> [N]ot every command issued by somebody superior in power is of a binding nature. . . . A command is binding, not because the individual commanding has an actual superiority in power, but because he is "authorized" or "empowered" to issue commands of a binding nature. And he is "authorized" or "empowered" only if a normative order, which is supposed to be binding, confers on him this capacity, the competence to issue binding commands. (GTLS, 31–32)

Whether a given command-norm does belong to a valid norm-order is an issue which cannot be settled by dint of

fact or force of muscle; nor can it be settled (except negatively) by examination of the conditions of norm-issuance.
It can be settled only by careful analysis—what Kelsen
calls "structural analysis"—of the norm's relationship to
the whole of its norm-order. This is the reason why the
pure-theoretic enterprise of "rational reconstruction" always appears to be broad-bore: the Pure Theory of Law is
an *organic* theory of law—it accepts the view that validity
of member-norms in a legal order is discoverable through
understanding the objective meaning—and this means the
logical interconnectedness—of the whole normative order.
This is a hard view, and certainly not a popular one in a
post-Hegelian age. But this *is* Kelsen's view, and we must
admit that Hart's portrait simply does not fit it. In the
prison-camp illustration Hart's attention is trained on *one*
way in which the descriptivity of Kelsen's "descriptive
ought" may be said to render legal norms more intelligible: compendious translation. What Hart misses, however,
is the way in which that same descriptivity may help to
bring out the normativity of norms; that is, to help confirm
or disconfirm their putative validity by demonstrating
their places in relation to other norms, norms which have
already been determined jointly to form an organic whole.

THE "LOGICAL" ORGANIZATION OF LAW IN PURE THEORY

Kelsen has insisted that a full account of the norm-relations that comprise a "legal system" must incorporate
"descriptive oughts." This insistence is his way of under-
scoring the constitutive capacity of the legal scientist's
reconstructive analyses. Unhappily however, Kelsen has
nowhere given his readers a detailed picture of the me-
chanics of these analyses, making assessment of the impact
of the "descriptive ought" difficult. On the basis of what
he has said, it seems clear that Kelsen wants the legal scientist's "presentation" to bring out a new view of the
meaning of legal norms, a view in which the notion of nor-

mativity is shown to be tightly connected with the notion of systematic unity.

The discussion to this point has provided a fairly simple picture of Pure Theory's presentational program. The leading assumption that gives the program its distinctive character is this: In determining the normative unity which is "meant" in a system of legal norms, the pure-theoretical scientist need not deal exclusively with norms in their "natural" systematic matrix. To be sure, he will examine the raw stuff of legal language which jurists have written into statute-books, and which has been applied in the adjudication of particular cases, and so forth, in order to locate a set of meanings, specifically meanings of "acts of will." But, working from these, he will try to construct *another* system of expressions, one which at once correctly depicts the logical-normative structuring of the prescriptions meant and *des*criptively asserts something which might be at least implicit in the originals; namely, that a series of determinate relations holds between legal antecedents (delicts) and legal consequents (sanctions). The legal scientist aims at representing the *norm-force* rather than the norm-expressions of a system. If he is successful in his mission, it will not be because he has revealed and clarified some hidden "subjective" meaning in normative acts of will. It will be because he has traced the binding force which constitutes the "objective" meaning of these norms outside themselves, ultimately positioning that meaning in a systematically unified structure of assertions, where it can be dealt with *logically*.

This simple picture clouds over rapidly, however, as we try to find the "logic" of this purportedly unified order of rules. There are, of course, many norm-expressions (in fact, an indefinitely large number of such expressions) through which a single norm of law might be enunciated. The varied language of statutes is adequate testimony to this fact. For every valid norm, though not for every normatively valid norm-expression, there will be one and only one true rule of law. And because rules of law, as opposed to norms, are true or false, logical principles can be applied to them to determine the coherence of the system they form. If a system of legal norms is by-and-large effective, if none of its component norms are in desuetude, and if derogating norms have been instituted to alleviate norm-conflicts, the validity of the norm-system will be indicated by the joint truth of all the rule propositions in the system which presents it. For this presentation to have its desired "constitutive" effect, however, it cannot be the case that assertion of the truth of a given rule of law is grounded simply on the prior recognition of the validity of the corresponding norm. Kelsen insists that the normative value of the norm-order comes from the legal scientist's discovery of the logical coherence of the order of rules; so the unity of the order of rules of law must be established in a way which is logically prior to all claims of the validity of corresponding norms. In short, any unity which is to accrue to the parallel orders must already be included in the presentational scheme. And since this scheme is in a real sense the invention of the legal scientist, a serious question arises as to whether the alleged unity is something that is recognized or imposed.

Kelsen's rather abrupt answer to this question is less than gratifying, since it relies in part on an outmoded psychologistic epistemology. Kelsen thinks that legal phenomena prior to the interpretive ordering of legal science are radically disorganized. The unity that Pure Theory brings to them is not artifically imposed on them; rather it is the chief requirement for understanding them. The idea here is that what confronts the observer as a mere panorama of disarray cannot be understood by him *as* anything. For an object to be understood as a legal object it must be "cognized," "seen *as*" an element or feature of something systematic. This process is partly a matter of definition: In every definition of "law" that Kelsen provides, the notion of "system" (alternatively, "order") is conspicuously present (for example, PTL, 31). Thus legal science, in order specifically to discern legal subject matter in the welter of norm and fact, applies the definitional criterion in an attempt to convert chaos into a comprehensible whole.

Still, however, we must wonder whether seeing legal phenomena as a *unity* is warranted by the thing itself, or whether it is something arising from the needs (compulsions, habits, hopes) of the legal scientist, and subject to his imperfections and rationalistic excesses. It is tempting to accept the latter explanation, and indeed many of Kelsen's critics adopt it as a line of attack. One writer (Tammelo) considers the notion of "unity" to be no more than a familiar "requirement of scholarly work."

> Kelsen's idea of the unity of juristic cognition . . . has a sound core. This consists in a long-and-well-established requirement of scholarly work that such work should strive for a good organization of acquired knowledge, so that its items will not be erratically disjointed, but will show, where possible, connections and interrelations between what is assured as known.[17]

Other writers have dismissed the doctrine as "so pathetically wrong that no further comment is needed." They argue that Kelsen's notion of unity is predicated on fallacious reasoning: "The fallacy, which is familiar to everyone who knows the history of philosophy, is the same as that involved in the following piece of reasoning: My thoughts of Vienna are wistful: therefore, Vienna is wistful."[18]

If this line of criticism is accepted, it is not difficult to view the unity concept as a symptom of a more pervasive ill, a kind of "reductionism," or even "mysticism."[19] Kelsen's account of legal-scientific cognition will not be open to these charges, however, if it is found that something in the legal phenomena themselves *demands* the particular mode of unifying interpretation Pure Theory undertakes. Kelsen clearly thinks there *is* such a demand in the legal subject matter; he thinks that it resides in the necessity—which all parties to the controversy recognize—of resolving norm conflicts.

> [S]ince the cognition of law, like any cognition, seeks to understand its subject as a meaningful whole and to describe it in noncontradictory statements, it starts from the assumption that conflicts of norms within the normative order which is the object of this cognition can and must be solved by interpretation. (PTL, 206)

Yet, having pointed this out, Kelsen does not seem to have appreciated how noncommital the demand is toward the character of the "meaningful whole." There is nothing in this which gives us reason to suppose that Kelsen's own idiosyncratic system of indirect analysis will prove to be the only, or even the best, means of settling these conflicts. Indeed, nothing forces us to conclude that two legal scientists doing their labors according to the canons of pure-theoretic methodology will resolve a given conflict of norms in precisely the same way. Nothing does, that is, unless we suppose that something in the nature of the norms themselves commits any number of objective reviewers to the same description of them. This Platonic assumption is ultimately just what Kelsen makes. Even though the determination of the validity of norms is (logically) posterior to the determination of the structure of rules of law, it is the *nature* of the former which gives shape to the latter.

Kelsen's version of legal science is committed to an interpretation which precludes discontinuity. No principle is more fundamental to Pure Theory than the following axiom: The reason for the validity of a given norm can be found only in another norm.[20] It follows from this principle that our knowledge of a singular norm cannot terminate in the norm itself. For a norm is nothing if it is not valid, and its validity depends upon other norms. This has led Kelsen to the conclusion that cognition of law is cognition of a system of what has come to be known as "internal relations." To know an element in the system it is necessary to know another element in the system; and this eventually means knowing the system itself as a whole. The standard criticism of theories of "internal relations" (one which Russell trained against Bradley with devastating effect) is that it is no use saying that the part can only be known in the whole if the whole itself cannot be an item of experience. This is certainly a good objection if the whole in question is (as in Bradley's case) "experience itself," or reality. But is the objection as good against knowing *law* as a unity? Kelsen thinks it is not. Law, he argues, can be known as a whole; but to do this it is not necessary, nor is it useful, to conduct detailed Baconian inspections of legal phenomena. The fact that legal norms, through reconstructive presentation, show themselves to have an organized structure which is as it were "closed at one end" precludes this. Disregarding all the particular legal contents, we are able to view the structure of law itself from this apex. And this, Kelsen thinks, will count as "knowing law as a whole." Kelsen gives a typically formalistic twist to Pure Theory's way of knowing the law: Legal contents are made extraneous, or rather, incidental, to scientific cognition of law, since they are what vary from system to system. The essence is what must be known—and it only—if true knowledge of the law is to be gotten; and the essence of law in Kelsen's reckonings is a matter of *structure*.

Clearly, a fundamental condition of the "knowability" of an order of elements having "internal relations" will be that the process according to which each element derives part of its meaning from other elements must come to an end somewhere. The alternative is a *regressus ad infinitum*; and such an outcome would radically undo the concept of unity Kelsen requires. Accordingly, Kelsen makes the notion of "legal order" definitionally dependent upon cloture by the "*Grundnorm*" at its apex.

> An "order" is a system of norms whose unity is constituted by the fact that they all have the same reason for their validity; and the reason for the validity of a normative order is a basic norm . . . from which the validity of all norms of the order of the order are [sic] derived. (PTL, 31)

It is with the introduction of this basic norm that Kelsen provides legal science with means for testing the normative validity of any prescriptive "ought."

> That a norm belongs to a certain system of norms, to a certain normative order, can be tested only by ascertaining that it derives its validity from the basic norm constituting the order. . . . An "ought" statement is a valid norm only if it belongs to such a valid system of norms, if it can be derived from a basic norm presupposed as valid. (GTLS, 111)

This last disclosure, however, has made Pure Theory an easy target for Realistic criticisms—the basic norm is *presupposed*. It hardly matters *who* presupposes the basic norm (although this has been an issue on which Kelsen has wavered considerably and on which he has yet to reach a fully satisfactory conclusion); *that* it is presupposed means that the unity it brings to the norm-order does *not* come out of the nature of the norms themselves.

Perhaps at this point it is necessary to introduce Kelsen's oft-repeated distinction between the "nomostatic" and "nomodynamic" perspectives on normative phenomena. These terms refer respectively to the norm-order as established (at rest) and to that order in the process of creation and execution. Seen from the static perspective, law is a system of valid norms, a stable system controlling conduct. Seen from the dynamic perspective, it is the human activity of making and changing its own controls.

Kelsen argues (PTL, 70-71) that the legal order is *essentially* a dynamic phenomenon; and that accordingly, the truest perspective for the legal scientist is the nomodynamic one. But he does not carry off this argument consistently. As Stone points out, Kelsen tries to classify the several jurisprudential concepts with which Pure Theory works under these two rubrics; so that "typical concerns of nomostatics are the concepts of law, validity, sanction, duty, responsibility, legal right, capacity, imputation, and legal personality." While "those of nomodynamics are the legal order, with the basic norm as 'its ground of validity' *(Geltungsgrund)*, and the hierarchy of legal norms *(der Stufenbau der Rechtsordnung).*"[21] But this is obviously a foredoomed division, inasmuch as both Kelsen's notions of *Geltungsgrund* and *Stufenbau* depend for their meaning upon the constitutive elements of sanction, delict, imputation, and the like. However many elements "at rest" are assembled, they cannot be made to "move." Kelsen conspicuously shifts perspectives at his convenience. Despite his frequent recurrence to this distinction, Kelsen obviously feels unrestrained in his development of norm-theory by the peculiarities of either viewpoint.

Yet, when it comes to the matter of "derivation" within the *Stufenbau*, Kelsen speaks as though the nomostatic/nomodynamic distinction were decisively illuminating. He maintains that regarding a system of *moral* norms, for instance, as a static order allows us to see all the particular norms in this order as "implicated in" the basic norm of the order.

> It is essential . . . that the various norms of any such system are implicated in the basic norm as the particular is implied by the general, and that, therefore, all the particular norms of such a system are obtainable by means of an intellectual operation, viz. by the inference from the general to the particular. Such a system is of a static nature. (GTLS, 112)

In the moral order, Kelsen says, this sort of "implicating" relation may be expressed by saying, "All specific moral injunctions are implicit in (part of the meaning of, derivable from) the Golden Rule."[22] But will this kind of rule and case relation hold in the *legal* order, where the *Grundnorm* is not God-given, but "presupposed"? When Kelsen chooses (for example, PTL, 178) to regard the legal order as *essentially dynamic* (that is, withholding itself from the static perspective), he uses this relation to distinguish the "logics" of moral and legal systems. He argues that the dynamic legal order does *not* exhibit the all-inclusive subsumption relation. And therefore, he holds, assessment of the validity of any particular norm in the system must take into account such "dynamic" features as norm-creation, the "authorization" which stands behind it, and so forth. When Kelsen chooses to regard the legal order as a system to which both dynamic and static perspectives are appropriate,[23] however, the issue of "implication" becomes most unclear. Kelsen certainly seems to be willing to make room for derivability in the (static) moral order. And this would suggest a collapse of meaning within the order into the basic norm (perhaps in the way all of arithmetic may be collapsed into Peano's postulates). What makes this prospect particularly worrisome, however, is Kelsen's acknowledgment of the fact that the basic norm is not something the legal scientist discovers in the world of *Sollen*; it is a *presupposition*—the very condition of the existence of that world.

If we now ask: *Who* presupposes the basic norm?, however, there are two distinct answers which Kelsen gives:[24] First, if we assume the nomodynamic standpoint, it is the legal subjects, or rather their constitution-producing customs, that make the presupposition.

> The norms of a legal order must be created by a specific process. They are posited, that is, positive norms, elements of a

positive order. If by the constitution of a legal community is understood the norm or norms that determine how (that is, by what organs and by what procedure—through legislation or custom) the general norms of the legal order that constitute the community are to be created, then the basic norm which is presupposed when the custom through which the constitution has come into existence, or the constitution-creating act consciously performed by certain human beings, is objectively interpreted as a norm-creating fact. . . . The basic norm is the presupposed starting point of a procedure: the procedure of law creation. (PTL, 198–199)

Although Kelsen allows that "to make manifest this presupposition is an essential function of legal science" (PTL, 46), he deliberately stresses that to *make* the presupposition is not its function.

As a norm the basic norm must be the meaning of an act of will. Hence it is not the *science* of law which presupposes the basic norm. The science of law, which is a function of cognition, not of will, only ascertains the fact: that if men consider a coercive order established by acts of will of human beings and by and large effective as an objectively valid order, *they*, in their juristic thinking, *presuppose* the basic norm as the meaning of an act of will. (ILR, 6)

The last statement puts Kelsen in something of a bind, however. For, if the basic norm is to count as a norm at all, it must clearly be, like all other norms, the meaning of a *Willensakt*. Yet precisely in the case of a *basic* norm—admittedly a hypothesis—it seems to make no sense to speak of *willing*, but only of *supposing*. Kelsen's attempts at escaping this bind are not very impressive. He tries to keep the normativity of something that is part of thinking *(Denkakt)* by insisting that there is in our thinking a "fictive" or "imaginary" will. So in presupposing the basic norm we are really *thinking* a *willing*, and the result is a most curious hybrid—something which is both *Denkakt* and *Willensakt*.

Unfortunately, Kelsen had already tied Pure Theory's technique for resolving conflicts between norms to this very distinction—the absolute *discreteness* of *Denkakt* and *Willensakt*:

> Since there is no analogy between the truth of an assertion, as the meaning of an act of thinking, and the validity of a legal norm, as an act of will, a conflict of norms cannot have the character of a logical contradiction; consequently a conflict of legal norms cannot be solved according to the logical law of contradiction. (LL,233)

Thus, in order to save the principle of normative noncontradiction (and this, after all, was the reason for introducing the notion of *Grundnorm* into legal-scientific cognition) Kelsen is forced to resign the thought-will hybrid. The necessity of this choice has finally appeared in Kelsen's latest work; and the conclusion he draws from it is nothing short of astonishing. He now admits that willing and thinking are entirely discrete functions, and concludes that because legal norms are strictly acts of will to which truth and falsity are inapplicable categories, logical principles are applicable only *analogically* (RLi, 422). Lest anyone misunderstand what he means by "analogical inference," Kelsen specifically singles out the constructional method of indirect analysis and torpedoes it. He expressly declares (RLii, 498) that he must now reject altogether the view that such rules as the Law of Contradiction and *Modus Ponens* are applicable to norms *through* their application to the correspondent rules of law. They are in fact neither directly nor indirectly applicable to norms.

This is clearly a case of Kelsen's throwing out the baby with the bath. If former confusions between prescriptive and descriptive use (or, what comes to the same thing, between *Willensakten* and *Denkakten*) are now seen to be incompatible with the indirect application of logical principles to normative orders, it is time to rethink the pernicious confusions—and a good starting place would be the "fictive act of will"—rather than repudiate the technique which appears to form the backbone of Pure Theory's representational construction. One can only presume that Kelsen fails to realize that to leap, as he does here, to an antiformalist posture on the basis of a logical discovery is to lose *all* of the "logical-formal" program of Pure Theory.

This brings us to Kelsen's second answer to the question: "Who presupposes the basic norm?" In the nomodynamic perspective, the jurisprudent's analytic interest lies principally in establishing the *fact* of norm-creation. Thus, when Kelsen expresses preference for the nomodynamic outlook in the execution of legal science his idea is that only by consideration of the *ongoing* development of norms from norms, according to systemic (that is, "positive") rules, can the differences between continually changing legal orders be cognized. The "basic norm" seen nomodynamically identifies particular norms as norms of a legal order, but only by affirming that the acts prescribed by the (logically prior) constitution-creating act were, in fact, effected. Hence, the question of an individual norm's validity is not a question of "logical-formal analysis," but of routine checking on norm-creating conditions. And Kelsen indicates that he thinks this "checking" will ultimately lead back to the *Grundnorm*.

> If the question as to the reason for the validity of a certain legal norm is raised, then the answer can only consist in the reduction to the basic norm of this legal order, that is, in the assertion that the norm was created—in the last instance—according to the basic norm. (PTL, 199)

Kelsen confuses matters further when he says that norms of the nomostatic order may be considered to be valid "on the strength of their content" alone, whereas norms of the nomodynamic order have a validity which

can, in the last analysis, be based only on a presupposed norm
which prescribes that one ought to behave according to the
norms created by custom. This norm can supply only the
reason for the validity, not the content of the norms based on
it. (PTL, 196)

But if considerations of content are dismissed, Kelsen says,
logical ordering of the normative system is made impossible. If one regards an individual legal norm dynamically,
and traces its "reason for validity" to other and higher
norms, it will not be possible to establish a logical connection between the norm that was the starting point and the
basic norm that is supposed to be the end point. (PTL, 197)

Who presupposes the nomostatic legal basic norm? It
appears that the answer *cannot* be, as it was for the
nomodynamic basic norm, the legal subjects and their customs. For it was the function of these to *will* into being the
process of norm-creation that makes *new* norms. They
cannot also be in the position of determining the validity of
norms in an already-existing, stable order. And this is for
two strong reasons: (1) As I have already stressed, Kelsen
regards the functions of *Willen* and *Denken* as absolutely
separate; and (2) The nature of the order itself cannot appear before the introduction of pure-theoretical cognition.
Hence, *if* a system of legal norms may be regarded as a
static order at all, it can only be he who exercises the function of legal-scientific *Denken* in regard to it, who "thinks"
it, that presupposes its basic norm. And this is the legal
scientist himself.

Kelsen is openly uneasy about nomostatic viewing of the
legal order. But this much is clear: To the extent that
"structural analysis" is possible, the nomostatic perspective is appropriate. For when Kelsen pronounced the
analytic aim of Pure Theory at the beginning of *General
Theory of Law and State*, the notion of *Grundnorm* he introduced in connection with it was surely *not* thought to

be something unearthed in the will of the legal community. Rather it is "to be established by a logical analysis of actual juristic thinking" (GTLS, xv). And it was clearly never in Kelsen's mind that ordinary legal subjects, the "willers" of law, were involved with, let alone capable of, this sort of "logical analysis." Logical analysis can only be analysis of what has-been-willed, and is, as Kelsen would have it, now at rest.

Thus, Kelsen's employment of the twin distinctions "form/content" and *"Denkakt/Willensakt"* forces him to give conflicting answers to the question of the origin of the basic norm. Recently, Kelsen has become aware of this problem. In the second edition of *The Pure Theory of Law*, Kelsen adds a footnote which offers a bold, succinct, but clearly unsatisfactory response:

> The question: "Who presupposes the basic norm?" is answered by the Pure Theory as follows: The basic norm is presupposed by whoever interprets the subjective meaning of the constitution-creating act, and of the acts created according to the constitution, as the objective meaning of these acts, that is, as objectively valid norm. This interpretation is a cognitive function, not a function of the will. Since the science of law, as cognition, can only describe norms, and not prescribe anything, hence cannot create norms, I have occasionally expressed doubt against the view that the basic norm is also presupposed by the science of law. . . . These doubts are eliminated by the distinction, presented in the text, between positing and presupposing a norm. (PTL, 204n)

This answer is unsatisfactory because the way in which Kelsen circumscribes the nature of legal-scientific presupposition renders impossible the role he gives legal science in showing the unity of the dynamic legal order. Time and again, Kelsen declares that the basic norm is a *logical*, or "transcendental-logical" presupposition. He claims, moreover, that the kind of unity this presupposition affords to legal orders is a specifically "logical" unity. As has just been pointed out, however, nomodynamic attention to norm-creation and its conditions confines the legal scientist's operations to the sphere of the prescriptivity of norms; and this, Kelsen has concluded, radically undercuts the application to legal-scientific cognition of the logical rules which are the backbones of logical unity.

Kelsen wants to say two irreconcilable things: (1) Because the legal scientist only *presupposes*, and does not *posit*, norms, he is thereby freed to present normative orders in a way that shows their true character, and shows it to be something other than what jurists and practitioners have thought; namely, a strictly logical unity. (2) Yet, because the norms themselves, even the basic norm, are products of acts of will (though, at least in the case of the basic norm, this may be a "fictive" will), they are the sort of thing which belong essentially to the world of *dynamic* phenomena, where the function of creating novel norms dooms the effort of exhibiting a strictly logical unity to failure. In trying to bring together these contrary objectives, Kelsen has tried two tacks. First, he has suggested the possibility of reinterpreting the basic norm itself in such a way as to combine the static and dynamic principles. He points out that this is effectively accomplished with some religious norms (for example, the Ten Commandments) and moral norms. In such cases, Kelsen observes, an authority "not only establishes norms by which other norm-creating authorities are delegated, but also norms in which the subjects are commanded to observe a certain behavior and from which further norms can be deduced, as from the general to the particular." (PTL, 197–198) The problem with this, however, is that the procedure of norm-deduction is created *by the norm-authority* in these cases; whereas Kelsen wants to make this "constitutive" function the property of the *legal scientist* when the norm-order is a legal one.

Kelsen's other tack has been to modify the sense of "logical" in which he holds legal orders to be logically unified. On the one hand, he is now insistent that Pure Theory is simply a theory of law and in no sense a logic ("Meine Lehre ist eine Rechts-Lehre, keine Logik," RRL, 551). On the other, he wants to maintain that both law and his *Rechtslehre* are in some sense part of the "sphere of logic":

> That it is not possible to apply the logical principle of the excluded contradiction to norms does not mean, that no logical principle at all can be applied to legal norms; that the law is outside of the sphere of logic. . . .That the question as to the applicability of logical principles to legal *norms* must not be confused with the question as to the—uncontestable—applicability, of these principles to the *science* as the cognition of law, is self-evident. (LL, 236)

This strategy, however, merely has the effect of shifting the problem back onto the thesis of presentational descriptivity. For, if law itself is something in which certain logical principles *do not* apply, and legal science seeks only to *describe* law, it seems that if these same principles *do* apply in the legal scientific representation, it can only be by dint of the scientist's imposition. Perhaps what Kelsen *really* wants to say here is this: Legal orders *do* have a logical unity that is logical in the *strong* sense that in the very process of reconstruction which *makes them* norm-orders (and hence for the first time shows their legal "essence") logical principles are nonarbitrarily employed. The employment of these principles is nonarbitrary *not* because of anything to do with the willing, creation, or effectiveness of law, but because of something in the *meaning* of legal norms which makes them conformable to the *meaning* of "order."

This may be the solution to Kelsen's problem with the notion of "logical unity" in the legal-normative order. It is a solution that *follows* from what he says about legal meaning and the role of legal science with respect to it; but it is a solution which Kelsen has never brought himself to formulate. Indeed, it is a solution which Kelsen does not express because it shifts the project of presentational analysis decisively, away from the dynamic order for which he holds special fondness. Yet this, ultimately, is the only place where the analysis can rest. "Logical unity," on this account, is something that does not belong to national legal systems, international legal systems, legal relations, persons, and the like, in their "natural," dynamic state. It belongs rather to the *meanings* of the norms and norm orders which are "embedded" in these phenomena, but which become real, which are "constituted," only by the legal scientist's structural analysis. The norm-expressions which legal practioners use (to make and apply positive law) may for one thing, contain contradictions. But though these contradictions may be *meant* (by the jurists and norm-issuing authorities), they cannot be part of the *meaning* of the norms themselves. To expose the meaning of norms, the legal scientist must "interpret" those norm-expressions in such a way as to show the contradictions to be "sham": "The specific function of juristic interpretation is to eliminate these contradictions by showing that they are merely sham contradictions. It is by juristic interpretation that the legal material is transformed into a legal system" (GTLS, 375). The meanings of norms are *not* the same thing as what-the-legislator-means when he makes law (that is, when he *pre*scriptively expresses a legal command, permission, or authorization). What one legislator means and what another means may well come into irreconcilable conflict; here there is no prospect of unity. Yet, after a law has been duly enacted, its norm-content has its own meaning; and this meaning is connected in some ways and unconnected in others with what the legislator said.

This realization—which Kelsen flirts with, but never

openly expounds—is of vital importance to Pure Theory's formalistic design. It is strictly analogous to the Wittgensteinian point that language, once created, "has a life of its own." To fail to see this is to subject legal theory to an endless confrontation with the welter of juristic intention, motivation, and interest. To see it is to commit legal theory to analysis of meanings which have already gone through the process of being legally meant and have therefore met all the *conditions* necessary for being legally meant—and are in this sense "static."

RAZ' CRITIQUE AND THE BASIC NORM

In *The Concept of a Legal System*, J. Raz has provided a detailed, extensive criticism of Kelsen's handling of the several concepts central to the discussion of the preceding section: the basic norm, presupposition, norm-validity, and the static and dynamic orders.[25] On many points, Raz' analysis converges with my own. However, there remain points of great importance on which our accounts diverge. It is worth our while to pause in our reconstruction of Kelsen's General Theory of Norms in order to scrutinize Raz' less sympathetic picture of these matters. Unfortunately, it will not be possible to make a very neat comparison of Raz' views and my own. Raz takes up the Pure Theory as part of a broader analysis of the existence, identity, and structure of legal systems; he is thus less interested in the inner ordering principles which characterize Pure Theory than he is in those of its features which align or contrast it with other theories of legal system. A great deal of what he says about the concepts we have been examining is colored by Raz' overriding interest in what he calls "the principle of individuation," a principle that has not played any important role in my own study. But the most profitable part of Raz' discussion, I believe, is that which deals with the basic norm. By dwelling especially on his attack on Kelsen's basic norm doctrine, we shall at once define the main differences between Raz' views and my own, and give needed amplification to that pure theoretic doctrine which is, by critical consensus, considered the most problematic.

Raz is certainly right on one count. To counter the objection that legislators often do not will the content of a given law (do not *know* its content, even), Kelsen holds that what is intended in the legislative act is merely the creation of a norm. Raz points out that this doctrine assumes exactly what it is meant to explain, the whole panoply of existing norms and conventionalized activities which make up ongoing legal systems. The only way Kelsen can escape the trap of assuming what his theory is meant to explain on this point is to pack a *tremendous* amount of content into the basic norm. This strategy averts the contest between what is presupposed and what is explained by stacking the side of the presupposed.

Following the lead of numerous critics, Raz attacks the vagueness of Kelsen's notion of "presupposition" involved here. But, he goes beyond most prior critics in recognizing the delicate relation the basic norm holds to other elements in Kelsen's theory. As Raz sees it, the basic norm does not impart existence, but, rather, unity and validity to a legal system (CLS, 65). And this, of course, means that the basic norm is, as I have argued above, essentially a device whereby legal science (rather than legal authority) imbues a legal system with meaningfulness. Raz calls this conclusion "astonishing"; I regard it as inevitable and sensible. If the basic norm is, as I have portrayed it, a "transcendental presupposition" initiated by legal science as the source of the objective meaning of norms in a legal system, those features of "content" which Raz finds objectionable may be seen as entirely reasonable consequences of Pure Theory's project. Raz blames Kelsen for absorbing into the basic norm all the conclusions of his theory of norms. The conclusions he enumerates are these: (a) the inner coherence of the legal system, (b) the absence of sanctionless norms in that system, (c) the determination of the basic norm's content by the facts through which a legal system is created and applied, (d) the composition of systematicity out of a multitude of norms, and (e) the criterial identification of norms within a system through the basic norm (CLS, 96–102). All of these points seem to me to be more aims than conclusions of Pure Theory; and, although they are undeniably linked with the doctrine of the basic norm, I am not convinced that they are, strictly speaking, "absorbed" in it. Moreover, Raz' attack on the capacity of basic norms to settle questions of identity of other norms within a given system seems to me to be more an admission of the inapplicability of his own scheme of criterial analysis than it is a demonstration of Kelsen's inadequacies. I cannot find anywhere in Kelsen a direct claim that the basic norm will *identify* the norms of a system. It is, of course, true that Kelsen has upon occasion argued that all norms of a given system are derivable from the basic norm. But this is not to say that norm N, which is derivable from the basic norm, *is* a member of the system L.

Raz claims that

> according to Kelsen, the question whether a certain norm, N_1, belongs to a certain system is settled by finding out whether the system contains a norm authorizing the creation of N_1. If it does—N_1 belongs to that system, if not—it does not. (CLS, 102)

This formulation puts a tremendous strain on the concept of authorization. It cannot be right, unless one assumes that some very peculiar notion of authorization prevails in the Pure Theory of Law. It is certainly true, as Raz points out, that Kelsen holds that every legal norm presupposes, as a condition of its validity, another norm authorizing its creation (CLS, 130). But one must be very cautious about the commitment entailed by presupposition in Kelsen's theory. Authorization is a necessary, but not a sufficient precondition of normative validity, as I understand Kelsen. So, contrary to Raz' view, N_1 may not belong to a given system, even if there is a norm of that system which authorizes its creation. And this conclusion, after all, accords with common sense: that the U.S. Constitution may be construed to authorize norms which would, in wartime circumstances, legitimate the incarceration of alien residents does not mean that norms to this effect exist within the American legal system.

It seems to me that Raz has attributed both too much and too little to Kelsen's notion of the basic norm. He says too little when he suggests that

> basic norms exist if they are regarded only as common bonds determining the identity of normative systems and the validity of orders as part of such systems . . . [T]he basic norm has nothing to do with the justification of norms. (CLS, 134)

This statement ignores Kelsen's repeated remarks to the effect that a particular norm is justified if the basic norm of its system is justified (and if the particular norm is derivable from the basic norm). He says too much when he equates Kelsen's basic norm with all the major conclusions of Pure Theory. Surely it is possible to accept a more moderate view of the basic norm than that to which Kelsen subscribed without sacrificing the sound theoretic conclusions based upon the basic norm postulate. Raz is driven by his critical appraisal of the existential status Kelsen gives the basic norm to accept the view that basic norms "do not help to establish the unity and identity of legal systems, nor do they help in arranging the norms of legal systems" (CLS, 138). But it is entirely plausible that one might give up altogether claims regarding the existence of the basic norm (that is, the existential legal status of that norm *qua* norm), and yet believe that the principle of unification and normative arrangement for which it stands is a reasonable expression of a reasonable aim for legal science.

This is really the core of my criticism of Raz. It seems to me that he is so distracted by the attention he pays to the issue of a norm's *creation* and *existence* that he fails to give proper attention to the norm's *function* in the scheme of the Pure Theory of Law. Raz admits initially that Kelsen "specifically denies that basic norms are created by being presupposed" (CLS, 65). But, having said this, Raz worries needlessly over the question of what accounts for the *existence* of basic norms. Presupposition, as he understands it, casts the norm into existence, seemingly in the way that wishing causes good fairies to appear. Oddly enough, it is because Raz indulges this pointless preoccupation that he is driven to ask a very sensible question. "Why," he inquires, "should legal theory be said to presuppose the basic norm and not merely to analyze and describe it, as it does the other norms?" (CLS, 137). One answer to this question is more or less obvious, if one stops worrying about the existential status of the basic norm: the basic norm must be presupposed in order to give meaning to the array of norms that cannot be understood other than as coordinated by a supervening norm. As I have maintained in the foregoing section, Kelsen thinks of the basic norm as a guarantor of "objective meaning" for the norm-order it supervenes. Assuming that the basic norm is valid is no more than assuming that validity can be distributed in a systematic way among those other norms that make up the body of the legal system.

Another answer to Raz' question might go deeper: There is no reason for legal science to do more than insist on the logical coordination and intersystematic coherence of member norms; there is, indeed, no further point in legal theory's "presupposing" a basic norm (if that means that one more norm would exist than would otherwise exist).

Raz, it seems, is very much disturbed by the apparent consequences of the existence of that which imbues the rest of a legal order with unity and validity, although he is not disturbed by the unity and validity of that order itself. I cannot help thinking at this point of a strange parallel between Raz' appraisal of Kelsen's basic norm and a popular philosophical view of the attributes of God. A familiar question to philosophical theologians is: Does anything more exist if God exists than if all the rest exists? The analogous question here is: Is anything more valid if the basic norm is presupposed than if the general validity and logical unity of the legal system is presupposed? It seems to me that Kelsen is aligned on this point with those who think that the difference alleged makes no difference. The existential status of the basic norm is, so far as I can make out, of no consequence whatever. The crucial issue is whether what the hypothesis of the basic norm achieves in the direction of systematicity in the appraisal of normative systems is of value or not. Because Raz is consumed with the issue of the basic norm's existence, he is drawn to the conclusion that it has "contrary to Kelsen's most firm beliefs, no real importance for the arrangement of the norms of a legal system" (CLS, 104). Raz shunts what is proper to the function of the basic norm to that of the "chain of validity." He claims that, assuming the propriety of this chain, the basic norm might be altogether eliminated from the legal system, with no loss to its structure and arrangement of norms, that is, its unity. But if the basic norm is understood as Kelsen's single instrument for securing exactly that systemic harmony which Raz hands over to his favored "validity chains," the loss of the basic norm would indeed be disastrous. In short, it appears that Raz' quarrel is not with the job Kelsen has his basic norm do, but with the thought that this job is to be done by something which has a suspicious ontological pedigree. Kelsen has, as I have observed earlier, the ungainly neo-Kantian habit of hypostatizing functions and relational notions. If one regards the basic norm as a *condition*, specifically a condition of meaningfulness, rather than a thing, many of Raz' objections evaporate. One need not, in this interpretation, be concerned with the *creation* of the basic norm (one of Raz' basic worries); meaningfulness-conditions are not created so much as they are *set*. And, of course, many of the considerations that go toward determining what conditions are appropriately set are those which Raz attributes to his "chains of validity."

I am generally in agreement with Raz' conclusions regarding Kelsen's troublesome management of the static-dynamic distinction. Raz chooses to regard the two perspectives as contrasting principles of individuation: On the static principle, every law is a norm imposing a duty by imposing a sanction; on the dynamic, norms are taken to confer legislative powers as well as duties. Raz does not, however, regard the two principles as independent. Taking his clue from GTLS, 144 (where Kelsen seems to discuss the projection of one static normative phenomenon onto another), Raz discusses the possibility of projecting static classification schemes upon dynamic schemes generally. He assumes (without argument) that such a projection is always possible for valid legal norms. And on the basis of this assumption, he argues that the static principle of individuation has primacy. It has primacy, because, as he sees it, dynamic norms are valid legal norms only if they are projectable onto a static representation of law. In fact, Raz goes so far as to say that "dynamic norms are, therefore, not norms at all" (CLS, 113). On the same page, however, Raz says (in a footnote) that "dynamic norms are one kind of dependent norms." These two statements are, despite appearances, reconcilable; for Raz does not think Kelsen's "dependent norms" deserve the title "norm." I disagree with Raz' downgrading of Kelsen's important doctrine of norm-dependency. (My discussion of dependent norms takes place in chapter four.)

I agree with his conclusion that static order has, contrary to Kelsen's repeated avowals, a kind of primacy. But I do not believe that this is due to any projectability of one order onto the other. Static and dynamic are, as Kelsen conceives them, discrete perspectives from which all legal phenomena may be viewed. They are as different as the views a cinematographer and an anatomist, say, might take of a running man. The primacy of the static perspective does not derive from the reducibility of the dynamic to it; it derives solely from the higher utility this perspective affords to the project of formal-logical presentation. Logical principles can be applied to norms only in their "rest state." Thus, nomostatic presentation gains ascendancy precisely to the degree that legal-scientific presentation does. And legal science has value only to the degree that it is capable of revealing the relations of meaning that bind together the norms of a normative order.

KELSEN'S DISCUSSION OF MEANING

What chiefly prevents Kelsen from drawing the conclusion I have drawn in the preceding section entitled "the Logical Organization of Law," and what forces him into the pitfalls and dilemmas I have exposed, is his own highly confused treatment of the subject of meaning. Kelsen distinguishes between two senses of meaning: the "subjective" and the "objective." Subjective meaning is the sense connected with an act of will purely on account of the intent of the willing person. The only conditions needed for subjective norm-meaning to take place are the willing itself, a publicly intelligible expression, and whatever material conditions (that is, a person to command, a practically possible condition to permit, and so forth) are required for the expression to be appropriate. Kelsen holds that " 'ought' is the subjective meaning of every act of will directed at the behavior of another" (PTL, 7). Consequently, the subjective commands of the judge, gangster, and tax-collector are not merely similar, but *the same*. Objective meaning, on the other hand, is the specifically "legal meaning" which results from interpretation of subjective meaning; it is "the meaning the act has according to the law" (PTL, 3). Kelsen sets three conditions on the objectivity of an "ought": (1) The "ought" must hold for the two parties involved, as well as for a third party; (2) the "ought" must exist even if the will of the party whose subjective meaning it is ceases to exist; and (3) the "ought" must be *authorized* (that is, "invested with objective meaning") by a higher norm. The last condition is the crucial one: It means that if A's will that B do a given deed can be brought under a valid authorizing norm, its subjective meaning is *identical* with its objective meaning. Indeed, as Kelsen sometimes puts it, to say that a norm is valid is just to say that its subjective meaning coincides with, or is the same as, its objective meaning.

What is profitable in this analysis is that it makes clear that the decision as to whether a given norm *has* validity is a decision about *meaning*, and hence a decision that can be made by "interpretation" according to legal cognition, rather than by fiat. Kelsen emphasizes that the *fact* that a law has been created according to constitutional procedure does not in itself guarantee that it will be valid ("acceptable as law"). What is further required is the ascertainment that the norm of that law fits into a valid order of norms, an order supervened by a basic norm. Since this judgment is one of testing internormative consistency, it passes from the hands of the jurist to that of the legal scientist, who alone can determine the *logical* coherence of the norm with a logically unified order (PGNR, 24; PTL, 204). What is *un*profitable in this analysis—and ultimately devastating to Kelsen's use of the subjective/objective distinction in respect to norms—is the conflation it permits between the sense of what is said and the intention with which it is said. If the major part of the subjective meaning of A's statement "B ought to go to jail" is A's *wish* that B go to jail, it makes no sense to say that this meaning may *ever* be identical with the objective meaning of the norm which says "B ought to go to jail" even when A is not willing it (and even after A has ceased to exist). Nothing at all is gained by saying that an objective meaning and a subjective meaning "coincide," "converge," or "are identical" if the willing that made the subjective meaning subjective is invariably dismissed from consideration by the interpreters of meaning. Kelsen's determination that norms embody the fusion of objective and subjective meanings amounts to a naïve misreading of the necessity of tagging norms for their prescriptive force; that is, of reminding the interpreter that they are not only meanings, but meanings of acts of *will*. Kelsen did not fully realize that the psychological fact of willing involved in "subjective" meaning is irrelevant to and in no way a part of the prescriptive "ought" of legal norms. There is no need to add the willed intention of a willing party to the norm, for prescriptivity—indeed, prescriptivity of a broader sort—is already part of the meaning of "norm."

The same point may be made by reductio ad absurdum: A legal scientist wishing to know whether the Riot Act of 1715 (I Geo. I, st. II, c.5) is (or was) valid will investigate the "objective meaning" of the norms it imposes by "describing" these norms in such a way that they be presented against the context of a legally valid order. This will perhaps involve "presenting" a host of other norms, checking them off against one another, invoking certain logical laws, and inquiring into the nature of the "basic norm" of some order. It will *not*, however, involve an investigation of the "will" of Parliament in 1715. But, if the subjective meaning of a norm is said to be identical with the objective meaning of that norm in case the norm is valid, then a determination of the validity of the Riot Act of 1715 *would be* a discovery about the psychological state of Parliament. To be sure, it might be a determination of a great many meanings (for example, that of "Felony without Benefit of Clergy," and of "Disturbance of the Publick Peace," and the like) which in one way and another cooperate in the meaning of the norm embodied in that Act. But the determination of the objective meaning itself will necessarily be the same as discovery of that which is identical to it—the subjective meaning. This makes the project of finding the validity of *this* norm a disaster. It will be recalled that the subjective meaning of any act of will is held by Kelsen to be the same as that of any other (namely, "ought"). But if this is so, success in the reconstructive project will amount only to finding something that is common to not only *all* laws, but to all expressions of acts of will directed at the behavior of others. Therefore, the subjective meaning of a norm and its objective meaning cannot be identical, at least not in the sense that the determination of one is identical with the determination of the other in the eyes of legal science.

It cannot be said of Kelsen that he was ignorant of the importance of "depsychologizing" legal meaning. The brunt of his attack on Austin's notion of "command" was a demonstration of various adverse effects of assuming the "subsistence" of subjective factors. That Kelsen should allow so conspicuous a vestige of "subjectivism" to survive in the core of his own theory of norms may be in part attributed to a nonlogician's understandable uncertainty as to the role of "ought" in normative inference. As I shall point out in the next chapter, Kelsen treats the "ought" in legal norms generally as a connective, rather than as an operator, with a given range. The compression this enforces may well have left him uneasy about maintaining the force of prescriptivity essential to the normative logistic. But even here an indelible difference between subjective and objective meaning stands out: Kelsen was clever enough to find several "oughts" in the fully expanded picture of a norm that the canonical form of its correlative "rule of law" provided. One of them is directed to the legal subject (to whom the sanction applies). Others are directed to various legal organs—requiring certain actions in case of nonimposition of sanctions. Now, whatever else may be unclear about the "subjective meaning" of an "ought," this much *is* clear: the "ought" willed in the act of will is singular. Only in the legal-scientific reconstruction of the normative order do the other "oughts" appear. Clearly, then, it will not do to stake the determination of normative validity on the identification of senses of meaning with such conspicuously different "logics."

Unfortunately, however, this is just the way in which Kelsen chooses to explain the "logical indispensibility" of the basic norm. This basic norm, Kelsen says, is logically indispensable because it provides the foundation for the objective validity of (all) positive legal norms; and it does this by being the *meaning* of an act of thinking. Kelsen will allow that legal science can ultimately say very little about this particular act of thinking.

> The science of law can state no more than: the subjective meaning of the acts by which legal norms are created can be interpreted as their objective meaning only if we presuppose in our juristic thinking the (basic) norm. (PTL, 204)

Thus, the basic norm is able to serve as catalyst for the fusion of the two sorts of meaning by being *itself* a meaning. But, of which kind, subjective or objective? Since it is specifically identified as the meaning "of an act of thinking," it cannot be subjective. But can it be objective in the sense in which other norms are, by dint of its agency objective? Clearly not. And to say, as Kelsen is fond of doing when he gets to this crossing, that it is simply a hypothesis, a presupposition that allows the rest of legal science to work, does not help to explain how, *as* a hypothesis, it has meaning (or *is* a meaning). Certainly not all hypotheses are meaningful. On this crucial point Kelsen is silent.

I have now brought out the two ways in which the *Grundnorm*, if it is to be regarded as a norm, must be conceded to be an anomoly: like other norms, the basic norm is supposed to be the meaning of an *act of will*; but, unlike them, it is not thought to be meant by a *real* will. Rather, it is a hypothesis, a "transcendental-logical presupposition," which, if it is to be thought of a "willed" at all, if "fictively" willed as a condition of the validity of all other norms in the order. Again, though it is the *meaning* of an act of will, it is not a meaning in the sense in which any other norm is. For it is neither a subjective meaning nor an objective meaning. To consider it to be the former would make it impossible to continue to regard it as something meant in a *Denkakt*. But it cannot be the latter for the yet stronger reason that the basic norm is itself the *condition* of the objective meaning of norms. Since it is the "reason" to which all norms in its order must appeal for objective validity, it cannot in the same sense serve as its *own* basis of appeal. It is not difficult to see that in the notion of *Grundnorm* Kelsen has expressed his realization of the *limit* of legal positivism. This is the place in Pure Theory where explanations come to an end.

III
The Logic of
Command-Norms

INTRODUCTION

Turning from the general outlines of Kelsen's theory of norms to its details, we shall assess the particular strengths and weaknesses of three "logics": (a) the logic of commands; (b) the logic of permissions; and (c) the logic of authorizations. This examination takes its trichotomous style from a trademark feature of Pure Theory. Kelsen insists that the "ought" of a legal norm cannot be comprehended as a mere command. It was, he thinks, a distinctive failing of previous legal theories that they *forced* the analysis of legal norms in general into the pattern appropriate to command-norms alone, thereby rendering ungainly and inaccurate the analysis of those norms which of their very nature resist this pattern. The key to Kelsen's attack on this widespread form of reductivism is his refocusing of attention on the "acts of will" from which he supposes all species of legal norms originate. In many instances, perhaps most, the act of will at work is a coercive directive whose imperative force is simply that such-and-such must be done if some sanction is to be avoided. In this case, the norm which is that act's meaning is properly called a legal command. But in other cases, its force may be to grant "license" or "concession" to a legal agent or agents, or in other distinctive ways "positively" to permit an action or type of actions. Kelsen is quick to point out that the "positive" kind of permission is substantially different in force from the more familiar "negative" permission. A permission of the latter sort means only that a specific action is not prohibited; it is thus simply the assertion of a "negative fact." By the former sort, however, any of a variety of positive acts of community organs may be meant. And Kelsen is adamant in his insistence that to construe the acts of will behind these as invariably translating into one or another sort of "reflex" of command norms is perniciously to prejudge them. Likewise with norms of authorization: the imperative force in the acts of will creating these goes toward conferring legal powers, typically powers of norm-enactment, on certain parties. To be sure, in some instances, these norms may have the effect of attaching sanctions to specific actions or omissions in respect of these parties; and in these cases there is the possibility of reinterpreting the authorizing norm as a package of commands. But, again, this will not always be the case. Because Kelsen has consistently stressed the importance of discrete analyses of these three types of norm it is appropriate to examine their analyses separately. At the same time, I should point out that Kelsen has been conspicuously sloppy in making and maintaining his threefold division. Frequently, where one of his discussions begins with application to commands alone, it concludes with results which quite evidently are meant to apply to legal norms globally. However, what Kelsen does say about permissions and authorizations independently presupposes the command-analysis as a base. I therefore follow Kelsen's lead on this score, treating commands specifically in this chapter, and portraying the dependent modalities as amendments to the command-analysis subsequently.

COMMAND-NORMS AS "DEUTUNGSSCHEMATA"

Raz has argued that Kelsen's exposition of Pure Theory makes norms of permission the primary legal norms. In fact, he goes so far as to claim that Kelsen's view entails that *every* norm, every law, is essentially a permission to apply a sanction.[1] On this point, however, Raz is altogether inaccurate. Kelsen, like the vast majority of jurisprudents before him, expends the bulk of his energies analyzing commands, and gives his readers no reason to think that the chief role of law is other than to coerce behavior by command. In the present chapter, I shall adhere to the traditional view that command norms are indeed the central "oughts" of Pure Theory.

In discussing Kelsen's logic of commands, it is well to bear in mind from the outset that Kelsen does not regard the designation of legal norms as "commands" in his system as allegiance to the *ordinary* sense of the term "command." The sharp discrepancy between the legal scientist's technical use of the term and what Kelsen likes to call its "proper sense" is most clearly revealed in the relations of these uses to the corresponding "acts of will." The difference consists not so much in the *intent* of the willing involved (what Kelsen calls its "subjective meaning") as it does in the existential condition of the will itself.

> A command, in the proper sense of the word, exists only when a particular individual sets and expresses an act of will. In the proper sense of the word, the existence of a command presupposes two elements: an act of will, having somebody else's behavior as its object, and the expression thereof, by means of words or gestures or other signs. A command is in existence only as long as both these elements are present. If somebody gives me a command, and if, before executing it, I have satisfactory evidence that the underlying act of will no longer exists—the evidence might be the death of the individual commanding—then I am not really faced with any command,

> even if the expression of the command would still be there—as it may, for instance, if the command is in writing. (GTLS, 32)

Now, it is Kelsen's point that in the case of legal command the coercive force involved persists, even if the act of will, the willing itself, has ceased. Kings die, parliaments and legislatures recess and change their membership. What is "commanded" by law at the initiative of these authorities, however, is contingent not on the existence of these men or of their wills, but on the validity of the corpus of norms to whose creation or sustenance they were party.

> A statute owing its existence to a parliamentary decision obviously first begins to exist at a moment when the decision has already been made and when—supposing the decision to be the expression of a will—no will is any longer there. Having passed the statute, the members of parliament turn to other questions and cease to will the contents of the law, if ever they entertained any such will. Since the statute first comes into existence upon completion of the legislative procedure, its "existence" cannot consist in the real will of the individuals belonging to the legislative body. (GTLS, 33)

This is the move which "depsychologizes" the specifically *legal* act of will, thus preventing legal science from becoming a psychology of persistent intentions. But is the difference stipulated enough to warrant Kelsen's strong charge that "command" in the legal sense "has hardly anything in common with a command properly so called" (GTLS, 33)?

Clearly, on the face of it, this is a paradoxical claim; for there is manifestly a great deal that commands in the legal sense and commands in the "proper sense" do have in common. Principally, they are both what (J. L.) Austin designated "exercitive performatives";[2] they carry with them the illocutionary force of obliging a course of conduct or its omission. Accordingly, as is the case with any performative, they are both forms of expression that are devoid of truth-value. They are both "coercive," though perhaps in different ways. It is not difficult to extend the catalog of similarities. Indeed, even the historical dominance of jurisprudents' selection of the term "command" to fit the legal notion seems to indicate a closer alignment than Kelsen wants to recognize. What, then, is the point of this remark?

Most likely, it is this: there is bound up in our ordinary thinking about the notion of "command" a large quotient of "intentional meaning"; that is, considerations touching the willing-state of the commander, his aim, the emotive strength of his imperative, and so forth. Kelsen wishes to preclude all of this—everything that would lead to an analysis of the phenomenology of commanding—from entering into our analysis of the legal command. To understand the "act of will" embedded in the legal command, he tells us, we must turn aside from the will of the commanding party, and find a unique imperative force within the martrix of a ponderous system of dyadic relations. The important point here is that this is a system whose shape (perhaps we should say "true shape") is determined by hands other than those of the command givers. It is because, within this system, "commands" must be seen as structural phenomena imbued with "formal content" that our ordinary, *in*formal understanding of commanding will be unilluminating here.

To bring into focus the structural analysis Kelsen wants to develop, it is necessary to clarify some of his groundwork assumptions. First, Kelsen explicitly identifies the notion of (legally) *valid* command with that of (legal) obligation: "To say that the behavior of an individual is commanded by an objectively valid norm amounts to the same as saying the individual is obliged to behave in this way" (PTL, 15). This is by no means counterintuitive. Our ordinary thinking tells us that if X commands Y to do something, our judgment that X's command is *valid* means that we are willing to allow that X was (for reasons which might need to be spelled out) *entitled* to make the command, and perhaps also that what X commands falls in with what we are inclined to regard as right. This amounts to saying that our judgments that X's command is a valid one and that Y ought to do what X has commanded are really only *one* judgment. Any differences, then, which arise between this ordinary account of command-validity and the specifically "legal-scientific" account must come in with what we might call the "certification" of the "ought" by whose force X aims to direct Y's behavior.

The "logical-formal" twist Kelsen gives to the legal-scientific account of "certification" amounts, broadly speaking, to this: until the "ought" which X directs at Y in a command is determined to be "objective" by our assessing its connections in a specific legal system with norms independently known to be valid, it is presumed to be merely subjective, and without legal status. To judge it "objective" it is necessary (though perhaps not sufficient) to specify and accredit the relevant intrasystematic connections. Everyone knows that what law "commands" has a radically different status from what the neighborhood bully and the stern schoolmaster "command." What Kelsen intends to show us is that which, in respect to the systems in which they are found, invests legal commands that are valid with their *special* objectivity. It is because Kelsen's account of this objectivity is strictly "formalistic" (in the sense indicated at the end of chapter one), that the command's "concrete performance" passes out of consideration at this stage.

A second key groundwork point is this: the analysis of command norms that reveals the basis of their validity is inevitably a presentation of systematic structure. The structure in point is, Kelsen reminds us, a structure of *meaning*; and as a consequence, questions concerning it must be given over to the special competence of the legal scientist. It is a distinctive characteristic of Pure Theory that the legal scientist's consideration of command-meaning has nothing whatever to do with the experience the command-giver has in "meaning it." This may perhaps best be appreciated by contrasting Kelsen's approach to one in which the phenomenology of commanding (the "concrete performance" of the command) *is* closely considered.

In *Directives and Norms*, Alf Ross considers an analysis of normative validity which is openly pyschologistic. He says, "I shall call any experience of obligation, rightness, wrongness, approval, or disapproval, the experience of validity. It must be made clear that this term designates certain psychological phenomena; 'validity' is nothing but the peculiar characteristic of these experiences."[3] As Ross admits, the result of tying validity to something which is *felt* in commanding, permitting, and so forth, is to make juridical behavior intelligible only by taking into account the existence of and force of feelings. And this means, ultimately, that the only kind of legal science that will be possible is a species of behavioral analysis. Kelsen rightly condemns this conclusion (especially as it is developed by the "sociological jurisprudents") as "metajuristic," and hopelessly subjectivistic. *Legal* validity, he says, is entirely apart from the feeling that enters as "subjective validity" into what judges and legislators mean when they make law. It is the convergence of subjective and objective validity, a juncture that resides in the *meaning of what is meant*. As before, the crucial point is the reminder that this meaning, seen as a product of legal science, is not to be regarded as a mere "replacement," nor as a "reproduction" of something already clear and exact in legal expression. Rather, it is a piece of "representation," a "reconstruction" which offers substantially more than the original.

This brings me to a third point. When, in the previous

discussion, we came to the distinction between an expression which is legally meant and the legal meaning of that expression, we found Kelsen saying that the latter is knowable only through a special "cognition," and that this cognition amounts to the discovery that, when a legal "ought" is valid, a determinate relation holds between given elements of a reconstructed formal order. It will be recalled that the relation in point was designated by Kelsen a "functional connection." Previously I have been concerned only with the role of this connection in deciding the adequacy of a norm's presentation by its correlative rule of law. Now it is time to examine the connection itself, both the elements it links and the relation that binds them.

To exhibit this "functional connection" as a jurisprudential construction, Kelsen introduces the technical notion of *"Deutungsschema."* In setting the object of legal-scientific cognition off from the "external facts" studied by sociological jurisprudes, Kelsen says this:

> what turns (the external fact) into a legal or illegal set is not its physical existence, determined by the laws of causality prevailing in nature, but the objective meaning resulting from its interpretation. The specifically legal meaning of this act is derived from a "norm" whose content refers to the act, so that it may be interpreted according to this norm. The norm functions as a scheme of interpretation. (PTL, 3–4)

The *Deutungsschema*, like Wittgenstein's "pictorial form," is a schema, a framework, built of that which a legal scientist's conception of the norm (his "rule of law") has in common with legal reality. Accordingly, the *Deutungsschema* displays a form common to all legal norms (valid as well as invalid). *On* this framework, the "functional connection" is exhibited; the role of the latter is that of "glue," holding or failing to hold together the parts of the norm structure. When the connection holds, the norm is valid; when it does not, it is invalid. Thus, there emerges

a distinguishing characteristic of the legal- scientific viewpoint; it amounts to a fixed style of "seeing-as."

Robert Vernengo, one of the few commentators to pay
significant heed to Kelsen's notion of *Deutungsschema*,
views the use of schematic structure in Pure Theory as the
beginning of a sharp departure from prevailing thinking in
the area.

> It is important to point out that norms, although a kind of
> modal sentences (ought-sentences, deontic propositions, im-
> peratives, or the like), are construed by Kelsen as understand-
> able enunciations, as linguistic structures endowed with
> meaning, an attitude which puts him in direct opposition
> with very influential trends of contemporary thought.[4]

This position, Vernengo argues, forced upon Kelsen the
responsibility of developing a set of criteria which, in actual practice, would effectively distinguish well-formed
legal-normative sentences and legally meaningless strings
of words. In his quaint neo-Kantian way, Kelsen calls these
criteria *"Geltungsbereiche"* ("normative spheres of validity"). They are what other positivists[5] would have called
"formation rules of the legal language," that is, rules for
making well-formed legal propositions. Following this
lead, Vernengo first formulates what he believes to be the
schematic form ("propositional function") of a meaningful
primary legal sentence (positive command), according to
the system adumbrated in Pure Theory. He then suggests
the need for deontic modalization of this schema, and
briefly indicates the way in which the four types of *Geltungsbereiche* Kelsen invokes work in determining its
meaning. He concludes that, despite Kelsen's best efforts,
the *Geltungsbereiche* he distinguishes will serve only as
"partial sets" of the sought-for formation rules;

> consequently, he must somehow restrict the ontological field
> to which those propositions can refer, a commitment that is
> not required by the nature of legal facts themselves, but is ac-
> cepted because of some practical reason that regards legal

theory. Furthermore, it must be stressed that the logical basis
on which Kelsen's theory works is not sufficiently developed,
as the very ambiguity of the normative spheres of validity
clearly proves.[6]

Vernengo's verdict is quite on target—particularly in
regard to the insufficiency of development plaguing
Kelsen's efforts toward a "logical basis." The argumenta-
tion by which this verdict is reached, however, is flawed in
at least three important respects. First, it is clear that the
"direct opposition" Vernengo speaks of appears, if at all,
only if one has in mind the earliest and crudest forms of
logical positivism. It is certain that none of the contemporary heirs of the Vienna Circle alluded to by Vernengo
holds that expressions rendered "noncognitive" by their
deontic neustics are thereby prevented from being "understandable enunciations." Vernengo seems here to be confusing propositional intelligibility with intrasystematic
clarity—the latter of which Kelsen's constructional approach aims for in a way that divorces it from Vernengo's
alleged conflict. In fact, the course of explication Kelsen
chooses brings Pure Theory into close alignment with the
general outlines of some influential programs of "neo-
positivism" (at least those of the "construction" wing).
For—and this brings us to the second point—Kelsen's interpretation of legal *Deutungsschemata* explicitly requires
a style of expression to a large degree in harmony with the
formulations of the latest efforts in the field.

It is wrong of Vernengo to suggest that Kelsen's treatment on this score is merely *noncommittal* with regard to
the modal status of well-formed normative expressions; he
apparently relishes the thought that Kelsen has left it open
for more technically adept formalizers (like himself) to
clear away the prevailing shadows with flashes of symbolic notation. There are indeed shadows enough in Kelsen's account, and judicious amounts of formalization
might help to dispel them; but, on just this point, Vernengo

has overlooked a glimmer already present. Far from being noncommittal about the modal status of *Deutungs-schemata*, Kelsen expressly embraces the relevant distinction between "modi," (PTL, 6) and openly, if laboriously, struggles toward a formulation adequate to the deontic modality. Vernengo's third error lies in his execution of the deontically modalized schematic form of a well-formed primary legal sentence. Vernengo's effort in this direction is especially disappointing; he misses all that is distinctive and revelatory in Kelsen's treatment; above all, he misses the *connective* in the "functional connnection" of the *Deutungsschema*.

In fairness to Vernengo, however, I should add that he has, in a very short article, perceived more of what is essential about Kelsen's style of formalization (in the specific case of schematized, well-formed norms) than have most other commentators on Pure Theory. The key to Vernengo's success is his simple recognition of the pervasive importance of *schematization* in Kelsen's account of legal norms. Kelsen wants to say that our understanding of the meaning of a norm is dependent on our successfully discerning in it a *schema*; this schema is part of the norm's own meaning, yet it shows upon analysis of a regular "functional connection"; and this connection is what allows the legal scientist to place the norm with others in a constructional order. Since the question of validity ultimately hinges on the makeup of this order, it follows that the "structural analysis" of "*Deutungsschemata*," the breakdown and display of their parts, is sine qua non for the objective determination of normative validity. Vernengo, it must be said, saw this, but saw it very dimly. In what follows, I shall try to get a clearer view.

THE CANONICAL FORM OF COMMAND-RULES

Among other early commentators, the only ones to sense the importance of the notion of "schema" in Pure Theory,

and certainly the only ones to come close to assessing correctly the role of the "functional connection" in *Deutungs-
schemata*, are Bergmann and Zerby. In discussing what
they called the "categorical" sense of "formal" in Kelsen's
writings, they fall as if by accident upon this appraisal:

> If we were asked what we consider the most plausible inter-
> pretation of Kelsen, we should say that he takes the category
> to reside in the schema as a whole; in other words, the if-then
> connection is considered as essential as the ought-
> clause. . . . To say the same thing in the language of contem-
> porary empiricism, on this interpretation Kelsen would deal
> with the *logic of imperatives* in general, not with a categorial
> determination of the law. This is in our opinion what he ac-
> tually does; the inclusion of the if-then connection into the
> category is redundant; it becomes understandable only as a
> rationalization of the desire to set law "formally" apart.[7]

When they speak of "the schema as a whole," what
Bergmann and Zerby have in mind is the following hypothetical form: "If there is X (delict), then there ought to be
Y (sanction)." When they say Kelsen takes "the category"
to reside in this schema, they are saying that he means for
there to be, as an essential property of this form, a new and
independently subsisting "epistemic necessity." It is, they
think, Kelsen's willingness to assert on behalf of this
species of categorical necessity a *special* status, a status
that will radically differentiate legal normativity from
ethical and other varieties, that runs his analysis on the
rocks.

Bergmann and Zerby are, of course, themselves convinced that the formalism legal theory partakes of is and
must be different from that of formal logic, "In whatever
sense—and this is a difficult problem in metaphysics—
logic may be said to be formal, analytical, or a priori, the
philosophy of law and the Pure Theory in particular are
not formal, analytical, or a priori in this sense."[8] And it is

Kelsen's alleged efforts to make Pure Theory partake of logical formalism that draw their hardest criticisms, "What is Kelsen's undoing is his ambition to dignify his brilliant analytical insights by elevating them to categorical, formal, or necessary determinations of the law."[9] What Bergmann and Zerby mean when they attack Kelsen's pernicious desire to "set law 'formally' apart" is this: if legal orders are (as they think) *in fact*, hierarchies of *Zwangsnormen* (coercive norms), it makes no sense to construe them as "formally determined," surely, at least, not in the logical sense of formal determination. Kelsen, in seeking to set law off from morals, and so forth, has chosen an inappropriate means of procuring the desired "special status"; for logic, though different from morals and the rest, is also different—and in quite the same way—from law.

The Bergmann-Zerby critique misses badly, however, on two counts. The first is its assumption that Kelsen's "categorial" formalism aims at appropriating *intact* the standard logical forms (and in particular, the "if-then" connective) for its analyses of legal norms. In a footnote, Bergmann and Zerby broach another possibility; but they immediately dismiss it.

> These remarks do not mean to deny that the if-then connection, if it occurs in the logic of imperatives, might have properties which are radically or, if you please, categorically different from those of the analogous indicative connective. . . . But it seems utterly unrealistic to assume that anything like this was in Kelsen's mind.[10]

Far from this being an "unrealistic assumption," it is a point of doctrine confirmed repeatedly in Kelsen's work. In Pure Theory, the connective corresponding to the logician's truth functional conditional is called "imputation." It is specifically identified as a "sui generis" form of structural link, and the properties with which it imbues the legal-normative hierarchy are differentiated from those that would have been imbued by the standard employment of the "if-then" connective. The second mistake lies in the Bergmann-Zerby interpretation of Kelsen's "schema." In their eagerness to cast doubt upon the status of the "category" in this schema, Bergmann and Zerby overlook an important point in connection with the *application* of the schema in pure-theoretic construction. It is, we may recall, the "rule of law" that gets hierarchically arranged in the "representations" of legal science, not the norm itself. And what is of interest in the rule of law—what it "abstracts" from the norm-schema—is the "functional connection," the determinator of its validity. Thus, whether or not norms themselves are to be regarded as *"Zwangsordnungen,"* the order of validation upon which their meaning depends may remain a system with its own style of cognition and—to some extent—its own style of formalism. When Kelsen shifts the field of legal-scientific operation from that of norms proper to that of the rules of law which describe them, he expressly avoids imposing a formal pattern on coercions as such; he insists that the order Pure Theory seeks can only be found in that which bestows upon coercions their *validity.* Since, as Kelsen puts it, this presentational order is only a "cognitive" order, an order finding its regularity in *Denkakten*, there is little threat of artificiality in the expression of its hierarchical arrangement. Bergmann and Zerby neglect altogether the all-important doctrine of *"Rechtsregeln."* Accordingly, they are considerably perplexed at the thesis of descriptivity which, as I have pointed out, is at its very core.

What is chiefly important in the Bergmann-Zerby account is the connection it adduces between the delict- sanction schema and the prospect of a "logic of imperatives." It is worthwhile following this suggestion in connection with the most evident species of imperative in law, the command. The simplest kind of legal command is a judicial order, or "individual norm," one which applies in a single, nonrecurring situation. Kelsen gives us an example of such a norm in *General Theory of Law and State*, "Suppose that a judge orders a debtor A to return $1000 to his creditor B. By expressly or tacitly threatening A with a civil sanction in case of non-payment, the judge here 'commands' A to pay $1000 to B (GTLS, 38)."

Here, it appears, is just the coercive element Bergmann and Zerby want: the judge "threatens" the debtor. But Kelsen is quick to neutralize this element when the command in point passes qua norm into the analytical consideration of the legal scientist. What makes this judicial order a *norm* is exactly the same thing that makes general norms norms; it is a matter not of coerciveness as such, but of form. Explaining the above example, Kelsen says,

> The decision of the judge is a legal norm in the same sense and for the same reasons as the general principle that if somebody does not return a loan then a civil sanction ought to be inflicted upon him on the motion of the creditor. The 'binding force' or 'validity' of law is intrinsically related, not to its possible general character, but only to its character as a norm. (GTLS, 38)

When it comes to specifying the command's "character as a norm," it is not the notion of *Zwang* that comes into play, but the notion of *schema*. In a passage immediately subsequent to the above-cited discussion of individual command-norms, Kelsen suggests as the defining feature the very schematic formula Bergmann and Zerby mention. General legal norms, he says, are essentially hypothetical statements stipulating sanctions under certain conditions. Finding the hypothetical *form* in command-norms is identical with the procedure of seeing them as *Deutungsschemata*. And since *all* norms share what is essentially one schema, it follows that the rules whereby all norms are represented must share a "canonical form." Now, what is it that canonical norms having the hypothetical delict/ sanction form share which, if it is indeed a "functional connection," will make the norms valid? An explication of norm-schemes for legal commands will show why Bergmann and Zerby are entirely wrong to characterize the "logic" that follows from this account a "logic of imperatives."

In the previous chapter, I took note of the fact that the expressions whereby law-making authorities issue norms may vary widely, while the rules of law corresponding to the norms they make are of just *one* form. This uniformity now appears as a function of schematic "seeing-as."

> It is the task of the science of law to represent the law of a community, i.e. the material produced by the legal authority in the law-making procedure, in the form of statements to the effect that "if such and such conditions are fulfilled, then such and such shall follow." (GTLS, 45)

The statements legal science produces are, of course, "rules of law," and not norms. Kelsen stresses that they are not prescriptive, and hence not imperative. So, whatever system is built of them, it cannot be a "logic of imperatives." But what sort of system *can* be built of them? So far, all we have is a barebones hypothetical schema:

$$(\text{Lc}^*\text{-}1) \quad \text{If} \ldots, \text{then} \ldots$$

When, in this formula, the first blank is filled by the "legal antecedent," or *delict*; and the second blank by the "legal consequent," or *sanction*, the result is a rule of law. Kelsen explains these terms as follows:

> Delict is a definite human behavior (an action or omission) which, because socially undesirable, is prohibited by the legal order; and it is prohibited insofar as the legal order attaches to it (or, more correctly formulated: to the fact that it is ascertained in a legal procedure) a coercive act, as this fact is made by the legal order the condition of a coercive act. And this

> coercive act is a sanction (in the sense of a reaction against a delict) and as such distinguishable from other legally established coercive acts only in that the conditioning fact of the former is a legally ascertained human behavior, whereas the coercive acts which have not the character of sanctions are conditioned by other facts. (PTL, 40–41)

It is essential to remember that the delict and sanction in a rule of law are *facts*, just as are the antecedent and consequent in a law of nature. Hence, the normativity that distinguishes the former from the latter must come in as a *supplement* to the facts.

Kelsen's way of injecting the normative component into the rule-schema is what gives his norm-"logics" their distinctive shape. It is at once the source of their considerable strengths and of their ultimate weaknesses. In the constructional system of Pure Theory *all of the normativity comes in with the connective.* This is what accounts for the sharp contrast between the conditionality of Lc*-1 and that of similar-appearing "natural" laws (we should say "scientific" laws).

> The rule of law and the law of nature differ not so much by the elements they connect as by the manner of their connection. The law of nature establishes that if A is, B is (or will be). The rule of law says: If A is, B ought to be. . . . The meaning of the connection established by the law of nature between two elements is the "is," whereas the meaning of the connection between two elements established by the rule of law is the "ought." (GTLS, 46)

Kelsen nominates the normative ("functional") connection "imputation" *(Zurechnung)*.[11] And, lest we forget, the sense of "ought" it carries is distinctively a "descriptive" sense.

> The science of law describing, e.g. the legal norm concerning murder does not say: "If a man commits murder, he will be punished," but: "If a man commits murder, he ought to be punished." In this statement the term "ought" has a descrip-

tive sense; and the connection between the condition and the consequence has not the character of causality, but of *imputation*. The sanction is not the effect of the delict as its cause, but the sanction is "imputed" to the delict. (ILR, 3)

We may therefore revise our previous "barebones schema" using the symbol "I" for the connection of imputation:

$$(Lc^*-2) \quad dIs$$

(This may be read "Sanction *s* is imputed to delict *d*"; alternatively, "If delict *d* is, sanction *s* ought to be.")

Kelsen insists that this formation, or something very much like it, is mandatory in the scientific representation of command norms. In it are contained all those elements which are both common and peculiar to all well-formed legal commands. Hence, the formula is really a *canonical form* for the rules which represent these norms, however various their material appearance. Kelsen stresses the universality of this form's application later on in *Pure Theory of Law*.

A rule of law describing a norm of criminal law must be formulated—much simplified even at that—approximately as follows: "If an individual has committed a crime determined in a general legal norm, then an organ designated in a general legal norm (a court) ought to order a sanction, determined in the former legal norm in a procedure determined in a general legal norm." (PTL, 231)

There is in this amplification of (Lc*-2) some indication of the connection between the ("formal") bond uniting the factual elements of antecedence and consequence and the ("material") bond of duty falling upon a legal organ according to the procedural rules of a given system. In the immediately subsequent text Kelsen elaborates upon this connection.

We shall see later that a still more complicated formulation is necessary, namely: "If an organ, whose nomination is deter-

mined by a general legal norm, has ascertained, in a procedure determined by a general legal norm, that facts are present to which a general legal norm attaches a certain sanction,
then this organ ought to order a sanction determined in the
earlier-mentioned legal norm, in a procedure determined by a
general legal norm." This formulation of the rule of law,
then, shows—and therein lies the essential function of the rule
of law describing the law—the systematic connection between the so-called formal and the so-called material law
(that is, between the determination of the delict and the sanction on the one hand and the determination of the law-
applying organ and his procedure on the other). (PTL, 231)

It is important to notice that Kelsen here includes in the expanded form of the universal command-norm schema explicit mention of four different "oughts": (1) the authorizing norm which "nominates" the norm-applying organ;
(2) the norm which imputes sanction to delict; (3) the norm
which, on account of this imputational connection, obliges
a legal authority to act; and (4) the procedural norm which
specifies the authority's course (or perhaps range) of action. The all-important "material-formal" connection in
which Kelsen finds the "essential function" of rules of law
concerns the relation of the second and third of these
norms. On this relation I shall have considerably more to
say shortly. Two things are particularly worth noting at
this point, however: first, the remarkable *complexity* of
normative interconnection which has sprung from an apparently simple schematic form; and second, the *independence* of the complex relation's several normative
parts: Each of the norms, it seems, could have been created
by different processes, and at different times; each is applied by a different organ and in a different way, as well as
at a different time. And perhaps most important, at least
three of the "oughts" apply to different subjects (that is, if
a procedure may be called a subject).

Since the "component norms" imbedded in an expanded legal norm do apply to different subjects, it is easy to suppose that between the norm imputing the sanction to the delict and the norm obliging an authoritative action (norms 2 and 3 above, respectively) there is no "unifying" connection. But Kelsen has been insistently opposed to this supposition. His constant underlying thought here is that the commission of a delict is never just the violation of an "ought" (individual or general) directed against the delinquent agent; rather it is always at the same time the implementation of a system-relative "ought" directed, not at the agent, but at the legal authority; and in the typical case this will involve not only a single "ought," but a series of "oughts" in which the possible nonapplication of the prescribed sanction as well as its application is taken into account.

To understand the peculiar compression of normative forces involved here, as well as the theoretic unification it allows, it is necessary to return to the notion of "imputation," a notion which Kelsen has recently called "one of the most essential contributions of the Pure Theory of Law" (RPS, 135).

"IMPUTATIONAL VECTORS";
THE ORGANIZATION OF NORMATIVE FORCE

When, for example, a norm in a given legal system says something to the effect that "if a man commits murder he should be hanged by the neck until dead," it seems to follow from what has been said to this point that the normative force contained in the imputational connective (if . . . , then . . . . should . . .) flows in two quite contrary directions. On the one hand, the norm seems to have the effect of requiring all agents subject to it to abstain from murdering; on the other hand, it seems equally clearly to have the effect of requiring legal organs of the system to apply the sanction of hanging in case of nonobedience. Now, it is entirely usual for us to think of the first of these imputational vectors as the fundamental one. Indeed, the brunt of the history of positivistic legal theory certainly supports the view that "to say 'a behavior is commanded' is synonymous (or roughly synonymous) with saying 'an individual has the obligation to behave in a certain way' " (PTL, 114). Naturally enough, Austin calls this kind of obligation "primary duty," and the corresponding individual-directed order "primary command." Austin regards sanction-stipulating commands and duties as "secondary," both in respect to temporal origin and to function in the legal system. Since, as he reasons, sanctioning duties and commands are *responses* to primary duties and commands, in that they aim at preserving or restoring the mode of behavior made obligatory in the latter, they are, strictly speaking, extraneous to the proper function of law.

Kelsen is quite right in saying that this view commits Austin to a position on the nature of law that is distant from his avowed aims; it is, in fact, tantamount to an outright identification of law and primary commands (duties, rights, and so forth). This comes out most clearly when Austin discusses the legal ideal. He says: "If the obedience to the law were absolutely perfect, primary rights and duties are the only ones which would exist."[12] And the question that Kelsen correctly raises here is: would such a system be law at all? Clearly, without the stipulation of sanctions, the legal order is without coercive force. And if law is defined as a specific form of coercive order, then the system which Austin describes—though it might be a system of duty—is simply not a system of law. In *General Theory of Law and State* Kelsen deftly shows Austin's many inconsistencies on this score (after all, it is a keystone of Austinian positivism that legal obligation is the same as liability to legal sanction), and proceeds apace to the reversal of Austin's analysis.

As Kelsen sees it, the sanction-stipulating norm (Austin's

"secondary") is primary, and the duty-specifying norm (Austin's "primary") is not only secondary, but ultimately epiphenomenal.

> That somebody is legally obligated to certain conduct means that an organ "ought" to apply a sanction to him in case of contrary conduct. But the concept of legal duty differs from that of moral duty by the fact that the legal duty is not the behavior which the norm "demands," which "ought" to be observed. The legal duty, instead, is the behavior by the observance of which the delict is avoided, thus the opposite of the behavior which forms a condition for the sanction . . .
>
> If it is also said that the legal duty "ought" is, so to speak, an epiphenomenon of the "ought" of the sanction. (GTLS, 60)

To make the reversal complete, Kelsen definitionally equates "law" and the system of primary norms (Austin's secondary commands, and so on).

> If one makes use of the auxiliary concept of secondary norms, then the opposite of the delict appears as 'lawful behavior,' or behavior conforming with the secondary norm, and the delict as 'unlawful behavior,' or behavior contradicting the secondary norm. When the delict is defined simply as unlawful behavior, law is regarded as a system of secondary norms. But this is not tenable if we have realized law's character of a coercive order which stipulates sanctions. Law is the primary norm, which stipulates the sanction, and this norm is not contradicted by the delict of the subject, which on the contrary, is the specific condition of the sanction. (GTLS, 61)

It is easy to see that hard conclusions must follow from this doctrine. It follows immediately, of course, that law so construed is a "closed system" in at least one sense: it contains no sanctionless norms. It also follows that the normative relation involves the agent subject only *indirectly:* "The imputation which is in question here is not the relation between an individual and an action of his, but the relation between the legal sanction and the action, and

thus indirectly the acting individual himself" (PTL, 92).
From the standpoint of legal-scientific presentation, however, the gravest consequence of the doctrine is this: If the
decisive vector in the imputational relation is, as Kelsen
says, coercion (the obligation to enforce a given sanction,
rather than the avoidance of unlawful agency) a legal
system composed of imputational relations will consist
wholly of laws that cannot be disobeyed by legal agents,
but only by the organs of enforcement. This is certainly a
most counterintuitive conclusion, requiring special critical
attention.

First, it is only fair to point out that Kelsen does not
shrink from drawing this remarkable conclusion himself.
On the contrary, he happily embraces it.

> Only the organ can contradict law itself, the primary norm,
> by not executing the sanction in spite of its conditions being
> fulfilled. . . . Only the organ can, strictly speaking, "obey" or
> "disobey" the legal norm by executing or not executing the
> stipulated sanction. (GTLS, 61)[13]

It is not difficult to see why Kelsen has taken his analysis of
command norms in this extraordinary direction. By re-
stricting the legal obligation incumbent upon the individual delinquent to an "indirect" and "epiphenomenal"
status, Pure Theory reduces the numbers and simplifies the
organization of normative relations in the constructional
order. In fact, the clearest prospect open to the legal scientist for a rigorous formalism relies on the arrangement of
connections between what Kelsen calls "primary" norms,
disregarding wholly whatever "secondary" norms may
follow from them.

Yet, understandably enough, Kelsen shows that he is
loath to lose sight altogether of the sense of personal legal
obligation connected with secondary norms. Indeed, when
he is discussing legal responsibility generally, and not
merely the representation of norm-structures, it is usually
the secondary, rather than the primary, which Kelsen

speaks of as "main obligation" (for example, PTL, 124). His way of recognizing the secondary norm in pure-theoretic construction is a transparently ineffectual *pis aller*. Kelsen insists that secondary norms, demanding the omissions of delicts, are strictly "dependent" on the corresponding primary norms, stipulating sanctions; but he quickly adds that this dependence is only a "convenience," and in no way shifts the weight of imputational fact. If the meaning of the secondary norm were properly part of the meaning of the primary norm—or even merely derivable from it—then clearly it would be possible for the individual legal subject to obey or disobey law in as strong a sense as that in which legal organs can. But Kelsen will have none of this. Even though he says "the representation of law is greatly facilitated if we allow ourselves to assume also the existence of the (secondary) norm" (GTLS, 61), he gives no indication of how the facilitation works. On the contrary, he repeatedly indicates that it comes to nothing; once he had admitted that obedience and disobedience of law is something restricted to legal organs, all the conceptual byplay with secondary norms becomes otiose. All of this is, in fact, merely a deferential nod to an annoying particle of legal fact left unhandled by Pure Theory; it points to a difference that makes no difference.

This situation makes it somewhat difficult to find a way of amplifying the crude command-norm schema Lc*-2 so as to bring out the fourfold complexity of component "oughts" indicated above. If to say that Smith ought to pay his taxes were the same thing as to say that a specific sanction ought to be imposed in the case of Smith's non-payment of taxes, an easy formalization would suggest itself:

$$O(x) \sim d = dIs(x)$$

(where "0" is the original (secondary) obligation upon Smith, "x" the agent and "dIs" the consequent imputational connection). But this will not fit Kelsen's scheme.

For while what appears on the right side of this equivalence has the requisite imputational connective, what appears on the left does not, since that connective necessarily joins sanctions to delicts, and the secondary obligation is secondary precisely in that it *lacks* the stipulation of a sanction. Even if it is suggested that this formula brings out the sense in which a sanction is *implicit* in the meaning of expressions of legal obligation (that is, as an element required if an "0(x) ∽ y" statement is to count as a *legal* norm), an insuperable problem remains: It would follow from the formula that if a failure to bring about what "I" dictates is a contravention of law, then so is a failure to bring about what "0" dictates; and this Kelsen will not allow. Nor will the weaker formulation,

$$0(x) \sim d \supset dIs(x)$$

do, and for a yet stronger reason. As I have pointed out, Kelsen insists that only a norm can be the reason for the validity of another norm; but if the above formula were sound, one would be able to infer something which is (or could be) a valid norm from something (for the reasons just given) which cannot be one.

It follows that the expansion of Lc*-2 we have been seeking must, if it is to comprehend the various "oughts" of the "material-formal" relation, exhibit these "oughts" as ingredients in the identification and regulation of legal *organs* and their operations, rather than legal *agents* and theirs. And, since styles of these arrangements differ broadly from system to system, about all that can be said here from the formal point of view is that, whatever is to operate as a legal organ in a system is subject to conditioning and certifying influences of intra-systemic regulations.

Although the "imputational vector" which leads in the direction of legal agency has been shown to be (in the context of Pure Theory) a shadow-force, it must not be assumed that the vector which leads to the imposition of a sanction ceases at that point to organize legal normativity. On the contrary, it is exactly what comes *after* the establishment of this link that provides legal science with the "prospect of unity" alluded to above. The stage for this development was set by Kelsen's insistence that only legal authorities can disobey the law. While this slogan takes the agent out of contention, it also underscores the contingent status of sanction-execution by the legal organ. This is where a fundamental distinction between the principle of imputation and the similar-appearing principle of causation comes into clearest focus.

Kelsen spends a great amount of time spelling out differences between causality and imputation, chiefly to counter the causalistic emphasis of sociological jurisprudence (WJ, 324–344; PTL, 76–81). The issue, however, is fundamentally a simple one. The distinction between the two principles is fully indicated in the relative effects of counterinstances. The causal rule that "if a baseball traveling at sixty miles an hour strikes an ordinary plate glass window (condition) the window will break (consequence)" is falsified when a baseball having the specified velocity *does* strike the window and it *doesn't* break. But the imputational rule of law concerning murder, that "if a man commits murder, he ought to be hanged by the neck until dead," is not invalidated upon the occasion of the first unpunished murder. This last- mentioned circumstance accounts for all of Kelsen's talk about the "a-temporality" and "inviolability" (for example, GTLS, 46) of legal norms. The point is only that, in order for a once-valid norm to be invalidated, yet another norm that has the force either of directly quashing or of derogating the former must become valid.[14]

This, of course, raises the question: What is the normative effect of a sanction's nonimposition? And while Kelsen very seldom addresses this question directly, what he does say suggests a most important expansion of $L^*c\text{-}2$.

THE IMPUTATIONAL HIERARCHY

Imputation shares with causation a temporally open-ended conditional form. That is to say, in both forms, what follows the "then" is unspecified, suggesting the possibility of the "then" becoming, at a certain point, the "if" for another conditional link. Thus, it seems plausible to suppose that both may form "chains," their consequence-elements becoming antecedence-elements for further relations. The notion of a causal chain is, of course, thoroughly familiar. But what of imputational chains? Here Kelsen takes a bold, direct approach. He willingly allows that there *are* imputational chains, and argues that they differ from causal chains chiefly in the matter of termination. Causal chains, he argues (PTL, 91) have no end points, no *primae causae*; imputation chains do. Now, obviously, the imputation chain has a *prima causa* analog in the delict. So, on the issue of the initial "end point" the distinction is clear enough. It is on the other end that crucial problems appear.

If a sanction that has been duly prescribed (and this takes into account residual questions of organ-legitimation, procedure, and so forth) is enforced, no further legal execution is in order. Thus, a clear-cut terminus to the imputational chain is reached. If, however, the sanction is not enforced, continuation of the chain remains possible. Kelsen takes up this possibility in *General Theory of Law and State*. There he allows that the nonexecution of sanction s may be the condition for the imposition of another sanction s':

The judge—or, to use a more general expression, the law-applying organ—can be legally obligated to execute the sanction—in the sense in which the subject is obligated to refrain from the delict, to "obey" the legal norms—only if there is a further norm which attaches a further sanction to the non-execution of the first sanction. Thus there must be two distinct norms: one stipulating that another organ shall execute a sanction against the first organ, in case the first sanction is not executed. (GTLS, 59–60)

This gives us the expanded schema:

$$L^*c\text{-}3 \quad ((dIs)\&{\sim}s)Is'$$

(which we may read "The sanction s' is imputed to the nonimposition of sanction s in the case of the commission of delict d").

Here, of course, the complex event $(dIs)\&{\sim}s$ is being treated as a species of delict; and it is only in the case that such a condition *is* a specified delict in a given system that the second sanction can be imputed to it. Similarly, as Kelsen points out (GTLS, 61), relative to the second imputational connection, what appeared as "organ" for dIs is only a "subject." This suggests the possibility of an indeterminately large chain of imputations, linked by successive nonimpositions of successive sanctions:

$$L^*c\text{-}4 \quad \ldots ((((dIs)\&{\sim}s)Is')\&{\sim}s')Is'' \ldots$$

Since the latter is an open-ended schema, it raises the question of whether the series of imputations might be *nonterminating*. The possibility that a never-ending series of sanctions might be called for to counter the nonimposition of sanctions prescribed for failures of law-enforcement was first recognized by Franz Brentano.[15] This specter of *regressus ad infinitum* has more recently been exhumed by Timasheff, who sees it as the keystone of an argument to defeat the view that every legal norm must impose a sanction.[16] Kelsen, arguing against Timasheff, defends a notion of legal normativity which makes sanction-stipulation an essential element. Kelsen's dodge is to allow that some norms in a legal order may not be "secured by other (and higher) norms" in that order.

> All the norms of a legal order are coercive norms; i.e. norms providing for sanctions; but among these norms there are norms the efficacy of which is not secured by other coercive norms. Norm n, e.g. runs as follows: If an individual steals, another individual, an organ of the community, shall punish him. The efficacy of this norm is secured by the norm n+1: If the organ does not punish a thief, another organ shall punish the organ who violates his duty of punishing the thief. There is no norm n+2, securing the efficacy of the norm n+1. The coercive norm n+1: If the organ does not punish the thief, another organ shall punish the law-violating organ, is not guranteed by a norm of the n+2nd degree. But all the norms of this legal order are coercive norms. (GTLS, 29)

There are two ways in which the language of this crucially important passage is potentially misleading. First, the focus here is on legal *efficacy*, that is, the empirical question of law's application in enforcing sanctions against delicts. This perspective takes the discussion away from the issue of *validity*, a nonempirical question which is the pivotal concern of imputational connections. Secondly, this discussion is framed (as is the bulk of *General Theory*) in the *suppositio materialis* of legal science ("norm-talk"), rather than its *suppositio formalis* ("rule-talk"), which alone is suited for constructional analysis.

Hart, who has recently aired certain "long entertained doubts" about this portion of Kelsen's treatment of norms,[17] seems to have been misled, and perhaps in both of these ways. In the course of explicating the idea that in some cases no norm n+2 "secures the efficacy" of its immediate inferior, Hart says: "Kelsen does not think that it is necessary that a sanction be provided for every legal rule . . ."[18] Now, if this interpretation relates, as the language suggests, to "*Rechtsregeln*," it is not born up by the evidence of the passage cited. In this case it is just a gratuitous and unaccountable remark, wholly extraneous to Hart's line of explanation. If, on the other hand, it relates to "*Rechtsnormen*," as seems more likely, it flies directly in the face of Kelsen's persistent dogma: Every independent legal norm, of its very nature, connects a sanction with a delict. What Hart apparently has in mind here is something more expansive. He wants us to see that Kelsen finds it unnecessary for every legal norm to have, as a conditon of its validity, a higher norm which will impute a sanction to the nonenforcement of the first, viewed now as delict. Hart wants to accept Kelsen's response to Timasheff et al. on the infinite regress problem; and he wants to agree with him that the pure-theoretic account of norm-coerciveness is invulnerable to the threat of regress. But nowhere does Hart recognize that Kelsen's argument is explicitly limited to the plane of efficacy; and nowhere does he hint at a suspicion that the legal-scientific presentation of *rules* constructed of this norm-situation might be a somewhat different, and possibly more revealing, picture. In fact, Hart drops the term "efficacy" altogether from his critical account, except where he cites Kelsen's own language or paraphrases it.

Hart's analysis has a twofold thrust. On the one hand, he bolsters Kelsen's resistance to the regress-argument by exposing a possibility of norm-construction Kelsen had not considered, but which further insulates the essential-sanction viewpoint from its critics. On the other hand, he undercuts the very cause of Kelsen's worry, the indefinite prolongation of the norm-sequence, by giving evidence of Kelsen's shortsightedness about normative self-reference. The key idea, as he puts it, is that "there is no reason why a rule should not provide a sanction for the breach both of other rules and of itself."[19] The example he gives is that of a judge ordered to punish any judge who fails to punish an individual who steals. Clearly, such an order entails the possibility of the judge's being obligated to punish himself.

On this point, however, it appears that Hart had confused a compounding of *persons* (the *one* judge both issues and is subject to the command-norm) with a compounding of *norms* (the "ought" that he directs to judges generally, and the "ought" that is imposed in the case of his own failure to punish). It is true, of course, that a law could be written in the manner Hart suggests, so as to rule against all judicial omissions of orders higher than that of n+2. But this would not mean that the logic of such a ruling's "interior relations," and hence of its rational reconstruction, would differ from that of the chain of norms which would have occurred in the absence of self-reference. Here Hart, unlike himself in other critical discussions of Pure Theory, seems strangely insensitive to the role left to legal science in the representation and hence, ultimately, the validation of norms.

If we turn away form the norm (and the question of efficacy) to face the rule that represents it (and settles its validity), we find Kelsen hinting at a more dramatic solution to the "norm-series" problem. This is a route of defense for which Hart has given Kelsen no credit. Let us consider a rule that represents a norm at the n+2-level. Regardless of whether this is a simple "series-initiating" norm or a Hartian recursive norm, the *meaning* of the norm is to place an obligation on some party in case of the non-execution of an act of prior obligation. Now, it is Kelsen's idea that this meaning will be revealed in the process of showing what it is with which the obligation it places connects. Again, if the obligation to be placed is that of a legal command, showing its connections will invariably involve showing a delict, a sanction, an imputational connection linking them, and a complex network of other sanctions, delicts, and imputations surrounding and supporting them (that is, providing a matrix of meaning within which its own meaning has an organic function). Obviously, wherever such a wide nest of imputations appears, the transferral of "duty" (that is, obligations to impose sanctions) is not a matter that is easily settled.

Yet—and this is the core of the matter—Kelsen does indicate that the work of legal science will come to a definite end in every case of norm-presentation. There must, as he puts it, be a "last norm" to every imputational chain, "This series of norms cannot be extended indefinitely. There must be a last norm of the series such that the sanction which it stipulates is not a legal duty in the sense defined" (PTL, 60). The key question regarding this statement is: what is the force of the "must?" It is possible, of course, to construe the statement as a commonplace empirical observation. It might, that is, be taken as meaning only that any actual legal system, bound by strictures of space and time, can only impute so many sanctions to so many delicts—its very finitude dictating an end to any given series of nested imputations. What stands in the way of this interpretation, however, is the "formal-logical" nature of the chain itself. As I have observed, the order in which the chain of imputations appears can only be the order of *Rechtsregeln*, not of *Normen*. This was made perfectly clear when Kelsen said that "imputation is a principle of order in human thinking . . . " (PTL, 103), a matter of *Denkakten*, not of *Willensakten*. It follows that the tasks of presentating the imputational order fall to the legal scientist, rather than to the lawyer, judge, or legal agent. Secondly, the complex of imputational relations in L*c-4 is in fact a "nest," rather than a chain; its connectives function superveniently, rather than linearly, in a way that mirrors the organization of organ-authority in the reconstructed legal order. Joining these observations, it is plain that nothing stands in the way of a *formally* endless piling up of imputation-relations. Quite to the contrary, the legal scientist might presumably wish to run the series out, in order to discover (or perhaps even reveal) the hierarchical organization or organ-authority in the particular system his reconstruction presents.

The other alternative is to regard Kelsen's "must" as a

logical compulsion, indicating the presence of a special norm, one which, not being a proper legal duty, does not (at least in the usual sense) imply an "ought." Reading along these lines, we may derive the following schema:

$$L^*c\text{-}5 \quad ...(((((dIs)\&{\sim}s)Is'...\&{\sim}s^{k\text{-}1})Is^k$$

(where s^k is the termination sanction implied in the "last norm," and $s^{k\text{-}1}$ is any sanction whose imputation to its delict is so *high* in the order of normative force (alternatively: issues from so high an organ) that its nonimposition calls in the special force of the "last norm").

Once this schema has been transcribed, however, a difficulty becomes immediately apparent. It is one thing to suppose that the "last norm" in the imputational series is "special," and another to say what it is that *bestows* the inviolability that is its distinction. That is, we may well ask: what is it about s^k that, in contradistinction to all sanctions previously discussed, makes it immune to the threat of nonimposition? Or what comes to the same thing: what is it about its possible nonimposition that makes it impossible for *that* to be a delict? It is perhaps tempting to regard this very question as pointing up a reductio ad absurdum of the whole "last norm" doctrine. We might, that is to say, regard the entire constructional "nesting" program as being vitiated by an inconsistency in the very notion of sanction it essentially incorporates. But a stronger interpretation, subtler but surer, is available.

Since there is nothing, apparently, in the notion of sanction itself to suggest that some one sanction (or set of sanctions) will escape the violable conditionality of the rest, it is reasonable to suppose that the answer to our question must lie *outside* the sanction, in the structural matrix in which the terminal sanction appears. Indeed, it must lie in the norm-system as a whole. As one traces the imputational chain up its hierarchical cone, one sees that the higher norms call up (and perhaps originate in) a progressively higher degree of authoritative force. And it is exactly at the stage of the terminal sanction that the norm-force of the whole string, the entire imputational series, is put in jeopardy. To put it briefly, for $\sim s^k$ (together with its implicit "background" nest of imputations) to be regarded as delict would be tantamount to the overthrowing (or perhaps the "dispensing with") the very system of law in which the preceding norms have their meaning. This is just the way in which a challenge to the "basic norm" is not a *legal* challenge (that is, a challenge *in* law), but an ideological challenge (a challenge *of* law). This last observation points to what is, in all likelihood, the clearest perspective on Kelsen's "last norm" doctrine. The "last norm" is by no means identical with or reducible to the *Grundnorm*; but it is the same *type* of formalistic unifying assumption. It is a *presupposition* required for the legal-scientific presentation of norms in their fully-expanded form. It is only through such a presupposition that the pure-theorist can make explicit the coherence of a given norm with other norms in the order, and with the hierarchy of organs issuing them. The idea is that each component norm is an imputational "nest" will perforce have a determinate internal structure, and an extrinsic reference as well; the "last norm" of the series differing from the others simply in having as its extrinsic reference not any supervenient sanction-conditioned norm, but, instead, the whole norm-series. No physical or logical obstruction prevents the nonimposition of the final sanction s^k; rather, to do so is, as Wittgenstein would have it, to change "games."

One of the weightiest assets belonging to this interpretation is the smooth transistion it affords between Kelsen's *Stufenbau* and his *Organtheorie*. Our analysis of the command-norm schema began with a static perspective; its interest lay exclusively in an order of meaning already laid down. Yet, as it developed, this analysis provided a strong link with the dynamic process of norm-creation and execution. In the end, the supervenience relations obtaining among parts of the fully articulated norm schema reveal something about the hierarchical shape of the order of sanction-imposing organs. To sloganize this outcome: norm-validity is seen to recapitulate norm-authority.

Typically, an imputation chain will be broken at some stage where the punishing authority is not required (that is, commanded) by law to punish an inferior delinquent organ, but is rather merely permitted or authorized to do so. Kelsen seems willing to regard such breaks as absolute termini: if a non-punishment is not itself the condition of a sanction-imputation, legal duty comes to an abrupt halt. There is *no* sense of obligation that extends residually beyond the break. But, as Raz has recently pointed out,

> it is possible to make sense of the concept of 'being required to behave in a certain way' without references to the concept of 'being liable to a sanction'. In such a sense it is customary to say that judges and other officials ought to apply a law, to execute sanctions, etc., even if they are not made subject to sanctions when they fail to do so.[20]

Kelsen does not consider this sense of requirement. What he says on related issues, in fact, suggests that he would regard the sense as legally irrelevant (PTL, 52). But this cuts him off needlessly from an extremely inviting prospect of presentational unity. The unity can come through Raz' extended sense of requirement, or it can come through permissory and authoritative norms. Since Kelsen holds that both permission and authorization have the prescriptive legal meaning "ought," the imputation chain shows, even when it is broken, the structure of norm-force underlying a system of legal norms. In tracing the chain of imputations, the legal scientist is tracing a series of "oughts" which define norm-authority levels; those levels in turn define a given norm system. In tracing a single imputation, the legal scientist is led to locate its place in the whole system of "oughts" that array themselves according to the pattern of superior-inferior stages of sanctioning authority in that system. These stages form an inevitable structure in legal systems: every organ who punishes another must be entitled to do so by authorizing norms; which is to say, by the procedural organization of "material" law even in the rare case when these organs are personally identical, though formally separate.

Thus, in representing the norm-order of positive legal systems, the pure theoretical legal scientist operates with a notion of unity that is imbedded in the organization of the systems themselves; namely, the indispensible norm-determined *staging* of sanctioning authority, a hierarchical principle without which it would be inconceivable to call them systems. The coherence which comes to the legal scientist's reconstructions is something which grows out of the nature of legal order itself. The "oughts" which the legal scientist describes are, in the end, not individual duties imposed on private citizens subject to law, but procedural or organizational duties that run the entire length and breadth of legal systems and cement their operations into wholes.

From what Kelsen has said, however (for example, PTL, 118, 119), it seems that nothing in the nature of a chain of imputations forces legal obligation to proceed link by link to the "last norm." This, presumably, will be a matter which varies from system to system; sometimes the legal authority will act under the aegis of a command-norm; at other times he will act under a norm of permission or authorization. And, if an organ is merely authorized to impose a sanction and does not impose it, this situation cannot form a delict to which an ulterior sanction may be imputed.

For the moment, then, L*c-5 must be regarded as the ramified schematic form of a special case of command-norm; namely, that in which both the original (secondary) norm and all organ-directed norms subsequent to it are commands. The question of *how* special this case is will depend on two considerations: (1) The latitude allowed the legal scientist in executing his reconstructions; and (2) the extent to which norms of (positive) permission and of authorization may be shown to be reducible to commmand-norms. Remembering that the "rationalized" order of legal rules will necessarily differ from the often-deceptive order of legal relations as they appear in the "raw state," it may be argued that the nonimposition of a sanction by a duly-appointed legal organ is in some extended sense (in the eyes of legal science) always delict, and hence bound into a chain as outlined in L^*c-5. And, if these permissions and authorizations which may take the place of commands in the imputation hierarchy can be "reconstructed" or otherwise translated into commands or command-complexes, the structural unity indicated in L^*c-5 will be preserved. Indeed, it will be preserved even if the permissions and authorization in question are logically independent from command-norms, but sufficiently like them to produce in the legal scientific cognition "chains" of their own which necessarily reach "last norms."

I explore this last possibility in the course of the next chapter, where I examine the two remaining norm "logics" of Pure Theory. And I shall return to the question of "constructional latitude" in the "Conclusion." But before preceeding to these matters, I should like to register a judgment on Kelsen's handling of the command-norm schema itself.

CRITICAL ASSESSMENT OF THE LOGIC OF COMMANDS

Perhaps the most glaring flaw in Kelsen's account of legal command-norms is the problem already mentioned in regard to personal obligation. Despite Kelsen's repeated and energetic insistence, it is really quite impossible to regard the sense in which an ordinary citizen, living in a system governed by laws, is said to be obligated by those laws as merely "epiphenomenal." It is certainly part of the meaning of "legal agent" that such a person be at least *able* to obey and disobey law; Kelsen's denial of this is simply too extravagant to be credible. Indeed, theoretic reconstruction which makes this counterintuitive claim would seem to discredit itself by explaining *away* one of the chief phenomena it was constructed to explain. Hart puts this criticism quite nicely in *The Concept of Law*.

> The idea that the substantive rules of the criminal law have as their function (and, in a broad sense, their meaning) the guidance not merely of officials operating a system of penalties, but of ordinary citizens in the activities of non-official life, cannot be eliminated without jettisoning cardinal distinctions and obscuring the specific character of law as a means of social control.
>
> We may compare the inversion of ancillary and principal, which this . . . theory makes, to the following suggestion for recasting the rules of a game. A theorist, considering the rules of cricket or baseball, might claim that he had discovered a uniformity hidden by the terminology of the rules and by the conventional claim that some were primarily addressed to players, some primarily to officials (umpire and scorer), some to both. "All rules," the theorist might claim, "are really rules directing officials to do certain things under certain conditions." The rules that certain motions after hitting the ball constitute a "run," or that being caught makes a man "out," are really just complex directions to officials; in the one case to the scorer to write down "a run" in the scoring-book and in the other to the umpire to order the man "off the field." The natural protest is that the uniformity imposed on the rules by this transformation of them obscures their function in the cooperative, though competitive, social enterprise which is the game.[21]

It is readily apparent that Kelsen is quite uncomfortable about this problem. A particularly glaring symptom of uneasiness is to be found in Kelsen's quixotic effort to make the agent's incapacity to obey and disobey law more attractive by dressing it up as evidence for "freedom of the will."

What Kelsen has to say about free will is hopelessly enmeshed in Kantian equivocality. On the one hand, Kelsen is quite willing to concede that human action, legal as well as extralegal, is strictly causally determined (PTL, 97). He says, in fact, that men always act under irresistible compulsion. This is "hard determinism" at its hardest. But, on the other hand—faithfully following Kant's lead—he wants to show that human normativity itself opens a prospect of genuinely free action, and does this by setting up an order of relations-among-facts different from the causal order, yet by no means in conflict with it. To show this, Kelsen stresses the fact that causal orders are nonterminating whereas legal (and moral) orders are not.

> The decisive point is: the behavior that, under a normative (i.e. a moral or legal) order, is the end point of an imputation, is, under the causal order, no end point (neither as cause nor as effect) but only a link in an infinite chain.
>
> This, then, is the true meaning of the idea that man, as the subject of a moral or legal order, that is, as a member of a society and as a moral or legal person is "free." That man, subjected to a moral or legal order, is "free" means: he is the end point of an imputation that is possible only on the basis of this normative order. (PTL, 93–95)
>
> Man is free because his behavior is an end point of imputation. And this behavior can be an end point of imputation even if it is causally determined. Therefore the causality of the natural order and freedom under a moral and legal order are not incompatible with each other. (PTL, 98)

One may conclude from this either that Kelsen has misunderstood the philosophical free will controversy altogether, or that, understanding it, he has accepted a monstrous sense of "free action."

"Man," says Kelsen, "is free because his behavior is the end point of imputation." What can this mean? Kelsen has already ruled out the possibility that the "end point" of imputation can be a locus of noncompulsory action. But if it is compulsory-yet-responsible action, is it not odd that the responsibility-chain which Kelsen educes from the imputational nexus leads not to the agent's action but to the organ's? Kant, at least, staked his claim for the possibility of free moral action on the ability of an agent to appropriate a law and subsequently obey it even if it should rule against him. Since Kelsen, however, has disqualified legal agents from the capacity to obey law, Kant's solution is unavailable to him. Yet, having followed Kant this far, it appears Kelsen has nothing with which to replace him. It is doubly odd that Kelsen should stress the notion of "end point" in this discussion, since the terminus in question is really only the delict-link, and not the unifying "last norm." The latter, entering at some distance from the agent's behavior, might suggest the prospect of a universalizable "moral order" in the Kantian sense.

It is tempting to conclude that, in his discussion of free will, Kelsen has slipped backward from the technical sense of *Zurrechnung* which he only shortly before introduced to the older, more familiar sense, in which it is acceptable to speak of "imputing" guilt, crimes, and the like, *to agents*. This possibility comes out most clearly when Kelsen, perhaps inadvertently, speaks of a *man*, rather than his delict as the end point of imputation. To take this tack, however, is to sacrifice all that has been gained for legal-scientific presentation by developing imputation as a dyadic relation, rather than a property-ascribing term. In any event, after Kelsen has submitted that "man always acts under irresistible compulsion," it is hard to see what can be gained by showing the legal action to be agent-terminating. The determinist position certainly does not depend upon the *infinite* character of causal chains; consequently, very much of Kelsen's libertarian attack is *ig-noratio elenchii*. Finally, one cannot help but ask: what sort of freedom is it that is confined to one's ability to do that which will make obligatory a coercive counteraction?

It would seem that Kelsen's efforts to assure us that we have not, under the rigors of Pure Theory, lost our precious freedom of willing are mainly backhanded attempts to minimize the cost of a very real loss: our incapacity, according to his account, to undertake legal obligation. There are, it appears, two forces working in the background to bring Pure Theory to this sorry state. The first is Kelsen's instinctive positivistic opposition to the notion of the secondary norm as it is generally formulated. It should not be forgotten that one of the key aims of legal positivism generally, and certainly a weighty consideration in the design of Pure Theory in specific, is to unburden legal theory of the sense of personal guilt it inherited from various religious and philosophical sources. If it could be shown that the only sense in which the legal agent can be said to be "guilty" is that of his creating a factual condition which is in a given particular legal system (though very likely not in some others) determined as "delict," perhaps much of the metaphysical mystery would evaporate from the plane of agency.

The standard positivistic picture, very much simplified, is this: legal agents enter into the scene of normative relations only as the creators of behavior. They do one thing and another, perhaps fully determined in their actions by causal laws. Occasionally they act in such a way as to trigger a rather complicated mechanism that creates an obligation upon an organ to react coercively, not against them personally (that was the "old" sense of "impute"), but against the delict which, as it happens, their action constitutes. Once the obligation—strictly an obligation upon the *organ*—arises, others arise around it, and the domain of *Sollen* gradually becomes furnished. Since all the legal relations in this picture obtain between organs and procedures within the mechanism triggered by, but otherwise not involved with, the agent's act, legal science (whose sole job it is to "present" and clarify these relations) is necessarily unconcerned with the delinquent agent himself and whatever sense of obligation he may feel.

The picture is neat enough; but what it leaves out is an explanation of how "guilt," which is either this "sense" of obligation or the obligation itself, is legitimately *caused* by complex machinations of the norm order. After all, it is a fundamental tenet of Pure Theory that law is an order of coercion; and it is clear that the *coercion* it involves applies primarily not to the organs it may obligate to enforce sanctions, but to the agents upon whom sanctions are coercively enforced. And it is an equally fundamental tenet that law is what legal science cognizes it as. It would seem, then, that in order to make intelligible the sense of coerciveness with which the norm-order essentially operates, legal science must account for an apparently real and causal relation between primary and secondary norms.

The reason for Kelsen's failure to provide the required account—and this brings us to a second source of awkwardness—is a logical mismanagement of the command-norm relation. The notion of "imputation," as Kelsen develops it, is strikingly effective in pointing up the complexity of systemic relationships which follow from the apparently simple connection of delict and sanction; but the cost of this constructional function is quite high. It has been shown that imputation, as a relational notion, is specifically contrived to exclude "direct" connection with personal legal obligation. Kelsen consistently deals with imputation as a "copula"—meaning by this a logical connection just like the truth-functional conditional, save that it bears the flavor of "ought." It is because the sanction stands in the position of consequence in the conditional relationship, a position that cannot be empty if the connective-*cum*-terms is to have sense, that the secondary, agent-directed obligation to sanction itself is left out of the logical picture. Kelsen's mistake here (and before the advent of "deontic logic" it hardly seems fair to call it a mistake) is to fail to "unpack" the imputational relation, so as to expose the "ought" it contains as an *operator* with a *range*.

Although it is true that Kelsen was quick enough to recognize in the difference between *Sein* and *Sollen* a distinction of modes, it cannot be said that he ever formulated a satisfactory modal schematization of the legal *Sollen*. By regarding the imputational connective as a unique, legally-flavored "copula," Kelsen was forced to stress its uniqueness—ultimately coming to regard it as a relation sui generis. But this conclusion radically undercuts the possibility of using available logic, built upon the nonnormative conditional, to organize legal-scientific constructions. The alternative—an option that Kelsen has never entertained—is to leave the "if . . . then" connection alone, allowing the adequacy of the truth-functional conditional for this job, and to develop the "ought" as a special normative operator, ranging over, in the primary instance, the entire legal consequence (the sanction-imposition), and in secondary (and tertiary, and so on) senses, its parts, "felicity conditions," and so forth.

The latter alternative recently has been extensively explored by the exponents of the so-called deontic logic.[22] To put it very briefly, the characteristic moves of deontic logicians in analyzing norms have been: (1) To construe the function of norms of all types as that of creating prescriptive primary hypothetical relations; (2) to regard the terms of normative relations as act-types, rather than "wills," "meanings," "duties," and the like; (3) to preserve the usual (truth-functional) sense of the "if . . . then" connection in the hypothesis involved; (4) to construe the prescriptivity at issue as "a relator concept, its function being to connect the concept of a legal subject with the concept of the object of a legal performance into the semantic unity of a legal norm";[23] and (5) to indicate various ways in which this "relator function" can be "transferred" so as to allow inferential connection between norms that are not merely logical translation of the same norm.

The strongest respect in which deontic analysis outstrips pure-theoretical analysis is its ability to articulate connections *within* the range of an "ought-relator" without requiring a covert sanction at every stage to complete an "imputational" relation. To return to an earlier example, if there is in legal system J a norm forbidding murder and attaching to the act of murder the sanction of hanging, a typical simplified deontic presentation might be:

$$L^*\text{-}cJ\text{:} \quad (O \sim d \ \& \ dx) \supset O(sy,x)$$

(where "d" stands for the delict of murder, "s" for the sanction-imposition, "x" for the delinquent agent, and "y" for the sanctioning organ). What is notable in this formulation is this: The *senses* of the two "O"-operators are identical, though their ranges are different (the first "O" must be understood to range over all agents subject to the murder-prohibition, the second to range only organs required to imposed the sanction). The role of the "personal norm" ($O \sim d$) in the formula is clear and far from "epiphenomenal": it is simply one of two conjuncts that jointly comprises a sufficient, but not a necessary condition for the "primary norm" obliging organ y to impose the hanging-sanction. Moreover, the way is left clear for a great many "oughts" following from Osy, x (that is, authorizing norms, procedural norms, and so forth) that would not follow from $O \sim d$ alone. That those normative relations would follow is clearly a matter of the specification and delineation of the *range* of Osy, however, and not a feature owing to its unique meaning or special force.

In this respect, at least, developments in deontic logic may be seen as an improvement on Kelsen's opening analytical moves. By freeing norm-presentation from the cramping limitations of the imputational "copula," yet retaining the essential features of delict and sanction in the obligation process, it is possible that deontic analysis will provide some advances upon Kelsen's project of rational reconstruction in the field of law. There are, however, decided limits to the capabilities of deontic logic in this area. As I have argued elsewhere,[24] key deontic terms have a somewhat different force in law than in other normative fields. In particular, norm force in legal systems seems to be distributed among higher-level norm-authorities in ways which violate axiomatic suppositions of deontic systems thus far devised (for example, what I have called the "Deontic Law of Excluded Middle," and the "Deontic Law of Contradiction"). It is thus no less naïve to suppose that deontic logicians will achieve the goal Pure Theory seeks than to suppose that Pure Theory achieves it without their help.

However much we are willing to allow deontic logicians to repair and extrapolate Kelsen's analyses, there remains at the heart of the pure-theoretic account of command norms a problem that no amount of logicising will avert. This has to do with the manner of hierarchical organization of norms. In plainest language, Kelsen's presentation seems to make the ordering of commands proceed in the *wrong direction*. It will be recalled that Kelsen's rather indefinite hopes for a nomostatic *Stufenbau* were tied to the development of subsumption-relations among legal rules (WJ, 221–222). He argued, in fact, that an inferior norm $Ln+1$ may be said to be deducible from its immediate superior Ln only if the rules describing them ($L*n+1$, $L*n$) form a valid syllogism (PTL, 74). In the present chapter, however, I have indicated that Kelsen's analysis of specific command-norms pays no attention whatever to syllogistic subsumption of norms under norms. On the contrary, what hierarchical organization there is comes from the layering of organs who enforce the norms. It is ultimately the order of rules for dealing with nonimposition of successive sanctions, and not any order of the original norms themselves, which affords the legal scientist's constructional system the prospect of hierarchic unity.

A specimen of law will perhaps illuminate this last criticism. The "Act against Popery" of 1700 states, in part:

> Be it further enacted by the Authority aforesaid That if any Popish Bishop Priest or Jesuit whatsoever shall say Masse or exercise any other Part of the Office or Function of a Popish Bishop or Priest within these realms . . . and such Person or Persons being thereof lawfully convicted that then every such Person shall on such Conviction be adjudged to perpetuall imprisonment in such Place or Places in this Kingdome as the King by Advice of His Privy Councill shall appoint. (II William, III, c.4)

In presenting the principal norm embodied in this law, the legal scientist will, according to Kelsen's account begin by describing the imputational relation which holds between the specified sanction ("perpetuall imprisonment") and the delict (Popery). His expression of this relation (dIs) will exhaust the pure-theoretic explication of the "internal logic" of the norm. But the greater part of the work still remains; for it is the strong claim of Pure Theory that a good part of the *sense* of the norm described comes from its relation with other norms in the organically unified system of British Law in 1700. Since the role of legal science is to "cognize" the norm in such a way as to expose its whole normative sense, further account must be made of the "external logic" binding the subject norm into its system.

Now, all that Kelsen says in regard to normative structure in general has prepared us to expect the explication of the "external logic" of the Anti-Popery norm to consist in a syllogistic or quasi-syllogistic detailing of connections between this norm and more general British legal norms governing the practice of religion and perhaps with less general norms regarding specific "Popish" practices. We expect, in short, to find legal science settling the claim of this norm to validity by exhibiting its ties with other norms already accepted as valid, and at the same time prepare to settle the validity claims of "inferior" norms by showing their ties with it. But much to our surprise, when Kelsen's discussion of specific norm-presentations actually appears (as indicated in the present chapter), nothing like the expected account of "external logic" is in evidence.

Whatever Kelsen says about this norm to suggest its "unification" with others has nothing further to do with legal agency and its governance, whether more general or less. Rather, it has to do exclusively with conditions attending the possible nonimposition of the specified sanction. This sort of explanation—that if a convicted Popish priest is not subjected to life imprisonment a sanction upon the nonenforcing organ becomes obligatory, and so forth —has an undeniable settling effect upon the system. By detailing the course of legal action consequent upon certain forms of legal non-action, it underscores the obligatoriness of the initial sanction. But this is scant payment for what we had been led to expect. For this account can tell us only what the norm's validity means vis-à-vis its enforcement; it cannot supply a legal "rationale" for that validity. The unity that comes of it is merely a display of the systematic dispositions of British enforcement-organs of 1700. It was certainly not this that we were seeking in our efforts to explicate the sense of the norm-order. Indeed, it would be perfectly possible for us to assess correctly the order of supervenience among organs of the eighteenth century British legal systems, and yet remain uninformed about the order of the norms they enforced.

There is, in fact, nothing in the Anti-Popery Act of 1700 to suggest what is to be done in case the sanction it specified is not imposed. Certainly, if the legal scientist is to find this connection, he must look far afield. If, perchance, he should find that *nowhere* in the statutes of 1700 is there any evidence of what ought to be done in this case, must he conclude that this legal order was "disunified"? Or, invalid? Or, perhaps, not a legal order at all? Suppose that Kelsen's legal scientist takes seriously the task of "rational reconstruction," and *provides* imputational connections wherever the system lacks them, up to the point where all "imputational chains" reach to the "last norm." If he may be allowed this much latitude, why should he not—in the interest of unity—foreclose the option of authorising-norms (rather than command-norms) within the "chain"? That is, why should he not insist that *every* nonimposed sanction is a delict, making obligatory a second-order sanction? The only way of blocking such questions as these is to reemphasize the purported *descriptivity* of legal science. Beyond a certain point, the interpretative construction we have outlined becomes altogether too farfetched. To be sure, the end-product of such a "presentation" may be a system of consistent and completely articulated, coherently related rules; but serious question arises as to whether these rules are any longer rules that faithfully reflect the British law of 1700.

IV
The Logic of
Dependent Norms

INTRODUCTION

According to Kelsen's usual division, legal norms that are
not commands are either authorizations or permissions.
Kelsen insists that these latter species of norm, or at least
certain of their members, deserve an analysis discrete from
that provided for command-norms. At the beginning of
chapter 3, I sketched a rough distinction between "negative" permissions, which can be recognized as "reflex"
statements of command-norms, and "positive permissions," which do not admit of this ready analysis. In *Pure
Theory of Law* Kelsen groups positive permissions, authorizations, derogations (which annul the validity of other
norms), certain "legal orders" (having the character of
"partial commands," directing forms of behavior, but failing to attach specific sanctions to opposite behavior), and
what we shall call "semantic norms"[1] under the rubric
"dependent legal norms." Their "dependence" consists in
a reliance upon command-norms for the stipulation of
sanctions. In one way and another, dependent norms work
to determine the conditions under which sanctions are to
be imposed, whenever their imposition is required by valid
independent norms.

It is not within the scope of the present study to present detailed discussion of the internal "logics" of each of the varieties of dependent norm. The principal concern here is the relationship their legal-scientific representations bear to those of independent command-norms examined in the previous chapter. One matter of special interest is the potential which presentational rules corresponding to dependent norms may have for filling out "imputational chains," either by their reduction to command-rules, or by otherwise determining connections with terminal sanction-omissions. In pursuing this interest, I shall concentrate attention primarily on norms of permission. I do this for two reasons: (1) Kelsen says somewhat more about permissory norms than he does about other dependent norms; moreover what he does say about them is said with comparative clarity; and (2) my discussion of permissory norms will reveal a *pattern* of divergence from the independent norm-analysis that is maintained consistently in other dependent modalities.

The position of norms of permission in Pure Theory is often misunderstood. Perhaps because the attention of critics has been captured by Kelsen's emphatic denunciation of the idea of lacunae in law (GTLS, 146–149; PTL, 245–250), it is usually assumed that Kelsen accepts as axiomatic a rule to the effect that the law permits whatever it does not explicitly forbid, and vice versa. Such a rule, delimiting what Kelsen calls the "negative norm" of permission, certainly does play a role in Pure Theory. It is conspicuous in Kelsen's writings from the earliest to the latest. But it is far from being the *only* norm of permission Kelsen recognizes.

In assessing the deontic independence of permissory legal norms, the crucial question is: should legal permission be regarded as an independent prescriptive modality, or should it be regarded as a reflex derivative of legal prohibition? Philosophical debate over this question has long

centered on what we may for want of established
nomenclature call the "Reflex Thesis": the position that all
legal norms of permission are merely assertions of the
absence (nonexistence, negation, or failure) of norms of
prohibition. Often this thesis has been confused with a
weaker claim (let us call it the "Reduction Thesis"): that
all legal norms of permission are in some manner
analyzable into norms of obligation. In the first account a
permission for X to do A must be the negation of an obligation upon X to do not-A (and no more); while in the second
a permission for X to do A might be an obligation upon Y
to refrain from interference with X's doing A; and it might
be some other yet more complicated arrangement of
obligations. Legal permission is said to be deontically independent if, and only if, both these accounts fail.

Since the Reflex Thesis asserts what amounts to a proper
instance of what the Reduction Thesis asserts, one clearly
may not accept one without also accepting the other. The
alternatives, then, are to accept both theses; to accept the
Reflex Thesis, but reject the Reduction Thesis; and to reject both. Each of these alternatives has its strengths, as
well as its supporters. The first alternative (accepting both)
is best represented in the current literature by Alf Ross;[2]
the second, though more approximately, by G. H. von
Wright;[3] and the third by Julius Stone[4] and Ilmar Tammelo.[5] Kelsen, unfortunately, never makes perfectly clear
his position in this dispute. It is evident enough that he rejects the Reflex Thesis; but he gives us no way of knowing
with certainty whether he regards all legal permissions
which are not reflex translations of commands (that is,
"negative permissory norms") as "representable" within
the parameters of the above-described "canonical form."
In several ways, Kelsen's position anticipates that of von
Wright. This happy circumstance affords us further oppor-
tunity to develop a theme of affinity between the "formal-
logical" approach of Pure Theory and the constructional
approach of the heirs of Vienna positivism.

NEGATIVE NORMS OF PERMISSION

Kelsen's discussion of "negative" permissory norms, those having the function of merely allowing the non-forbidden, bears a direct and obvious connection to the familiar (and ancient) doctrine of reflexivity between rights and duties. In the *General Theory*, Kelsen's very brief discussion of permission (which takes no account of varieties other than the "negative") is followed by an entirely standard exposition of this relationship.

> If the legal order determines a course of conduct to which a certain individual is obligated, it determines at the same time a corresponding behavior of another individual to which—as it is usually termed—this other individual has a right. In this sense, to every obligation there corresponds a right. A "right" in this sense is nothing but the correlative of a duty. (GTLS, 77)

As has been frequently observed, this doctrine affirms the redundancy of either of the two "correlative" notions: "legal duty" or "legal right." And, as we expect, Kelsen argues in *General Theory* for the same sort of redundancy in regard to "legal permission."

> The right to behave in a certain way is often interpreted as a permission. That I have a right to do or to omit doing something, is also expressed by saying that the law allows me to do or omit doing it. Accordingly, a distinction is drawn between legal norms which command or forbid, on the one hand, and legal norms which permit, on the other: "Law is imperative or permissive." But the distinction does not hold. The legal order gives somebody a permission, confers on somebody a right, only by imposing a duty on someone else. . . . Law is imperative for the one, and thereby permissive for the other. (GTLS, 77)

Here Kelsen has openly accepted the Reflex Thesis. Some critics argue that he holds the same view as late as the second edition of *Pure Theory of Law*.[6] But, as I shall demonstrate shortly, such is clearly not the case. It is necessary therefore to seek clarification on two counts: (1) What—in terms of the broad constructional picture of norms he presents—did Kelsen *mean* by his early affirmation of the Reflex Thesis; and (2) Why did he ultimately choose to reject this account?

The answer to the first of these questions is to be found in Kelsen's intention to display the presentational order of legal science as a *closed system*, a system without gaps and unrelated to other systems of normativity. Reflexivity, as he develops it, is the application in *Organtheorie* of the "unification" which Pure Theory provides for the legal system. There are, of course, in any society a number of actions which, though considered from various normative viewpoints are "wrong" or "forbidden," have not been explicitly proscribed by the system of positive law governing that society. It is Kelsen's aim—an aim that he particularly promotes in connection with the legal maxim *"nullum crimen sine lege"* (GTLS, 52–53; PTL, 112)—to rule out the possibility of "deontic neutrality"[7] in respect to these actions. Here the Reflex Thesis becomes a normative "Law of Excluded Middle"; it means that all sections not explicitly regulated by positive law are thereby "negatively" regulated "by default." Thus *all* societal action, possible as well as actual, is brought into the range of existing legal norms.

> As a sanction-prescribing social order, the law regulates human behavior in two ways: In a positive sense, commanding such behavior and thereby prohibiting the opposite behavior; and, negatively, by not attaching a coercive act to a certain behavior, therefore not prohibiting this behavior and not commanding the opposite behavior. Behavior that legally is not prohibited is legally permitted in this negative sense. Since human behavior is either prohibited or not prohibited, and since, if not prohibited, is to be regarded as permitted by the legal order, any behavior of an individual subjected to a

legal order may be regarded as regulated by it—positively or negatively. (PTL, 42)

The account of the logic of commands given in the previous chapter will allow us to recognize a certain indirectness in this statement. Here, when speaking of "positive regulation," Kelsen describes the normative function of law as simply commanding behavior x by attaching a sanction s to its omission. But I have pointed out that this agent-directed function is, at best, secondary, and "epiphenomenal." The *real* command-function consists not in the setting of an obligation on the agent to do x, but rather the setting of an obligation on some legal organ to impose sanction s in any case of x's omission—together with a terminating series of obligations on other organs to control possible nonimposition of successive sanctions. The emphasis in the above citation is on *mala prohibita*; properly, it should be on the imputation (and proliferation) of sanctions. The difference may not at first seem large. But recognizing it is a first step toward placing the task of "closing" the legal order in the only hands capable of determining the construction of imputations involved; namely, those of the legal scientist. This clarification is of utmost importance in countering a common line of attack upon Pure Theory.

Bergmann and Zerby, putting together what Kelsen has said regarding the "negative norm of permission" with what he has said about *nullum crimen*, conclude that Kelsen wishes to defend a doctrine of system-cloture which excludes *non liquet*.[8] They consider it an essential dogma of Pure Theory that "all legal-systems are, in matter of fact, comprehensive . . . in the sense that the organs are not allowed to refuse decision on any issue whatsoever."[9] Such a conclusion *might* have been in order if Kelsen had been arguing that legal commands and their correlative negative permissions were jointly exhaustive of legally modalized action-types in actual judicial practice. But, as I pointed out earlier, Kelsen, at least in his more recent writings, disavows any direct linkage between the cognitive order established by legal science and the prescriptive order applied by organs. Kelsen's discussion of *nullum crimen* and system cloture does not bear upon the order of norms; at least, not directly. Rather, it has to do exclusively with the rules of law by which norms are "presented." If anywhere, it is in the constructional system created by legal-scientific analysis, not the coercive order of norms, that commands and permissions exhaust the range of legal action. Any reference, therefore, to what legal organs are in fact allowed or obliged to do consitutes an illegitimate extension of Pure Theory's theoretical scope.

A similar form of criticism—principally explored by Stone and Tammelo—concerns Kelsen's denial of the possibility of "deontic neutrality." The opening moves in this attack were suggested by H. Kantorowicz, a prime early exponent of "legal realism." He observed that wherever there is a legal system, rules of some degree of specificity must operate. And for this to happen, it is necessary for norm-authorities ("organs") to have been enabled to distinguish subject-matter which is and is not "fit" for the application of these rules. By deciding whether any subject-matter is "fit," these organs determine the "justiciability" of legal rules.[10] In thus linking the range of legal applicability to particular judgment, however, Kantorowicz opens the possibility (which he does not critically elaborate) of norm-situations occurring which escape all justiciable law. Against this possibility, of course, proponents of the Reflex Thesis will argue that, since nonjusticiable situations are nonforbidden, they are *a fortiori* permitted. But, if Reflexive expressions are regarded as contingent cloture rules, dependent upon the determinations of system-relative norm-authorities, it becomes possible for legal systems left "open" by their organs to construe nonjusticiable subject-matter as neither permitted nor not-permitted.

Tammelo and Stone follow Kantorowicz' lead by arguing that no reason can be found why legal orders cannot be logically open normative systems.[11] Stone defines the "deontically neutral" state as one in which no norm obliges agents either to do or not to do something; one in which the legal order is simply silent as to the given behavior. Hence, a claim that some matter enjoys legal neutrality is not the expression of a norm at all, but the radical absence of norms; it refers to a logical space outside a given law field. Tammelo and Stone, like Bergmann and Zerby, state their cases for the possibility of deontic neutrality on the operation of the *non liquet* principle in international law.

It is, of course, true that certain international tribunals have declined to decide cases brought before them for lack of applicable rules. Yet, controversy remains as to whether such a declaration of *non liquet* is ever justified. Recently, the balance of opinion on this question has favored those holding it justifiable. Even so, as was said in response to Bergmann and Zerby, to introduce the consideration of *non liquet* when weighing the merits of the Reflex Thesis for legal science is to remove the controversy from the plane of constructional analysis to that of juridical operation. This shift is particularly apparent in the way Kantorowicz set the problem. He began, not with the legal theorist, but with the norm-authority deciding questions of "justiciability." Kelsen does not, of course, exclude *ab initio* the possibility that legal-scientific constructions may be of use to legal organs in making such decisions. But it will not do at all to *begin* with the fact of the decision-making to give shape to legal science.

The alternative to straightforward empirical generalization in theoretic system-building—the alternative Kelsen has steadfastly defended throughout—is analysis of the nature (the "essence") of the thing. If the question of the adequacy of the Reflex Thesis for representing relations between permission and command in law cannot be settled by examining the roles of *non liquet*, "allowability," and so forth, in actual legal practice, it must be settled by analysis of the terms themselves. What Kelsen seeks, then, is a "real definition" of "legal permission"; and his vacillation in respect to the Reflex Thesis must be seen as a record of his uncertainty about this definition.

Kelsen's thinking in this direction, though cluttered with prolixity and irrelevancies, is fundamentally simple. To understand legal permission of any kind, negative as well as positive, he cautions, one must begin with an understanding of the legal command. And this, of course, means that one must come to grips with the complex, interwoven structure of normative relations in which commands have their meaning. Such a broad theoretical prerequisite is in order, Kelsen thinks, because the legal function of permission presupposes a system of commands with prior function: "A definite human behavior can be *permitted* only within a normative order that *commands* different kinds of behavior" (PTL, 16). It follows that there can be no legal permissions in the absence of legal commands. And the kernel of Kelsen's doctrine of "negative" permission is contained in the obverse of this: wherever some portion of human conduct is made obligatory through the issuance of a (valid) command, a *remainder* is thereby created; whatever portion of this remainder is also not included in the conduct of any other command-norm in a system is, in respect to that system, a *pure residue*.

Now, if one conceives of this situation wholly from the viewpoint of the *secondary* norms involved (that is, those directing the conduct of agents), it may appear that the residue is an admixture of two species of conduct: that which law specifically allows (through writs of entitlement, declarations of rights, and the like), and that in respect to which law is simply "absent" (that is, the question of liability in law prior to 1950 in the collision of artificial satellites). However, Kelsen's position on the cognitive priority of command-norms is designed to undercut this dichotomy. It is a fundamental point of his analysis of legal commands that their primary function is to prescribe the sanctioning behavior for legal organs, not of agents. Where law has not attached a sanction as a consequence to a specific type of conduct, no imputational chain follows from it. And since the meaning of "ought" as law applies it to conduct is that an "imputational chain" follows from its antecedence, the normative status of all conduct free from such chains is purely and simply "non-ought"; that is, freedom from the sanctioning action of legal organs. "Negative permission," then, is Kelsen's convenient shorthand for the residual "non-ought" status of conduct-types. The distinction between conduct specifically allowed by law and that with respect to which it is silent does not apply at this stage. For in order to distinguish these varieties within the "non-ought" state, one would have to consider *other* commands (upon third parties) by which law gurantees the execution of actions it "allows" (GTLS, 77). And this is no longer a matter of a command-*free* residue.

Perhaps the most important thing to notice in this account of the nature of "negative permission" is that the term denotes a non-normative *status*, rather than a species of enacted norm. This is to say, a legal organ cannot "negatively permit" a type of conduct by issuing a norm of the form "We permit x," or "X is hereby permitted." To assert this would be to say only that no sanction is attached to x; and though this might clarify an already existing normative situation, it could not create anything new. We should also notice that no grandiose assumption of "completeness" or "unification" is contained in, or derivable from, the doctrine of negative permission. Legal science simply has to have a name for the domain of actions to which no sanctions have been imputed. Again, nothing follows from this choice such as would prevent a judge's declaration of *non liquet* and nothing follows touching the meaning of legal norms which can be and are created using the language "*X* is hereby permitted."

Kelsen's early mistake, then, was not to conceive of negative permission as imposing artificial judicial restraints, but to suppose that the *only* sense in which law may "permit" is this "negative" sense. In accepting the Reflex Thesis, Kelsen was, like so many theorists before him, blinded by the command-form from seeing an essential multiplicity of permission normativity. He simply fell prey to a "mental cramp" resulting from overattention to a single, but nonexclusive variety of usage. Kelsen had in his early writings assumed that the "real definitions" of "negative permission" and "legal permissory norm" would coincide. All that backed this assumption was the conviction that law was essentially limited in its power to prescribe "oughts" to the independent mode of commanding detailed in the previous chapter. The mere fact that Kelsen has recently stressed a *tripartite* analysis of norms—one in which some permissions as well as authorizations call for independent explication—indicates a rejection of the trivialization of permissory modality implicit in this early dogma.

Regarding the Reflex Thesis as a real definition has a stultifying effect on efforts to make clear what *causes* disputes about it. According to the real definist, inspection of the "nature" of legal permission reveals its identity with nonprohibition. The terms of the Reflex Thesis only reflect this natural connection. So, to know the meaning of "permission" is to know the meaning of "nonprohibition," and to know either is to know directly the truth of the Thesis. It follows that a person who disputes the Reflex Thesis necessarily does so from ignorance; he must have failed to procure a clear understanding of the facts to which it refers. Since, as the definist believes, truth in this matter is a relation of facts, he is committed to the view that agreement can be procured only by a consensual grasping of the facts. If the disputant alleges the existence of exceptions to the equivalence the Reflex Thesis asserts, he must, according to the definist, deny the facts or be factually mistaken. In the real definist's view, one cannot even begin to find exceptions to the Reflex Thesis: to find a permission that fails to fit the rule one must first understand what it is for something to be a permission, and to understand this is to know immediately that the Reflex Thesis is true and exceptionless.

It is easy to see that advocacy of the Reflex Thesis as a real definition cannot but lead to a familiar philosophical stalemate. Whenever exceptions to it are alleged, charges of delusion or miscomprehension on one side will be matched with charges of dogmatic myopia on the other. Increasingly, philosophers have come to circumvent this impasse (which they regard as the unhappy heritage of Platonism) by casting into disrepute the underriding notion of "essence" upon which real definitions depend. And recently the broad frontal attacks initiated by G. E. Moore and Wittgenstein in the realm of metaphysics (or what used to go by that name) have been carried into the realm of jurisprudence by the nominalistically inclined Legal Realists. Glanville Williams struck what may prove to be the final blow in the celebrated article "The Controversy Concerning the Word 'Law' "[12] by taking a Wittgensteinian inventory of the kinds of fallacy that support juristic real definism.

Defending the Reflex Thesis as a preferred arrangement of conventions, rather than an observation about the nature of things, has the advantage of admitting the knowledgeability of one's opponents. As the camp of opponents swells, it becomes more difficult for definists to insist with conviction that all of these otherwise informed men either are ignorant of the meanings of the terms at issue, or, knowing those meanings, are speaking of things as "permissions" that are other things altogether. Accordingly, it has become the prevalent strategy among definists to regard the Reflex Thesis as a stipulative, rather than a real definition. At the very least, this shift has improved the quality of the debate by ridding it of appeals to fictive understandings of hypostatic essences.

As the nominal definist sees it, the Reflex Thesis expresses a conventional rule for dealing with legal permissions that is probably superior to alternative rules. The proof is pragmatic: no one denies that *some* legal norms of permission are simply assertions of the absence of norms of prohibition. It is in fact generally agreed that *most* legal permissions are of this sort. As a means, then, of simplifying our already cluttered juristic language, the nominal definist urges adoption of the Reflex Thesis as the rule of usage for "legal permission" which extends our prevailing usage minimally. Plain Occamite parsimony seems to dictate this course, since any other would entail recognition of anomalous permissions, permissions whose analyses would only divide the logic of legal systems from those of other normative systems.

Not surprisingly, an outpost for the nominal definist defense of the Reflex Thesis has developed recently among deontic logicians. The Thesis or a rule equivalent to it has been taken by them to be a "deontic law of the excluded middle," an axiom which may be challenged only by espousing intuitionism. It is well to remember, however, that deontic logics were originally devised for the formalization of nonlegal normative systems (moral orders in particular), and that the extent of their application to law is an as-yet unsettled issue. To be sure, a number of deontic theorists have argued that a generalized deontic calculus does have positive law as an interpretation; but the support they give this claim is far from convincing. A. R. Anderson, for instance, resorts to the introduction of ad hoc principles by which it is understood that parties to legal relations may *assume* that all possible acts will have some deontic status, that is, will be permitted if not forbidden.[13] This, however, is a plainly artificial means of system-cloture, a *pis aller* without basis in systems of positive law. Although such a metasystematic rule might be useful in demonstrating something about possible legal systems, it certainly cannot be useful in supporting claims about current law. Deontic logic, in short, cannot provide the kind of support that will convince jurists that the Reflex Thesis represents a legal reality.

What the deontic theorists have generally failed to appreciate is the problem of descriptive accountability which besets all formal analyses in legal science. Within purely conventional systems (for example, mathematics, geometry), introduction of nominal definitions is indispensible and relatively unproblematic. But, in systems that avow correspondence to preexisting relational structures, stipulation will not settle disputes. A nominal definition introduced into a system of legal norms does not thereby become a valid rule of the system; and it cannot be used to support claims as to the legitimacy of those norms, or itself. As Kelsen puts it, only another legal norm can be the reason for a legal norm's validity. Clearly, the Reflex Thesis qua nominal definition will not do what its proponents wish it to do. For no claim that permission *really* is the absence of prohibition, or that a system without such a rule is incomplete, can break the seal of conditionality on such a definition's application.

Any definistic defense of the Reflex Thesis raises hard questions. First, in what sense of "are" are legal permissions nonprohibitions? On reflection, it is difficult to maintain that the "are" is simply the "are" of identity. For plainly, the absence of a norm is not a norm. To make it into one is to rule out a priori the possibility of "deontic neutrality," that legal state of affairs which is neither permitted nor forbidden, a condition which some jurisprudents (for example, J. Stone, I. Tammelo) have forcefully argued is a real and important part of existing legal systems. If norms of permission are thought to exist wherever norms of prohibition do not, it follows that legal systems possess an infinitude of norms (since there are countless nonforbidden acts in any system). It also follows that the law at any time contains norms to cover all possible actions (since those acts that are not even contemplated are *a fortiori* not forbidden). Clearly, these implications are unattractive.

If it could be shown that the Thesis correctly reports actual juridical usage, it might be defended as a true inductive report. Here, the warrant for it would be empirical, rather than logical. Inductive reports can be verified, recommendations cannot. To defend the Thesis as a report, then, one must determine either (a) that all legal systems do happen to have principles identical or equivalent to it, or (b) that it accurately depicts prevalent rules of use current in judicial discourse about legal systems.

The first reportivist alternative may be disposed of at once: it is readily demonstrable that not all legal systems institutionalize the Reflex Thesis, or any rule to the same effect. This is particularly apparent in systems of international law and customary law (if these two can be said to comprise "systems"), as well as in common law. The second alternative, however, enjoys a certain gnawing attractiveness. Clearly many lawyers, jurisprudents, and others, do use the words (or concepts) that compose the Reflex Thesis in the way it describes. It is therefore tempting to thing that occasional aberrant uses might be dismissed as solecisms, making the Reflex Thesis true in the way rules of etiquette are true, as criteria of correct usage born of established practice.

In *Directives and Norms,* Alf Ross accepts what amounts to this second option. It is this that he falls back upon ultimately during his debate with von Wright over the modal status of legal permission. Ross attacks von Wright's employment of two deontic operators (one for obligation, one for permission) by affirming the Reduction Thesis and offering the Reflex Thesis as justification. At first, the justification presented in turn for this is the thin pragmatic claim that "telling what I am permitted to do provides no guide to conduct unless the permission is taken as an exception to a norm of obligation."[14] But later, the substance of Ross' support for the Reflex Thesis appears to be the extent of its application in legal discourse. Ross admits that his version is derived from Hohfeld's well-known table of jural relations. And his final, telling claim against von Wright is that he (Ross) has employed Hohfeld's doctrine "for many years without encountering any instance of legal speech in which the term 'permission' (and derived expressions) could not without difficulty be interpreted as the negation of obligation."[15]

What is lacking in the reportive view is, of course, precisely that feature which vitiates inductivism, but which alone makes advocacy of the Reflex Thesis controversial and interesting: the systematic exclusion of exceptions. Without this, the position of those who deny the Thesis is self-certifying, since, qua universal inductive report, it is overthrown by the first counterinstantial use. Obviously, everyone who denies the Thesis takes exception to Ross' parting allegation about the ease of interpretation it uniformly provides. Thus, to prove the inadequacy of Ross' position, it is enough to show that there are such things as "positive permissory norms," and that these do not accomodate themselves to facile conversion into obligatory norms. Since "positive permission" is an indispensable part of Pure Theory, at least in its mature form, we may proceed apace to an examination of this independent modality, relying on Kelsen's account for an answer to Ross.

Whoever denies the Reflex Thesis holds either that there are (or at least could be) legal permissions which are not merely absences of legal prohibitions, or that there are (or at least could be) absences of legal prohibition which are not legal permissions. And whoever accepts the Reduction Thesis, while denying the Reflex Thesis, holds that whatever these differences may be, they are tractable to the extent that some complex analysis will allow permissory norms to be eliminated in favor of command-norms, or vice versa. The important questions now arise: to what extent did Kelsen embrace this latter position? And, what were his grounds for doing so?

"Positive permission," as Kelsen presents it, is not merely a residual normative status left in the wake, as it were, of independent norms. Rather, it is the product of specific positive acts of will, providing various kinds of legal response for certain actions. Among positive permissions there are two broad types: (1) "entitlement" *(Berechtigung)*—the freedom of action of one party may be defended by attaching sanctions to actions of other parties which have the effect of interfering with or preventing that action; (2) "validity-limiting" permission—under the condition that the permission is given by an authorized legal organ, a positive norm may have the effect of *exempting* an otherwise forbidden action from the legal sanction that is its legal consequence (PTL 16, 55–56). Kelsen calls this process "limiting the sphere of validity" of a command-norm. Kelsen explains the former sort of guarantee as follows:

> "To permit" is also used in the sense of "to entitle (berechtigen)." If A is commanded to endure that B behaves in a certain way, it is said that B is permitted (that is, entitled)

to behave in this way. And if A is commanded to render a certain service to B, it is said that B is permitted (that is, entitled) to receive the services of A. In the first example, then, the sentence "B is permitted to behave in a certain way" says the same as the sentence: "A is commanded is endure that B behaves in a certain way." And in the second example, the sentence: "B is permitted to received a certain service from A" says the same as the sentence: "A is commanded to render a service to B." (PTL, 17)

There is no question here of the "endurance" required by norms of "entitlement" being coincident with the "negative" state of nonobligatoriness discussed earlier. Kelsen emphasizes the distinction between the two species of "freedom" involved.

The freedom left to the individual by the legal order simply by not prohibiting a certain behavior must be distinguished from the freedom which is positively guaranteed to the individual by that order. The freedom of the individual which consists in permitting him a certain behavior by not prohibiting it, is guaranteed by the legal order only to the extent that the order commands the other individuals to respect this freedom; the order forbids them to interfere in this sphere of freedom, that is, the order forbids a behavior by which an individual is prevented from doing what is not prohibited and what therefore in this sense is permitted to him . . .

However, not every behavior so permitted—in the negative sense of not being forbidden—is safeguarded by the prohibition of the opposite behavior of others; not every permitted behavior of one individual corresponds to an obligation of another individual. It is possible that a behavior is not prohibited by the legal order (and therefore, in this sense, permitted), without an opposite behavior being prohibited by the legal order, so that this opposite behavior is also permitted. (PTL, 42)

By arguing for the logical independence of the negative nonforbidden state and positive "entitlement," Kelsen makes it clear that he rejects the Reflex Thesis; by suggesting that the entitlement of A to do x is identical with the command to B (presumably a class of B's) to endure A's doing of x, he shows that he affirms the Reduction Thesis. Here, then, the issue is relatively clear and aboveboard. Positive permissory norms of the "entitling" variety, at least, are reducible to complexes of command-norms applying to parties other than the agent. At this point, it seems that no formal amplification of the analysis of independent norm structure given in the previous chapter is required, only an extension of its range. That is, the commands issued to norm-organs must in this case be occasioned by delicts involving "secondary norms" obligating certain conduct by all agents *other* than the "entitled" agent. The issue is not so clear, however, in the case of "validity-limiting" positive permissions.

Kelsen holds the function of "limiting the sphere of validity" especially important in revealing the "positivity" of positive permissory norms, "The positive character of a permission becomes particularly apparent when the limitation of the sphere of validity of a norm that forbids a certain conduct is brought about by a norm that permits the otherwise forbidden conduct. . . ." (PTL, 16). Perhaps the assumption here is that acts of will can be moderated only by acts of will; hence, the permissory incursion against a command-norm's range must be "positive" in the same sense in which the original command norm is. In any event, Kelsen indicates that the operation of "limitation of a prohibition's sphere of validity" takes place through the same instrumentality as that by which the independent norms makes its effect; namely, by attaching sanctions to opposite behavior. So far, this suggests that the "imputational-chain" model, or something like it, is involved here too. But, far from specifying a clear connection of "excusing" permission with his previous formalism, Kelsen undertakes at this point an altogether confusing excursion.

Kelsen provides three examples of "validity-limiting" permissory norms: (1) a norm permitting individual self-defense in the context of a general prohibition against the use of force by individuals; (2) a norm permitting national self-defense in the context of a general prohibition against the use of force by nations (for example, Article 2, paragraph 4 of the UN Charter, taken together with Article 51 of the same charter); and (3) a norm licensing the sale of alcoholic beverages in the context of a general prohibition against the sale of alcohol (PTL, 55–56).

Common to these examples, Kelsen argues, is a certain combinatory relation among the original (independent) prohibitory norms involved and the subsequent (dependent) limiting-permissions. In each case, he says, the permissory norm makes possible a rewriting of the prohibitory norm which it modifies: a new statement of the command-norm, including the permissory exception as a "without . . . " clause is now in order. To take Kelsen's third example, the two apparently incompatible norms prohibiting (all) liquor sales, and permitting (licensed) liquor sales may be combined into a single norm: "If someone sells alcoholic beverages without a state license, he ought to be punished" (PTL, 56). But this policy of norm-combination raises serious problems with Pure Theory's constructional program—problems of which Kelsen was apparently largely unaware.

One of these problems is the simple question of whether the expression that results from combining the prohibitory and permissory norms is itself a *norm*. Although it may be perfectly clear that the two component norms are products of *Willensakten*, it is certainly not clear that *anyone* wills the compound normative proposition, namely, that everyone who sells liquor without a state license ought to be punished. The answer that this proposition is (implicitly) willed by *both* of the norm-authorities who issued the component norms does not square easily with the conviction of the strict prohibitionist who, having willed a universal obligation to temperance, considers any permissory exception given to licensed sales a contradiction of his will, and no part of it. Yet, the answer that the combinatory norm is willed only by the authority issuing the permissory norm fares no better. For, this would make it the case that the latter authority wills *two* norms whenever he issues one. It seems reasonable to suppose that the authority who issues a norm permitting licensed liquor sales might view a prior norm prohibiting all liquor sales as contradicting his will (the reverse of the situation just considered). But the permissory norm has the function of creating an exception to this prior command-norm by *leaving its intrinsic validity unchallenged* while limiting its scope. So to view the permission-issuing authority as simultaneously willing the permissory and "combinatory" norms is to assume his complicity in willing the residual validity of a norm quite unacceptable to him. To extend this illustration: the authority who issues a norm permitting licensed liquor sales may very well be opposed to all restrictions on liquor sales whatever. Such an attitude of opposition is, in any event, compatible with his willing the legalization of licensed sales. But it is *not* compatible with a will that some liquor sales (the nonlicensed ones) be forbidden. This shows the futility of attempts to "unpack" from a simple permissory will a prohibition-will covering the ground the former leaves uncovered. The truth of the matter is that the permissory norm makes *no* commitment regarding the possibilities of action outside its scope. The authority whose will it is that licensed liquor sales be legally permitted may *wish* unlicensed liquor sales to be permitted or forbidden; but this wishing is not part of his (objective) willing. "Objective willing" is a matter of a norm's meaning, and hence of its validity. And a norm's validity derives in part from its position in relation to other norms. The "combinatory norm," in short, may be the legal effect of the convergence of two norms that are authoritatively willed, but it cannot be said to be willed itself in the willing of either, or both.

The problem here is evidently partly one of misleading terminology. What Kelsen calls a "single norm" is, as I have indicated, an expression that does not embody the meaning of any one act of will. The unitary but qualified normative force it expresses comes to it, not directly, through some compound willing act, but indirectly, through "rewriting," or "re-presentation," of the separate normative expressions that go into it. This "combinatory" norm is really a norm-*construct*. It is the epiphenomenal norm-correlate of a rule of law in which two other rules of law have been combined. Its "without . . ." clause, a clause which cannot have been part of the meaning of either constituent will, is an unmistakable fingerprint of the legal scientist. Here, it is the theorist, not the norm-authority, who "combines" the norm-contents of two counter-directional norms into a "single norm," precisely in order to show the way in which their "ought-functions" interact. The "single norm" itself has only the role of clarifying the routing of normative force in a system, not of creating that force.

This sort of "combinatory norm" is, in fact, one of the plainest examples of "rational construct" Kelsen provides. By careful attention to the effects that two norms actually have upon a preestablished system of sanction-imputing relations, the pure theorist is able to show a cooperative nexus between them, even though their "face value" appearance was one of incompatibility. Yet, this clarification leads to larger questions still: is the whole, complicated arrangement of "combinatory norms" to cover "validity-limiting" permissions a necessity in the program of Pure Theory? Or is it merely a gratuitous thrust of overeager formalism obscuring an easy and already available analysis? Certainly it would be simpler by far to *accept* the apparent incompatibility of a general prohibition and a permission which makes exception to it. One might, in this case, regard the permissory norm as nullifying the preceding command-norm, according to the familiar principle *lex posterior derogat priori*. And this effect would certainly be compatible with the establishment of a *new* command-norm, one that wills the former prohibition excluding the exception made by the permission. As long as one is willing to allow that a"combinatory" norm might be valid without having been willed by anyone, what is to prevent one's allowing that this constricted command-norm (whose meaning is not directly meant by anyone, but is "constituted" out of what has been meant) is valid instead?

The answers to these questions do not come easily. For I am now calling into criticism one of the most deeply-rooted dogmas of Pure Theory. Kelsen has consistently maintained that no legal-scientific representation (specifically, no "rule of law") may enjoy prescriptive effect. But at least one such representation, a validity-limiting permissory norm-construct, can be "constitutive" to the extent that the norm-relation it expresses is said to have valid force in a legal system, even though this relation is not the product of any "act of will." How can we know if this is a transgression of the concept *"Rechtsregel"* (the construct's conceptual basis) unless we are given a clearer notion of the limits of legal-scientific constitutivity than Kelsen has provided?

It is instructive to observe, at this point, that G. H. von Wright's analysis of norms of permission leads him to what amounts to the same nest of problems. Von Wright, of course, divides the domain of permissory modality somewhat differently than Kelsen. Moreover, his treatment profits from recent gains in deontic logical theory and does so without the notorious "Kelsenisms" which occasionally stifle efforts at elucidation. Yet there are deep-running similarities in the two analytical perspectives; and this makes it worthwhile to refer to von Wright in essaying Kelsen's position on permissory-norm construction.

PERMISSION AND PERFORMATIVITY

Apostates are perhaps no clearer in their reasoning than others, but, forced by conversion to justify their ways, they are often clearer than others in expressing their reasoning. This may be why von Wright's examination of legal permission in *Norm and Action*[16] has become the *locus classicus* of opposition to the Reflex Thesis. In the course of a dense though abrupt analysis, von Wright admits the mistake of his former acceptance of the Thesis, and seeks to correct it by considering in detail one reason for its rejection. (He tells us that he has others; but unhappily he does not tell us what they are.)

Von Wright's chief point is that "permission" is an ambiguous term in law; for *one* of its senses (what he calls the "weak" sense) the Reflex Thesis is a perfectly adequate rule of use; but for another (the "strong" sense) it is not. The argument for this is worth rehearsing. Von Wright begins by acknowledging a familiar point from Legal Realism: new kinds of acts are forever emerging upon which legal norm-authorities must make permissory or prohibitory judgments. Now, there is, he thinks, nothing misleading in saying of acts which in this sense have not yet "come before the law" that they are for that reason nonforbidden. Permissions in this sense are certainly not to be regarded as having an independent norm-character. But once a norm authority has had a chance to consider the normative status of an act, he *may* deal with it in (at least) three ways which could only misleadingly be called (merely) "nonforbidding." In issuing a "strong permission," von Wright says, a norm-authority may declare that he will (a) "tolerate" an act (that is, announce judicial indifference to the doing or not-doing of the act), (b) do one

or more things which have the effect of "enabling" someone to do the act (thereby making the act possible, rather
than not making the act impossible), or (c) do one or more
things that have the effect of preventing interference with
someone's doing the act (what Kelsen calls "entitlement").[17]

Von Wright, like Kelsen, sees no special difficulty in the
reduction to command-norms of "entitlements." These, he
agrees, expressly involve the issuance of nonpermissory
norms to third parties. "Enabling" norms are perhaps
somewhat trickier; but not impossible to reduce. An example will serve to show this: By establishing the corporate
category "hui"[18] an authority creates the possibility of
legal property negotiation through this instrumentality.
And by commanding legal recognition of this category in
contractual actions, and the like, the court "enables" a
style of conduct, in a minimal sense. Any further commands by which legal authorities might "enable" the
member of a "hui" to execute conduct will presumably
blur the lines of distinction between this and the other two
types of "strong" permission. Thus, von Wright concludes,
if some feature of permission-modality will require special
treatment, treatment that does not amount to more or less
direct translation into the command modality, it must be
sought in the class of "tolerations."

Clearly, as von Wright recognizes, a "strong" sense of
permission is not obtained if tolerations amount to no
more than declarations of intention; that is, mere psychological reports about the state of mind of norm-authorities
issuing them. He allows[19] that volitional reports lack altogether the normative weight required; and this, he says,
means that we have no other course than to treat them as
promises of noninterference. By introducing the notion of
"promising," von Wright aims to certify tolerations as sui
generis, by appeal to reputedly *performative* characteristics of their use.

If legal tolerations are, like promises, *performative* expressions, we can discover the different functions which
these permissions serve in their systems only by attending
to the varieties of performative character in the expressions through which they are made. To say that "strong"
permissions differ performatively from other norms and
differ performatively one from each other is to say that
they are irreducible to other norms and untranslatable
among themselves. Von Wright comes closest to making
this observation when he points up a systematic ambiguity
in certain "deontic sentences," among which permissions
have a special place: the same forms of words that are used
to formulate (that is, create) legal norms can be used to
form existential statements about those norms.[20] The expression, "You may park your car in front of my house,"
for example, can be used either to grant a permission, or to
give information about a normative state-of-affairs (namely, that there is no regulation forbidding parking there). If
such an expression is used to give existential information
(that is, describe a state-of-affairs) it will be either true or
false: a permission statement will be true if, as it says, prohibitory norms are absent; otherwise it will be false. If,
however, such an expression is used to create a norm, it
cannot be either true or false; it can only succeed or fail to
achieve its end (that is, it can either perform or misfire).

On this last point Kelsen and von Wright reach substantial accord. In the final analysis it is not the specific norm-
character of "strong" (or "positive") permission that cap-
tures their attention. Rather, they base their claims for the
special status of this sort of norm on observation of its performative connection with other features of the norm-
system. There are two regards, frequently confused, in
which performativity-in-use bears significantly upon norm
analysis; these are: (1) the variety of means at norm
organs' disposal in creating norm-situations through expression, and (2) the variety of conditions prerequired for

the success of these linguistic performances. Neither Kelsen nor von Wright manages to keep these regards wholly separate; but both theorists are manifestly sensitive to each of them.

Kelsen's awareness of the matter of "means" is most clearly indicated in his discussion of positive permission's validity-limiting capacity. He speaks of not one, but an indefinite number of ways in which a community organ can clarify and reshape the situation of legality in a preexisting juridical framework. When Kelsen's discussion of the issue is vague, it is due to an unwillingness to catalogue the various performative means at the organs' disposal. Under the rubric "positive permission" are gathered a host of what Austin called "exercitives," as well as "commissives," and even "expositives" (all of these neologisms appear in *How to Do Things with Words*). A norm-authority may "license" an act, grant a "right" or exemption, waive a requirement, bestow a privilege (or a title or power), and so forth. The list is indefinitely large. The forms of positive permission are, in short, as various as the performative instrumentalities given to norm-authorities for the determination of particular orders.

The distinctions among these varieties of permissory norm are not merely differences of style in norm-issuing performance. If a norm-organ in system S issues a "right" instead of a "privilege," it may be that incursions against the right will be responded to in an altogether different way than if the privilege had been granted. To illustrate: in the one case, commands might be issued to organs to fine the violators; in the other, commands might be issued to make laws attaching as yet unspecified sanctions to the acts of violation. Any number of responses, in fact, might be in order. It is this, rather than any unwillingness to unify the pure-theoretic presentational system under the concept of command, that gives rise to Kelsen's recognition of permission as a special normative modality. And it is this which goes a long way toward preventing the pure-theorist

from reaching exhaustive schematic representation of permissory rules.

It is not, however, the variety of performative *means*
which provides the decisive blow against a narrow reductivism in permission modality; it is the variety of conditions permissory use demands. The success of performative
expression depends upon the presence in the situation of
utterance of certain factual conditions without which the
performance intended is said to "misfire." The performative expression "I pronounce you man and wife," for
example, misfires if the person uttering it is not either an
ordained minister or a duly authorized functionary of the
state, or if his license to marry has expired, or if one of the
parties to be married is ineligible because of age, or sex, or
previous marriage, or if no witness is present, and so on.
Now, since these "felicity conditions" are empirical in
character, generally conventional, and entirely system-
relative, no construction that pretends to "purity" (system-
indifference) in the manner of Kelsen's theory of norms
can account for them. The regulations which stipulate
these conditions may form a highly complex, multileveled
interweave. There is no question of a single "higher" norm
taking them all as content, authorizing the marriage-con-
secrating norm-expression by exhaustive specification of
its validity conditions. Since the "misfiring" of a performative norm-issuance renders the proposed norm *invalid*,
no construction that pretends to rationalize the organization of validity within a norm-system without taking the
"felicity conditions" into account can succeed.

Kelsen is manifestly aware of the performative character of legal norms generally. Early in the *Pure Theory* he
pauses to underscore the diversity of performances
through which norms can be "meant."

Acts whose meaning is a norm can be performed in various
ways. For example, by a gesture: The traffic policeman, by a
motion of his arms, orders the pedestrian to stop or to con-

tinue; or by a symbol: a red light constitutes a command for the driver to halt, a green light, to proceed; or by spoken or written words, either in the imperative form—be quiet!—or in the form of an indicative statement—I order you to be silent. In this way also permissions and authorizations may be formulated. (PTL, 7)

In his 1962 article, "Derogation," Kelsen explains the *presentational* consequences of the discrepancy between expressions and performance:

The law often makes the expression of certain words or phrases a condition to legal consequences. It provides, for example, that a document is a valid will only if it is entitled "last will" or "testament." Another example is that for a marriage to be valid, the minister must utter the words: "I hereby pronounce you man and wife." From the grammatical point of view, the words "last will" and "testament" are merely descriptive, and the words spoken by the minister are descriptions of a legal consequence. But at law, they are not mere descriptions or assertions, but conditions for legal consequences. (EJRP, 342n.)

In this same article, Kelsen explicitly refers to the theory of performatives adumbrated by Austin in "Other Minds." Kelsen's understanding of Austin is somewhat marred by his evident confusion over the reputed inability of performative utterances to be true or false. He argues, for instance, that the marriage pronouncement, for example, can be *true* if uttered under appropriate circumstances inasmuch as *part* of its function is descriptive (EJRP, 342n.). But it is clear that Kelsen accepts Austin's view that legal consequence (what the legal scientist aims to present) is conditional upon the "true" (that is, "felicitous") performance of appropriate acts, rather than on the grammatical form of expressions employed.

Kelsen is moreover aware of the "phrastic/neustic" distinction by which R. M. Hare attempted to separate the constative portion of expressions from the portions bearing illocutionary force.[21] In fact, he makes his own distinction between the normative character of an expression and its "content" or "subjective meaning" by borrowing the very example ("The door's being closed"/"The door ought to be closed") with which Hare introduced the neustic/phrastic distinction (PTL, 6). But, at least in the case of command-norms, it is Kelsen's view that the conditions necessary for the valid enunciation of a particular norm are completely provided for in a higher norm which "authorizes" its specific "ought"-neustic (PTL, 8). For command-norms, then, Kelsen is willing to argue that whatever features of a legal system are to contribute to a particular command's performative success—these features must be somehow incorporated into the meaning of higher "authorizing" norms. This view obviously facilitates the hierarchial norm-construction that Kelsen wants legal science to undertake. For, on this analysis, in order to determine fully the validity of any command- norm of a given system, it will only be necessary for the legal scientist to present it in such a way as to show the order of successively higher authorizing norms which speak for its validity-conditions, and for each other's, on up to the one norm whose "objective validity" is presupposed—the *Grundnorm*.

I have discussed the rationale for such a project in chapter 2, above. But now, in the domain of "positive permission," there appears a system of normative relations in which the project is obviously and decisively thwarted. And Kelsen himself evidently senses this. When he discusses the use of the term "right" in bestowing an official permission he says:

> The "right" may also consist in that an activity, for instance the exercise of a business, in order to be lawful, is conditioned by a permission called "concession" or "license" given by an organ of the community, a governmental authority, either

within its free discretion or only if some requirements are fulfilled. To carry on the activity without this official permission is prohibited, that is, subject to a sanction. This permission does not consist in the mere negative fact of not being prohibited, but in the positive act of a community organ. . . . This right, based on an offical permission, is not a reflex right: it is not the function of a corresponding obligation. (PTL, 138)

Clearly here is the case of a proper norm, specifically a "positive permissory norm," for which not all (if any) of the validity-conditions are provided in "higher," authorizing norms. Kelsen has directly admitted here that the valid expression of such a norm is sometimes a matter of "free discretion," and sometimes a matter conditioned by "some requirements." It is not easy to see what Kelsen might have in mind by "free discretion"; it is unlikely that a norm-authority is ever completely free of the control of system-specific conditions on the exercise of his permissory power. But it is perfectly obvious that the "some requirements" of his oblique reference are just the sort of problem-makers I have spoken of as "felicity conditions." There is no pretense that they are referred to the permissory norm by an authorizing norm. They are simply part of the matrix of performance that must be established for the norm-expression to succeed. Indeed, there may be other and higher norms at play; but here Kelsen has at last recognized that the entirety of the normative situation—the sum of conditions for the success of the norms at issue—is not fully determined by the order of norms themselves, however carefully enunciated, however organized. This I believe, is the reason why no schematization of positive permissory norms is attempted in Kelsen's works. And it is the reason why Kelsen insists on regarding permissory norms as constituting a "special modality," even while adhering to the analytic dogma of the Reduction Thesis. He wants to regard the various legal relations that arise in the permission-context as being like relations supervened by the independent command-modality in that they stipulate obligations through imputing delicts to sanctions (though the breakdown of relations here may be remarkably complex), but unlike them in the manner of the provision of the conditions providing for the validity of those stipulations.

NORMS OF AUTHORIZATION

Kelsen regards norms that "authorize" various kinds of conduct and various kinds of legal response as "positive" norms, in the sense in which commands and "positive" permissions are "positive." The kinds of legal relation which he subsumes under the rubric "authorization" are extremely diverse.

> Human behavior is positively regulated also, when an individual is authorized by the normative order to bring about, by a certain act, certain consequences determined by the order. Particularly an individual can be authorized (if the order regulates its own creation) to create norms or to participate in that creation; or when, in the case of a legal order providing for coercive acts as sanctions, an individual is authorized to perform these acts under the conditions stipulated by the legal order; or when a norm permits an individual to perform an act otherwise forbidden—a norm which limits the sphere of validity of a general norm that forbids the act. (PTL, 15–16)

I have already discussed the last of these varieties; it is the same as "validity-limiting" positive permission. The other varieties Kelsen regards as more-or-less direct bestowals of power upon legal agents and organs (PTL, 8). Among the powers bestowed, it is clear that the powers to create and enforce norms are of paramount significance. Here Kelsen has in mind not only particular delegations of power at relatively inferior levels of the norm-hierarchy (for example, a governor's empowerment of National Guard personnel to enter a riot area and make summary arrests), but also the general delegation of power provided by the "basic norm."

> The basic norm merely establishes a certain authority which may well in turn vest norm-creating power in some other authorities. The norms of a dynamic system have been authorized to create norms by some higher norm. This authorization is a delegation. Norm creating power is delegated from one authority to another authority; the former is the higher, the latter is the lower authority. The basic norm of a dynamic system is the fundamental rule according to which the norms of the system are to be created. A norm forms part of a dynamic system if it has been created in a way that is—in the last analysis—determined by the basic norm. (GTLS, 113)

It is clear that we are approaching once again (but now from the viewpoint of normative *dependency*) the question of what it means for a normative order to be "hierarchically structured." In discussing the pure-theoretic logic of commands, I pointed out that although Kelsen speaks of independent norms as forming a *Stufenbau*, the only "steps-and-stairs" order of ascendance he is willing to defend formally is the order of supervenience among imputations consequent to the nonimposition of original sanctions. Now, however, there emerges the suggestion that relations of authorized empowerment (both to create and enforce norms) have their own hierarchical structure, a structure in some way "determined" by the *Grundnorm*.

Two crucial subordinate questions appear at this point: (1) How and to what extent is the hierarchy of organ-authority *correlated* with the imputational hierarchies we have discussed?; and (2) What is the role of legal-scientific presentation vis-à-vis the hierarchy of authorization? As was indicated earlier, Kelsen opposes the traditional division of general legal norms into norms of "formal law" (regulating court procedure and the organization of legal authority) and "material law" (determining the "contents of judicial and administrative acts") (PTL, 230–231). He thinks that (at least in the "mature" legal system, one that contains explicit rules of law-creation and application) the two "orders of law" are in reality complementary normative functions embodied in the meaning (and hence in the "presentation") of every legal norm in its application. He argues that this functional integration is most clearly exposed in the rules of law by which legal science describes these norms:

> Material and formal law are inseparably connected with each other. Only in their organic combination do they constitute law that regulates its own creation and application. Each rule of law that completely describes this law must contain the formal as well as the material elements. (PTL, 231)

In the previous chapter, discussion of the "ramified schematic form" of rules of law in which Kelsen attempts to combine "material" and "formal" elements, revealed a multiplicity of "oughts," only one of which was later found to be "primary," in the sense of directing a norm-organ to impose a sanction upon the occasion of a specified delict. It was pursuit of this "ought" that led to the development of the "imputational hierarchy" binding together sanctions to be imposed in the case of prior sanction-omission. Now, however, it is possible to see the way in which this "ought" is supposed to "combine organically" with the others.

What Kelsen has done—to put it as boldly as possible—is this: where prior theorists have insisted that *two orders* of law (the formal, the material) interact in the operation of mature legal systems; Kelsen has held out for *one* order; but he has retained the *effect* of the division by distinguishing two normative functions in the rule of law through which any norm is presented: the "independent" function (corresponding, roughly, to the "material") and the "dependent" function, generally characterized as "authorization in the wider sense" (PTL, 57) (corresponding to the "formal"). I have indicated how the independent "ought" directed at a norm-organ is systematically linked with other and higher "oughts," directed to norm-organs (which, except in the case of self-referring imputational relations, will be *other* norm-organs); and I have indicated how system-relative "felicity-conditions" are incorporated into the working of dependent "oughts" governing the details of norm-application. It remains only to combine these observations in order to reveal the systematic connection between the formal and material law which Kelsen believes allows him to speak of the legal order as *one* order.

This may be done most efficiently by means of an illustrative example. The "Seditious Meetings and Assemblies Act" of 1795 (36 Geo. III, c.8) provides that the members of any gathering numbering greater than fifty persons who fail to disperse upon the command of specified officials shall be adjudged felonious in action, and shall suffer the penalty of death. The language of this Act is both cluttered and prolix; but one may assume that a legal scientist given the task of describing it would without difficulty isolate for presentation the primary independent norm it embodies: this is the command to specified organs of the court attaching the sanction of capital punishment to the delict of unlawful assembly. The question of (willful) nonimposition of this sanction is explicitly covered in articles VII, VIII, and X of the Act: official failure to impose the prescribed sanction is grounds for the capital punishment of "obstructing magistrates." The further question of nonimposition of this secondary sanction (designated s' in the foregoing analysis) is not treated in the Act.

The legal scientist entrusted with the job of presenting in ramified form the rule of law corresponding to the primary legal norm embodied in this Act will record this much at least (following the pattern of L^*c-3):

$$(d \text{ (unlawful assembly) I } s(\text{death}) \text{ and } \sim s) \text{ I } s' \text{ death})$$

But, what more might he say? He might, as was suggested in chapter 3, proceed to the matter not mentioned in the Act itself, but perhaps latent in the system of laws of which the Act is a part; namely, the issue of official failure to impose s'. It is at least arguable that this consideration is part of the meaning of the norm embodied in this act, inasmuch as that meaning is organically linked to that of rules governing official action throughout the system. If, in fact, another rule were to be found, valid concurrently with the Seditious Meetings and Assemblies Act, which stipulated penalties for official disobedience to sanctioning commands generally, it would seem quite reasonable to consider that rule as contributing to the meaning of the present rule by way of establishing part of the meaning of the terms "magistrates," "justices," "justices of the peace," "sheriffs," and so on, in short, the meaning of the terms designating authorities through their functions. It is this latter sort of determination that Kelsen wishes to make over into various dependent norms, replacing what had formerly been called "formal law." Specifically, these relations are to be represented as "authorizing" norms governing the execution of coercive acts designated in the Act.

The legal scientist might, moreover, incorporate into his ramified rule other extrinsic considerations, touching points of procedure, identification of "facts" as indicated in the language of the Act, and points of the English law of 1795 otherwise bearing on terms of the Act.[22] It is because Kelsen views this sort of undertaking as a legitimate, perhaps essential, function of scientific presentation that he insists on the "complicated formulation" of rules of law mentioned earlier. Let us recall the generalized form of ramified *Rechtsregeln* he suggested:

If an organ, whose nomination is determined by a general legal norm, has ascertained, in a procedure determined by a general legal norm, that facts are present to which a general legal norm attaches a certain sanction, then this organ ought to order a sanction determined in the earlier-mentioned legal norm, in a procedure determined by a general legal norm. (PTL, 231)

Now, the "general norms of procedure" in this formula are certainly dependent "norms of authorization," as he has portrayed them in *Pure Theory* I, 6,d. And it is just as certain that the procedural features of the legal order to which they point are largely matters of contingent detail, matters to be settled only by inspection of the whole of English law at the time of the Act's enactment. So, to the extent that legal-scientific representation of the 1795 Seditious Meetings Act demands determination of dependent normative relations extrinsic to the language of the Act itself to settle the felicity conditions of its principle norm, this representation will be a project of empirical research, and not one of "transcendental-logical" formalization.

It is true, at the same time, that it was in part the role of "formalistic" rule-presentation (determination and amplification of the independent norm-schema) to show how the analysis is and must be taken *outside* considerations wholly determined in the Act itself. But it cannot reasonably be argued that the presentation which includes all relevant extrinsic norm-relations (rules designating circumstances which are conditions of the successful "performance" of the primary norm) will be "pure" in the sense Kelsen requires. Such a presentation will, of necessity, contain features which are not common to all legal systems, but which are, by Kelsen's own admission, essential to the determination of the full meaning of a given norm.

This last observation exposes a fundamental shortcoming of Kelsen's pure-theoretical approach to the logic of legal norms. If under the title "norm" Kelsen wants to allow dependent "oughts," rules shaping the framework of meaning of santion-prescribing norms while prescribing no sanctions themselves, the spell of "formal analysis" is broken, and a descriptive accounting of system-relative normative relations at specific times and places takes its place. If, on the other hand, he confines his analysis to independent norms (and at times he certainly seems to regard sanction-stipulating norms as the only norms *proper*), he loses the connection with the hierarchy of authorization (the so-called formal-material nexus) which held the promise of connecting the imputational hierarchy belonging to independent norms with the *Grundnorm*, and hence with a principle of validity overriding the entire system.

It is the second horn of this dilemma that is the more hurtful to Kelsen's theoretic ambitions. For, as I suggested earlier, what gives the notion of an "imputational chain" its special appeal is the idea that the order of successive sanctions imposed against official omissions might be connected with the order of norm-organs who impose them; and the related idea that the "last norm" of the imputational hierarchy might thereby share in the force (that is, the threat of counteraction to the system-as-a-whole) of the "basic norm" which heads the hierarchy of authority. It was in this way that Kelsen hoped to explain that the norms of the constitution (being, in the case of the historically *first*, those whose obedience is commanded by the "basic norm") participate organically *throughout* the system of independent norms, and do not merely supervene from a remote apex.

> The norms of the constitution which regulate the creation of general norms to be applied by the courts and other law-applying organs are thus not independent, complete norms. They are instrinsic parts of all the legal norms which the courts and other organs have to apply. . . . The norms of the material constitution are law only in their organic connection

with those sanction-stipulating norms which are created on their basis. (GTLS, 143–144)

This idea of "instrinsic" participation through the means of a "formal-material connection" is radically undercut, however, by Kelsen's admission that the "last norms" of imputational chains may be norms of permission or authorization. For Kelsen has made it abundantly clear that those norms have the limited function of fixing conditions under which independent norms may be applied. In the case of independent norms the norm-authority alone is capable of obeying or disobeying the command that is meant; and he does this by executing or failing to execute the prescribed sanction. Obviously, however, nothing corresponds to this sort of obedience in the case of permissory and authorizing norms. If norm-organ 0 is merely permitted (in the "positive" sense) to impose sanctions upon the occurrence of a certain action, and 0 fails to impose S, there simply is no further legal consequence. The termination of the "chain" here is simple and complete. And likewise with norms of authorization: that organ 0 is authorized to impose a punishment upon the occasion of a certain action cannot, in the absence of a command-norm to that effect, obligate 0 to do so, in the sense that his failure to impose the punishment will be the ground of a sanction to be imposed against him (PTL, 25, 118).

This radical limitation of the imputation-chain model in presenting independent norm-relations is perhaps most clearly demonstrated in connection with the most general condition under which legal power may be conferred (authorized); namely, the general "effectiveness" of the legal order. Kelsen repeatedly insists that the validity of any individual norm in a system is *conditional* upon the effectiveness (that is, the regular application of norms and their regular obedience) of the system-as-a-whole.

A norm is considered to be valid only on the condition that it belongs to a system of norms, to an order which, on the whole, is efficacious. Thus, efficacy is a condition of validity; a condition, not the reason of validity. (GTLS, 42)[23]

Since effectiveness is here considered to be a condition, rather than a cause of the validity of independent norms, and since those norms which set the conditions of other norms' validity are generically termed "dependent" norms; it follows that effectiveness is the highest, most general authorizing norm of any system. Yet, Kelsen is quick to point out that this norm need not be directly enunciated at any time for it to have effect. Rather, the principle of effectivenness is presupposed in the "dynamic" cognition of the legal order. At GTLS, 42, Kelsen argues that the relationship between effectiveness and validity is cognizable only from the dynamic, and never from the static, viewpoint. Even if it is indiscernable in positive legislation, the effectiveness-norm may be discovered through "analysis of juristic thinking."

> An analysis of juristic thinking shows that jurists consider a constitution as valid only when the legal order based on it is effective. This is the principle of effectiveness. That a legal order is "effective" means that the organs and subjects of this order by and large behave in accordance with the norms of the order. . . . The principle of effectiveness is the general basic norm that juristic thinking assumes whenever it acknowledges a set of norms as the valid constitution of a particular state. This norm may be formulated as follows: men ought to behave in conformity with a legal order only if this legal order as a whole is effective. (WJ, 224)

When the principle of effectiveness is thus considered as a (dependent) norm, it is perfectly clear that contravention cannot be the grounds of a sanction: if men ought to behave in conformity with an effective order, but fail to do so, their failure does not become a delict (that is, a violation *in* the system); rather, it is a repudiation of the system itself. In such a case, Kelsen says, what started out as a system of norms is no longer that. It is in this sense that the

norm of effectiveness is a sine qua non of the legal order
(GTLS, 119). Here, however, it is perfectly apparent that
the threat of ineffectiveness to the system-as-a-whole bears
no consequential relation to the "last norm" of imputational chains within the system. Instead, this threat must
be answered *before* the validity of norms within their imputational matrices may be determined.

It is clear that the norm of effectiveness is not the sort of
norm that could fit into an imputational chain (that is, a
norm-organ could not be authorized to punish according
to that norm). It is, if a norm at all, a *dependent* norm; and
considering it a dependent norm makes it entirely impossible to produce the kind of formal analysis of validity
within systems of legal norms generally which Kelsen had
promised. In the end, Kelsen is forced to admit that *any*
norm of a positive system can be rendered invalid if it is
largely ineffective. This latter condition is designated
desuetudo (desuetude).

> [A] norm is not regarded as valid which is never obeyed or ap-
> plied. In fact, a legal norm may lose its validity by never be-
> ing applied or obeyed—by so-called *desuetude. Desuetudo*
> may be described as negative custom, and its essential func-
> tion is to abolish the validity of an existing norm. If custom is
> a law-creating fact at all, then even the validity of statutory
> law can be abolished by customary law. If effectiveness in the
> developed sense is the condition for the validity not only of
> the legal order as a whole but also of a single legal norm, then
> the law-creating function of custom cannot be excluded by
> statutory law, at least not so far as the negative function of
> *desuetudo* is concerned. (PTL, 213)

Once it is admitted, however, that the validity of any given
norm in a system is *not* conditional wholly upon the validity of other norms (given the appropriate framework of
norm-enactment, organ-authority, and so forth) but is,
rather, to some extent effected by *custom*, the prospect of a
complete, rigorous "formal-logical" accounting of the

system's normativity is lost. By allowing that "negative custom" can have a law-denying effect, Kelsen has undercut all possibility of displaying the organization of normative force in the system by means of rules which describe only norms. *Desuetudo* is, after all, a condition of *fact (Sein)*, not of obligation *(Sollen)*. For Kelsen, who makes the Humean-Kantian division between *Sein* and *Sollen* a fundamental tenet of positivism in legal theory, the invalidating potential of desuetude is therefore a crushing admission. Once this intrusion of fact is allowed, the hermetic seal is broken, and the "structural analysis" of norms promised by Pure Theory collapses.

NORMS OF DEROGATION

This brief discussion of the validity-nullifying effect of custom leads us unavoidably into an equally brief discussion of the validity-nullifying effect of certain positive dependent norms, called by Kelsen "derogating norms." In many ways, Kelsen's presentation of this species of norms makes derogation appear to be simply the extreme case validity-limiting positive permission (where all, rather than merely some, of the conduct forbidden by a prior norm is now allowed). But Kelsen is clearly eager to attribute to derogating norms a *special* status in respect to their peculiar range and unique transitoriness.

> Derogation is in addition to commanding, permitting, authorising, a specific function of a legal norm. A derogating norm is a norm, which repeals the validity of another norm. It differs from other norms, commanding, permitting, or authorising a definite behavior, insofar as it does not refer to a definite human behavior, but to the validity of another norm, the norm whose validity it repeals. (L & L, 233)

Derogating norms are, according to Kelsen, the only legal norms that do not refer to behavior, but to the validity of other norms. Since they do not prescribe behavior, they can be neither violated nor obeyed. Their sole function is to create "non-ought" states by repealing valid norms. Once the norms to which they refer lose their validity, derogating norms also lose validity (EJRP, 339–40).

And these differences between derogating norms and other norms purportedly add up to a final, formal difference.

> Since the derogating norm stipulates neither the "ought to" of a certain behavior, nor the "ought to" of the forbearance of a certain behavior, but the "non-ought" of a certain behavior, it cannot be expressed like other norms in an imperative or ought-sentence. (EJRP, 341)

There are several puzzling features in Kelsen's account of derogating norms. The reasons for his insistence that derogations comprise a separate normative category are, in the end, far from clear. Where he argues that these norms require a new style of presentation Kelsen shows that he has forgotten the main lines of analysis he had previously so painstakingly laid down. To begin with, Kelsen's insistence that derogating norms are uniquely inviolable comes as a surprise. After all, these norms have been introduced as a species of *dependent* legal normativity; and it is clear from what Kelsen has said to this point that *all* dependent norms are inviolable. The sole function of dependent norms is to determine conditions under which sanctions are to be imputed, and not to impute these sanctions themselves. There is a sense, of course, in which one may be said to "violate a permission," or "violate an authorization" when one "oversteps" the guidelines of action these norms determine. But in either case one "violates" the dependent norm only if some independent norm antecedently applies to the conduct "in excess" of the permission or authorization. One might, for instance, be permitted to stay out of the country for one month, then "violate" this permission by staying abroad for two months. But this action violates the law (is subject to sanction) only on the condition that some prior command-norm forbids one to stay abroad for such a period. (The permission here is said to "limit the validity" of the prior command if exception is made through the permissory norm to a blanket prohibition against foreign travel.)

Kelsen clearly wants to attribute the inviolability of derogations to their ephemerality, rather than their dependence. The derogating norm, he tells us, ceases to exist (that is, to be valid) when the independent norm which it seeks to annul becomes invalid. Here one might well ask: when does the derogating norm *begin* to exist? Kelsen's answer is that it begins to exist (become valid) at the very moment it ceases to exist (EJRP, 340, 352). It is in this manner *a*temporal; and since it allows no occasion for violation, it is (logically) inviolable. The whole meaning of a derogating norm is the repeal of a prior norm; and because the actualization of that meaning comes simultaneously with the termination of the need for the derogation, it passes into and out of existence without regard to agent-behavior (which *is* temporal). Thus, the derogation remains inviolate in the face of all conduct.

A brief examination of Kelsen's own example of a derogating norm, however, will show the inadequacy of this account. Kelsen chooses a norm which derogates a command of military conscription.

> For instance, a valid norm is that all men shall serve in the military who have reached the age of 21 years and who have been found physically fit. The legislator can terminate the validity of this norm by a legislative act whose sole function is the repeal of the validity of the said norm. By this norm, military service of qualified men is not prohibited. No definite behavior is prohibited or ordered. (EJRP, 341–42)

Surely Kelsen's previous analysis of command norms makes it abundantly clear that such a norm *can* be violated, and precisely because a definite behavior is prohibited (or ordered) by it. The primary reference of independent norms—lest we forget—is to the conduct of legal *organs*, not agents. That the derogating norm in question does not rule out or make mandatory any agent- conduct does not mean that it neither prohibits nor orders *any* conduct. On the contrary, it orders legal organs to refrain from imposing sanctions upon the occasion of conduct determined as delict in the conscription norm. Unless this sort of prohibition were implicit in the derogation, it is hard to see what legal effect the repeal of the conscription norm would have. Indeed, unless such an order were implicit in the derogation, it is hard to see why it should be called a "norm" at all.

Derogating norms, then, refer to judicial conduct, not to legal agency. By removing certain delicts from the norm-order, they prohibit organs from imposing sanctions on the condition of those delicts. Thus it is true, if awkward, to say that the derogating norm creates a "non-ought" in respect to a piece of agent-behavior; but by doing so, it creates an "ought-not" in respect to organ-behavior relating to this behavior. Kelsen's proposed "logically correct formulation" of the derogating norm fails to recognize this.

> Suppose the legislature were to formulate the following norm: "Men who have reached the age of 21 years and who have been found physically fit ought *not* to serve in the military." That norm would not repeal the validity of the norm prescribing that qualified men ought to do military service, but would establish a separate norm in conflict with the former. The derogating norm, however, does not conflict with the norm whose validity it repeals. To formulate the derogating norm in a manner which is logically correct: "men who have reached the age of 21 years and who have been found physically fit, non-ought to do military service" is, however, linguistically impossible. Therefore, derogating norms assume the form of assertions such as "the norm according to which men who have reached the age of 21 years ought (etc.) . . . is hereby repealed." (EJRP, 342)

It is only in respect to their "secondary vectors" that the two command norms concerning conscription are in conflict. If both these norms are valid, both military service and its omission are delict. And this means that the norm-organ finds himself in no "conflict" in enforcing them; he simply attaches the prescribed sanctions in both cases. Elsewhere, Kelsen has argued that the mutual exclusiveness of delicts does *not* entail the logical contradictoriness of norms imputing sanctions to these delicts:

> [W]ithin . . . a normative order the same behavior may be . . . commanded and forbidden at the same time, and . . . this situation may be described without logical contradiction. This is the case if a certain conduct is the condition of a sanction and at the same time the omission of this conduct is also the condition of a sanction. The two norms: "*a* ought to be" and "*a* ought not to be" exclude each other insofar as they cannot be obeyed or applied by the same individual at the same time; only one can be valid. But the two norms: "If a is, x ought to be" are not mutually exclusive. These two norms can be valid at the same time. Under a legal order a situation may exist in which a certain human behavior and at the same time the opposite behavior is the condition of a sanction which ought to be executed. The two norms can be valid side by side. (PTL, 25)

In such a case, Kelsen says, the rules of law describing the "conflicting norms" will not themselves be in contradiction. One will state the imputation of a sanction to the *commission* of act *a*; the other will impute a sanction (perhaps the same one) to the *omission* of the same act. This suggests that there is no pressure within the norm-order which compels derogation of one or the other norms. Kelsen equivocates on this. In the article, "Derogation," he says "derogation is required if norms stand in conflict with each other" (EJRP, 349). In *Pure Theory of Law*, however, he concedes that there is no formal "requirement" in such a case, but only a "teleological conflict" resulting from a "politically unsatisfactory situation" (PTL, 26).

Once "*primary* norm-vectors" are considered, however, it becomes clear that derogating norms *do* conflict with the norms whose validity they repeal. Moreover, the conflict here is a case of straightforward logical contradiction (at least at the level of *Rechtsregeln*), and not mere "teleological conflict." The norm which derogates the norm requiring military service of able-bodied 21-year-olds has the function of denying a formerly operative imputational connection. And this means that the organ who was formerly under obligation to impose sanction *s* in the case of certain conduct *d* is now forbidden to impose *s* in the case of this conduct. The primary norm exhibited in the rule of law describing the derogation will "logically exclude" the primary norm in the original conscription norm in exactly the way Kelsen described in *Pure Theory of Law:* The one says "*a* (in this case, the sanction *s*) ought to be"; the other says "*a (s)* ought not to be."[24]

Our discussion has now uncovered a subtle truth about the norm-character of derogations. To present this truth in the clearest light it will be useful to consider the question of whether a derogating norm may be regarded as the asymptotic limit of a series of validity-limiting permissions of increasing scope. A permissory norm toward the beginning of this series might, for example, excuse from the general requirement of military duty those able-bodied 21-year olds who are students. Another might exempt students; and so on. Each of these permissory norms may be unproblematically regarded as nonobligating and hence dependent; they only confine the range of the original independent norm, leaving its validity untrammeled in all cases other than those to which they make specific exception. However, if the end of the series appears as a "blanket permission" having coextensive range with the original conscription not by enumerating exceptions which jointly exhaust its scope, but by declaring as the necessary and sufficient condition of its validity the invalidity of the former norm, its force is no longer unquestionably that of a dependent norm. Now it appears that the derogating norm has the same force, exercised in a contrary "direction" to that of the *primary* (organ-directed) force of the original norm; and it has therefore every title to the status of independence as does that norm.

Kelsen's reluctance to regard derogations as independent organ-directed norms should not, however, have prevented him from recognizing the mistake in his denial that they can be expressed, like other norms, in imperative form. Dependent or independent, derogating norms enjoy the same potential diversity of expression-forms other forms do. Kelsen seems to have forgotten here his former recognition that it is the function of the norm-expression not the style of performance that matters. I have already indicated one way in which a derogating norm can be framed in an imperative (the ought-sentence directed to the norm-organ forbidding his imposition of sanction against the commission of conduct formerly regarded as delict). If one should wish to criticize this construction as retaining intact the original validity of the conscription norm, while merely forbidding its enforcement (arguing that so long as the original norm is valid, the derogating norm has failed to do its work), it only need be said in response that (as Kelsen himself has consistently argued elsewhere) a norm whose enforcement is systematically thwarted simply *ceases* to be valid *(in desuetudo)*. Whether the invalidity of the original norm is to be regarded as an indirect function of desuetude or a direct function of derogation is, in this case, clearly inconsequential. The normative situation in either event is the same.

Kelsen makes a final claim in connection with derogating norms which we cannot allow to go unchallenged. In the "Derogation" article, he says:

> In contradiction of a widespread opinion in the field of jurisprudence, the question whether norms exist which cannot be derogated must be answered in the positive if the ques-

> tion means: whether there are norms whose validity—according to their own meaning—cannot be repealed by a derogating norm, and if the question does not mean whether not every norm may lose its efficacy, and thereby its validity, and be replaced by another norm regulating the same subject matter in a different way. (EJRP, 343–344)

Kelsen allows that the latter formulation of the question must be answered in the negative, out of regard for the inescapable invalidating effect of desuetude: "A norm can exclude its derogation by another norm, but it cannot prevent the loss of its validity by the loss of its efficacy" (EJRP, 344). But what means, we must ask, has a norm, any norm, of excluding its own derogation by a later norm? Kelsen's argument on this question is conspicuously thin. He says:

> Without doubt, a norm, especially a legal norm, cannot only relate to specific conduct but it can also affect its own validity. It can, for instance, prescribe to be valid for only a certain length of time, for only a certain space, or for certain persons. It can prescribe to be valid for an unlimited time, for an unlimited space, and for all persons until another norm formulated by the same authority becomes valid which is in conflict with the first one. It can provide that it may be repealed only in a certain manner prescribed by itself or by a norm of the same order. There is, therefore, no reason to assume that it cannot provide that it should not be repealed by another norm. (EJRP, 344)

What Kelsen fails to recognize in this statement is the possibility of extending the same powers of validity-regarding self-reference to general norms governing the systematic derogation of earlier norms by later norms—for example, the principle *lex posterior derogat priori*, conceived not as a logical principle or customary presupposition, but as a genuine norm of positive law. If a norm which claims for itself immunity from repeal also asserts the repealability of all other norms (according to a systematic prescription), what becomes of the self-declaration of one such norm that *it* is immune to repeal? To be sure, nothing will prevent a norm (any norm) from providing that it should not be repealed. The only question is: what is the effective force of such a provision in the face of a posterior norm asserting its derogation?

Here it is evident that Kelsen has left essentially unanswered the challenge he cites from Regelsberger; namely,

> There is no law which cannot be changed. A legislator can make a change of the repeal of a legal norm very difficult by imposing conditions and limitations, but he cannot control the unchangeability of a legal norm, even for a limited period of time.[25]

Regelsberger's conclusion follows directly from the recognition of the possibility of a *lex posterior* rule as a positive norm in any norm-system. It is simply another way of expressing the essential "open-endedness" of legal systems, a condition that Kelsen has elsewhere defended. Kelsen's recalcitrance on this point is not merely a lapse in an otherwise carefully prepared analysis of positive norm-force; it is a needless, unjustified abandonment of a fundamental tenet of positivism—the tenet expressed in the opening pages of both of his major theoretical works: Laws are what men make them to be; legal theory can clarify and organize the complex meanings these laws involve, but it is powerless to set conditions on their development and revision.

SUMMARY CONCLUSION ON THE
LOGIC OF DEPENDENT NORMS

I began the present chapter by asking the question: what relation is there between the logic of independent legal norms and the pattern of presentation laid down by Kelsen for independent legal norms? My findings have been disappointing. Rather than providing a separate formal schematization for the various sorts of dependent norms he discusses, Kelsen merely indicates—with considerable hand-waving—that the "ought"-value of these norms consists in setting the conditions under which sanctions are to be imputed to delicts through independent command-norms. Since these conditions, the "felicity conditions" of the commanding performances, are stipulated by norm-authorities with specific reference to the aims and needs of each particular legal system, we cannot expect the dependent norms that reflect them to fall under a universal "formal" rule. Kelsen has made the meaning of independent norms depend in part on the meaning of dependent norms; but the transfer cannot be extended. At some point, the meanings of dependent norms turn upon matters of fact; and this is the end of "logical-formal" analysis. The limits of "purity" in Pure Theory are most clearly shown in the case of the dependent norm of effectiveness. Kelsen is fully willing to allow that customary neglect may annul the validity of norms, and that the condition of desuetude is a contingency that cannot be comprehended within the order of norms themselves. But once this is admitted, the principle that the validity of any norm has as its sole reason the validity of another norm has to be abandoned.

I have shown that Kelsen was led to abandon a simplistic rule of reduction for permissory norms due to his tardy realization of the "positive" force some permissions undeniably have. And, in pursuing the analysis of these positive permissions, I have indicated that Kelsen conceives the normative effect of "validity-limitation" to be the establishment of a "formal-material" nexus, in which the conditions and procedures of organ-authority are brought to bear upon the functioning of independent norms. This interpretation, which forces the legal scientist to look outside any particular norm to condition-setting rules scattered throughout legal systems, radically undercuts the style of analysis suggested by the "imputation chain" model which Kelsen applied in connection with commands. For, ultimately, it is the *whole* of the legal order, and not just the chain to which a command-imputation belongs, that settles a norm's validity. This was made clear in discussion of the Seditious Meetings Act of 1795: here, in order to determine whether a norm-authority's action should be counted as "obstruction" a variety of rules concerning title and procedure in connection with a host of offices have to be considered. Moreover, "semantic norms" which set the parameters of application for the terms employed in all the other norms must be brought into account. Once these considerations are made, it becomes clear that the prioristic and formalistic program which Pure Theory promised, tracing the validity of legal norms through the narrow channels of hierarchically arranged "ought" relations, simply cannot be achieved.

General Conclusion

What will be the final verdict on Kelsen's efforts to formulate a scientific jurisprudence? No unequivocal answer to this question is possible. This study has shown that the program of formal norm-analysis developed in the Pure Theory of Law cannot reach its announced goals. But it has also shown that it wins various smaller victories along the way. The anti-ideological, anti-metaphysical bias conspicuous in Kelsen's writing does insulate Pure Theory from many of the germs of partisanship and parochialism which debilitate other theories. It is only fair to admit, in the end, that the Pure Theory of Law is very nearly as pure as Kelsen says it is. Its accounts of Law are uniformly general, schematic, and descriptive. It does not waver from regarding law as a species of norm, and rightly sees normative structure as the foundation of legal order. It identifies the functional elements within legal norms and goes some distance toward describing the composition of these elements in articulated legal systems. Even where its analyses falter, they provoke improved analyses, rather than outright abandonment. Kelsen's insights, retooled and refined, have become indispensable parts of worldwide scientific jurisprudence.

What is perhaps the most impressive gain in Kelsen's Theory comes in quietly. It is his suggestion that legal science may circumvent the classical rift between formal and material law through a process of reconstruction involving "imputation chains." Imbedded in this suggestion is the bold hint that legal norm-hierarchies might be better understood if they are taken to be ordered, not by some vague scheme of subsumption, but by a principle reflecting the staging of norm-authority in particular systems. Kelsen does not exploit this suggestion fully. But if it *can* be exploited, Kelsen's quest for an organic whole of legal meaning in all legal systems will no longer seem to be quixotic.

Ironically the most glaring shortcomings in Kelsen's account derive from his zealous adherence to principles which are, taken independently, beyond reproach. Surely, the theory of positive law does require a descriptive legal science. Surely, the legal order itself is a structured arrangement of norms. And, just as surely, familiar principles of logic should be applied in determining the consistency and coherence of sets of descriptions. But once Kelsen combines these principles in a program of "constitutive" representation, a conflict results which radically undercuts his war against naturalism. As this study has shown, Kelsen's effort to provide a purely *descriptive* account of normative validity runs headlong against his effort to exhibit legal systems as orders in which norms are touched only by norms. To support his theory of independent norms, Kelsen was forced to devise a companion theory of dependent norms. And to support this theory of dependent norms, Kelsen was forced to admit conditioning factors that break the normative seal.

What is bad for Pure Theory may be beneficial to a broader concept of legal science. Perhaps legal scientists should not be disheartened by the fact that rigorously pursued formalism leads to its own downfall, forcing its practitioners to look beyond norms to determine normative validity. If this means that the whole of legal orders—norms, norm-organs, conditioning rules, agents' behavior, and so on—must be taken into account in settling questions of validity, it need not be taken as a sign that formal-logical analysis is a forlorn enterprise. Rather, it can be taken as an invitation to join the forces of pure-theoretical science with those of allied empirical and analytical disciplines in a cooperative effort to grasp law holistically. Seen in this light, Pure Theory's failings are but challenges for new developments in sociology, history, legal logic, and the like, and its achievements are the secure foundation stones for even more ambitious constructions.

Notes

NOTES TO CHAPTER 1

1. Kelsen's employment of the natural/non-natural distinction is faithfully Kantian. By "natural" Kelsen intends whatever is spatio-temporal, and by "non-natural," whatever is not. The Kantian metaphysical strain conspicuous in this doctrine is evident in all of Kelsen's works, from the earliest (see HS, 6–9; PGNR, 23–25, 63) to the latest (see PTL, 2–10; ILR, 1, 4).

2. This is M. Knight's designation ("Translator's Preface," PTL, v).

3. It is important to remember that in all of his early writings Kelsen emphatically insists that his theory is essentially a theory of *knowledge*. Both the language and the structure of his theory draw heavily from Kant's *Critiques*.

4. Kelsen has gone so far as to suggest that the proper legal scientist is distinguished by his anti-ideological personality type. We find an extreme, indeed an incredible statement of this view in PGNR, 63. Such a statement is quite surprising in light of Kelsen's repeated invectives against psychologism in jurisprudence (e.g. his attacks upon Austin's notion of "command"). The motivation behind it is clear, however. Kelsen wished to sever legal science cleanly from *Realpolitik*; he was not unaware of the direction the ideologization of Continental Legal Theory was taking. This feature of Pure Theory was emphasized and warmly received in the earliest reports on Kelsen's work to the Anglo-American jurisprudential community.

5. R. von Ihering, *Law as a Means to an End*, p. 380.

6. "The Pure Theory of Law and Analytical Jurisprudence," *Harvard Law Review* 55 (1941): 44–70 (reprinted in WJ, 266–287).

7. The same may be said for Savigny's followers (Vanegrow, Puchta, et al.), collectively known as the "Pandectists." It is worth noting that Austin was very strongly attracted to this aspect of Pandectism. He cites with great favor Savigny's discussion of the "mathematical" (syllogistic) method as it was applied in Roman jurisprudence (*Lectures on Jurisprudence* 2: 1116).

8. *Juristische Logik.*

9. *Einführung in das Juristische Denken.*

10. See HS, 42, 92–94, 268–270; "Juristischer Formalismus und Reine Rechtslehre," pp. 1723–1726; "The Pure Theory of Law and Analytical Jurisprudence," pp. 49–51.

11. C. K. Allen, *Law in the Making*, 7th ed., pp. 56–57, 58.

12. W. Jöckel, *Hans Kelsens rechtstheoretische Methode*, p. 3.

13. See, e.g., J. Prévault, "La Doctrine Juridique de Kelsen," pp. 32–42.

14. F. Gény, *Méthode d'interprétation et sources en droit privé positif*, vol. 1 (Paris, 1899).

15. H. Lauterpacht, "Kelsen's Pure Science of Law," pp. 106–107.

16. C. Boasson, "The Use of Logic in Legal Reasoning."

17. H. Kelsen, "Recht, Rechtswissenschaft und Logik," p. 548.

18. The term "transcendental-logical" predominates in Kelsen's early writings (e.g., PGNR, 64), where the influence of Kantian jargon is most conspicuous; the term "logico-juristic" appears mainly in later work (e.g., GTLS, 370), while "logical" appears throughout (e.g., GTLS, xv). The term "formal-logical," which occurs early (e.g., HS, 4–7), hints at a connection with Carnap's *Aufbau*. (See the use of this term in *The Logical Structure of the World*, p. 28.)

19. O. Bondy, "Logical and Epistemological Problems in Legal Philosophy," p. 81.

20. Ibid., 83.

21. Ibid., 86.

22. "The Formalism in Kelsen's Pure Theory of Law," pp. 110–130.

23. R. von Mises hints at a positive relation (*Positivism*, p. 332. This is essentially a translation of *Kleines Lehrbuch des Positivismus* [1939], written in the heyday of the *Wienerkreis*), while Bergmann and Zerby explicitly deny it ("Formalism," p. 125).

24. W. Ebenstein, "The Pure Theory of Law: Demythologizing Legal Thought," p. 625.

25. R. Carnap, *The Logical Structure of the World*, p. 28.

26. G. Bergmann, *The Metaphysics of Logical Positivism* (Madison, 1967), p. 32.

27. F. E. Oppenheim, "Outline of a Logical Analysis of Law," *Philosophy of Science* 11 (1944): 142–160.

28. Ibid., 158.

29. A. Wedberg, "Some Problems in the Logical Analysis of Legal Science," p. 246–275.

30. M. Golding, "Kelsen and the Concept of 'Legal System,' " p. 359.

31. Ibid., 361.

32. Ibid., 385–386.

33. R. Carnap, *Logical Structure*, p. 19.

34. Ibid., 107.

35. I might add that the same sort of revealing transformation can be done with various works by other logical positivists (e.g., M. Schlick's *Problems of Ethics* [New York, 1939]), changing "ethics" for "legal science."

36. References to Wittgenstein's *Tractatus Logico-Philosophicus* are taken from the standard Pears and McGuiness translation. The citation numbers refer to passages according to Wittgenstein's idiosyncratic numeration system.

NOTES TO CHAPTER 2

1. J. Stone, *Legal System and Lawyers' Reasonings*, p. 102.

2. The reader must be warned that Knight's translation is somewhat misleading here. The original term (German, 2d ed.) for "described" is *"bezeichnet,"* which would be more accurately rendered "designated," or "referred to." Obviously *"Recht," "Droit," "Lex,"* etc. do not describe anything. This error does not, however, affect the analysis that follows. It is worthwhile to contrast this passage to the parallel passage in GTLS, (pp. 4–5). In the latter, Kelsen is not so keenly interested in getting from the use of the term "law" in connoting factual phenomena to its use in pure-theoretic analysis. Accordingly, the factual sense predominates. The point of the discussion turns out to be the contrasting of positive law with "the philosophy of justice."

3. The direction of analysis intimated here is one which a number of recent legal scholars have taken (see esp. G. Williams, "The Controversy Concerning the Word 'Law,' " pp. 134–156). The idea, popularized by

the later Wittgenstein, is to find "family resemblances," "clusters of meaning," instead of "senses," "univocal meanings." Kelsen's doctrine of the "social-scientific cognition" is, of course, a strictly essentialist position, and an outright rejection of Wittgenstein's approach.

4. Kelsen does not (as some writers do) take "X ought to be" (or "Let X be," etc.) as the form of a legal command-norm and "X ought not to be" as the form of its correlative prohibition-norm. Had he done so, the two would indeed have been straightforwardly contradictory. Rather, for reasons I shall discuss later, Kelsen considers these norms to have the forms "If Y is, X ought to be" and "If non-Y is, X ought to be" (though putting it just this way oversimplifies some important features of Kelsen's account). Accordingly, he concludes that the two norms are not mutually exclusive; they "can be valid side by side. They can be described without logical contradiction." (PTL, 25)

5. Although there is nothing *prima facie* wrong about this treatment of the notion of "legal meaning," it will be subsequently shown that a fundamental ambiguity about "meaning" in these contexts seriously blurs the point Kelsen is after. A typically Continental "intentional" account of meaning lies at the bottom of Kelsen's theory of presentational analysis. This perspective ultimately leads him to inflated claims about the role of legal science vis-à-vis its twofold object.

6. Both of these theses are variously stated throughout Kelsen's writings. Among the clearest enunciations are to be found in GTLS, 45–48, 163–164; PTL, 22, 70–75, 78–80. A caveat about Kelsen's work prior to GTLS: The term "rule of law" is sometimes used in earlier expositions of "normative jurisprudence," but generally without the special sense indicated in these theses. Even in the second edition of *General Theory*, the term is occasionally used to denote a particular legal requirement in the "factual sense" (see section [a]); e.g., "Every rule of law obligates human beings to observe a certain behavior under certain circumstances. . . . A rule of law may oblige neighbors to lend assistance to the victims of an inundation" (GTLS, 1). That the sense "rule of law" has in these occurences cannot be identical with the sense it has in theses (1) and (2) is made undeniably clear by Kelsen's stipulation that "rules" in the latter sense are without prescriptive force (PTL, 74–75).

7. I use the asterisk (*) throughout this study to flag rules of law, distinguishing them from the norms to which they correspond.

8. The clearest statement of this doctrine appears at PTL, 73. It is a position that Kelsen has increasingly stressed in his latest writings (LL, 232; RLi, 422; RLii, 496–497). While Kelsen does not, even in his most

recent essays, speak of "alethic" and "deontic" systems, he does refer to the difference between them as a difference of "modi" (PTL, 6).

9. Strictly speaking, of course, it makes no sense to speak of verifiability of what cannot be true; but this term is appropriated from alethic use due to a lack of corresponding deontic expressions. The neologism "validitability" would do nicely were it not such an ungainly departure from usage. Kelsen frequently speaks of the "verification" of norms (e.g., PTL, 73).

10. The doctrine of performatives was enunciated first by J. L. Austin in the William James Lectures at Harvard (1955); later transcribed and edited by J. O. Urmson and published as *How to Do Things with Words.* Some elaboration was provided in a BBC Third Programme talk in 1956, which is printed (with minor alterations) in Austin's *Philosophical Papers.* In a telling aside Austin says, "[W]riters on jurisprudence have constantly shown themselves aware of the varieties of infelicity and even at times of the peculiarities of the performative utterances. Only the still widespread obsession that the utterances of the law, and utterances used in, say, 'acts in the law,' *must* somehow be statements true or false, has prevented many lawyers from getting this whole matter much straighter than we are likely to. . . . " (*How to Do Things,* p. 19). From this it is plain that Kelsen deserves some measure of credit for leading jurisprudents to escape from the "obsession" Austin decries.

11. The word "performative" does not, of course, appear in Kelsen's work; it was, after all, coined by Austin long after the main lines of Pure Theory were developed. But the recognition of performative affects is undeniable there.

12. Typical of the critics is Alf Ross, who maintains that Kelsen's notion of a descriptive "ought" can be maintained only at the expense of a collapse of the crucial distinction between *Seinswissenschaft* and *Sollenswissenschaft.* See his review of WJ, *California Law Review* 40 (1957): 364–369; *On Law and Justice,* p. 10.

13. M. Golding, "Kelsen and the Concept of 'Legal System'," 364–365.

14. Or what amounts to the same thing; Hart admits that at the time of the Berkeley debate with Kelsen (November 1961) he had not read Prof. Golding's article.

15. H. L. A. Hart, "Kelsen Visited," pp. 714–715.

16. Ibid., 715.

17. I. Tammelo, review of *Reine Rechtslehre* (1960), *Journal of Legal Education* 15 (1963): 354–355.

18. G. Bergmann, L. Zerby, "Formalism," p. 116.

19. Tammelo makes both these charges, and even compares Kelsen's image of the world of law to Plotinus' vision of the moral universe (!).

20. This point, expressed in the same language ("reason for validity") is to be found throughout Kelsen's work: GTLS, 111; WJ, 219; ILR, 5; PTL, 193, etc. The phrase "reason for validity" is ambiguous, however. As members of the "good reasons" school of contemporary meta-ethics have pointed out, there are a wide range of ways in which something may be adduced as a "reason" or "good reason" for something else. Sometimes Kelsen seems to want to say that the validity of L-n+1 is a reason for the validity of L-n in the logical sense of "sufficient condition"; this claim can, of course, only be made indirectly: L*-n+1 implies L*-n. At other times he seems to want to say that L-n+1 is the *right answer* to be given to one or another party's question as to why a given sanction should be imposed, or why a certain act should be regarded as delict. In this sense, L-n+1 functions as a *justification*, rather than a sufficient condition, and the considerations at play are of a quite different character. The ambiguity at work here can be seen in what Kelsen says about the influence of "efficacy" on the validity of norms. It would seem that if only a norm can determine another norm's validity, then only a norm can determine another's invalidity. But Kelsen hastens to tell us that this is sometimes not the case. Plain facts of court operations, enforcement conditions, even general public behavior may have an invalidating effect on legal norms (see PTL, 10–12; GTLS, 118–119). If these matters of *fact* are to be regarded as "overriding reasons," or something of the sort, then it will no longer make sense to say that norms are the reasons for the validity of other norms. But to say that they are merely "reasons-among-others" would be to cast them into a weak middle ground where their service to rational reconstruction is at least questionable.

21. J. Stone, "Legal System," p. 102.

22. The moral rule that Kelsen chooses at GTLS, 112, and PTL, 195, is: "Live in harmony with the universe."

23. This position seems to be the stand Kelsen takes whenever challenged on the point (see "Reine Rechtslehre und Egologische Theorie," *Oesterreichische Zeitschrift für öffentliches Recht*, 5 (1953): 449–492.

24. To say that there are *two* is to simplify the picture somewhat. This is a problem which Kelsen has grappled with throughout the development of Pure Theory, and one point at which numerous critics have sensed that he is vulnerable. Only recently has he come to realize how much hinges on the issue, and how unclear his prior efforts toward ex-

plaining the point have been. Later we shall examine Kelsen's "official" compromise settlement, which we shall show to be unsatisfactory. Identification and criticism of the two divergent thrusts which go into this settlement (and which Kelsen has, at various times, tried independently) will help to show *why* the solution which Kelsen seeks is foredoomed.

25. J. Raz, *The Concept of a Legal System*. Hereafter referred to in the text as CLS.

NOTES TO CHAPTER 3

1. J. Raz, *Concept of a Legal System*, p. 85. Apparently Raz has a distorted sense of the force of permissory norms in Kelsen's scheme. It is, of course, true that Kelsen holds that legal norms invariably apply sanctions against delicts. It is also true that Kelsen admits that legal authorities are not always required, but sometimes only permitted (Kelsen also says "authorized") to impose sanctions. What Raz fails to recognize in this is that the fact of an authority's having been permitted to impose a sanction does not militate against his being commanded so to do. Permission to sanction is the exception, rather than the rule. Typically, the legal system (or the basic norm), or some authority higher than himself, will *permit* a norm authority to impose sanctions in a general way and *command* him to impose a specific sanction whenever the conditions specified in a delict-describing norm-antecedent occur. To construe all directions from higher norm-authorities to lower as mere permissions is to wreak havoc with Kelsen's notion of imputation-chains (see below).

2. J. L. Austin, *How to Do Things with Words*, p. 154–156.

3. Alf Ross, *Directives and Norms*, p. 86.

4. R. J. Vernengo, "About Some Formation Rules," p. 341.

5. It is evident that Vernengo has Carnap primarily in mind from remarks made elsewhere in the article.

6. R. J. Vernengo, "About Some Formation Rules," p. 346.

7. G. Bergmann and K. Zerby, "Formalism," p. 115.

8. Ibid., 130.

9. Ibid., 115.

10. Ibid., 115n.

11. Kelsen admits that he is here employing an old word in a new sense (PTL, 8), and hastens to disclaim in his later writings the traditional sense in which he employed it in the earlier ones.

12. J. Austin, *Lectures on Jurisprudence*, cited by Kelsen, GTLS, 63.

13. H. L. A. Hart voices particularly strong criticisms of this feature of Kelsen's program in *The Concept of Law*, pp. 35–41.

14. The one exception to this rule is the situation called desuetude; here a norm is invalidated by prolonged ineffectiveness. For more on this, see chap. 4, "norms of derogation," below.

15. F. Brentano. *The Origin of Our Knowledge of Right and Wrong*, trans. and ed. R. Chisholm and E. H. Schneewind. (London, 1969). (Translation of a work first published in 1889, with revised editions appearing in 1921 and 1934.)

16. N. S. Timasheff, *An Introduction to the Sociology of Law* (Cambridge: Harvard University Press, 1939), 264. (Cited in GTLS, 28.) Timasheff attributed the general form of the argument to Petrazhetsky and Stoop.

17. H. L. A. Hart, "Self-Referring Laws," p. 302.

18. Ibid., 308.

19. Ibid., 309.

20. J. Raz, *Concept of a Legal System*, p. 84.

21. H. L. A. Hart, *Concept of Law*, pp. 38–39, 40.

22. This branch of modal logic draws its name and fundamental ideas from G. H. von Wright's article, "Deontic Logic," pp. 1–15. Von Wright's system was greatly elaborated in his subsequent *Norm and Action*, and "An Essay in Deontic Logic and the General Theory of Action." The most ambitious and most rigorous general developments of deontic logics have been executed by A. R. Anderson and N. Rescher. Attempts at applying their results to the formal analysis of legal systems have been made by J. Kalinowski, C. K. Cobb, I. Tammelo, and A. Ross. For an excellent short history of the deontic logic movement, see N. Rescher, *The Logic of Commands*; for an interesting discussion of the application of deontic logic to legal theory, see J. Kalinowski, *Introduction à la Logique juridique* (Paris, 1965). Both contain extensive bibliographies.

23. I. Tammelo, "Sketch for a Symbolic Juristic Logic," p. 290.

24. R. Moore, "The Deontic Status of Legal Norms," pp. 151–158.

NOTES TO CHAPTER 4

1. ". . . those that further determine the meaning of other norms, by defining a concept used in a second norm or by authentically interpreting a second norm otherwise." (PTL, 57)

2. A. Ross, *Directives and Norms*, chap. 5.

3. G. H. von Wright, *Norm and Action*, chap. 5; "An Essay in Deontic Logic and the General Theory of Action," chap. 4. Von Wright clearly rejects the Reflex Thesis, but seems equivocally disposed towards acceptance of the Reduction Thesis.

4. J. Stone, "Legal System," chap. 5.

5. Ilmar Tammelo, "On the Logical Structure of the Law Field," *Archiv für Rechts-und sozialphilosophie* 45 (1959): 95–101; "On the Logical Openness of Legal Orders," *American Journal of Comparative Law* 8 (1959): 187ff; *Outlines of Modern Legal Logic*, chap. 3, 4.

6. E.g., I. Tammelo, Book Review, *Journal of Legal Education* 15:355.

7. This is the term Stone and Tammelo use to indicate the condition of an act's being neither permitted nor forbidden.

8. I.e., in the present day, the refusal of a legal organ to render a normative verdict, either of command or permission. The term is usually applied in international law. It should be noted that this usage differs considerably from the ancient usage (see *Black's Law Dictionary* 4th ed. [St. Paul, 1968], p. 1203).

9. Bergmann and Zerby, "Formalism," p. 120.

10. V. H. Kantorowicz, *The Definition of Law*, ed. A. H. Campbell (Cambridge, 1958), pp. 70–74.

11. I. Tammelo, "Sketch for a Symbolic Juristic Logic," pp. 188–192.

12. G. Williams, "The Controversy Concerning the Word 'Law'," *British Year Book of International Law* 20 (1945): 146–199 (reprinted in *Philosophy, Politics, and Society*, pp. 134–156).

13. A. R. Anderson, "The Logic of Norms," *Logique et Analyse*, pp. 84–96.

14. A. Ross, *Directives and Norms*, p. 120. (It is to be understood that the obligation here is one to *omit* a given act, hence a norm of prohibition.)

15. Ibid.

16. G. H. von Wright, *Norm and Action*, especially pp. 85–92. (Von Wright has touched lightly on this subject since, in "The Logic of Action: A Sketch," in *The Logic of Decision and Action*, ed. N. Rescher [Pittsburgh, 1968], esp. pp. 133–136; and in *An Essay in Deontic Logic and the General Theory of Action*, Acta Philosophica Fennica, fasc. 21 (1968), chap. 5. His position has not, however, substantially changed in the later discussions; the early account remains the best statement.)

17. *Norm and Action*, p. 86.

18. "Under the law of Hawaii, an association of persons in the owner-ship of land, members of which ordinarily hold the property as tenants in common." *Black's Law Dictionary* rev. 4th ed. (St. Paul, 1968), p. 874.

19. Von Wright finesses, rather than concedes, this point. He states the claim of non-normativity against declarations of intention, then sug-gests that his alternative is all that remains "if this is accepted." (*Norm and Action*, p. 91).

20. Ibid., 104–105.

21. See R. M. Hare, *The Language of Morals* (New York, 1964), pp. 17–22.

22. It is unclear how many of these Kelsen wants to consider "semantic norms" (PTL, 57–58) and how many he wants to distribute under other titles of norm-dependency.

23. This thought is echoed at GTLS, 118–119; PTL, 11, 26, 211–214; WJ, 224; ILR, 2.

24. Of course, it is possible to view this conflict as a "teleological con-flict" at the secondary level, entailing the imposition of a secondary sanction upon the occasion of *either* a sanction-imposition or its omis-sion by the norm organ in the face of the conduct prohibited by the original conscription norm. In this case, assuming a minimal extention of the imputational chains involved, the conflict appears roughly as follows:

$$L^*c \text{ (the conscription norm):} \quad \ldots ((dIs)\&{\sim}s)Is'$$
$$L^*d \text{ (the derogating norm):} \quad \ldots ((c{\sim}Is)\& s)Is' \ldots$$

(where c is conduct extensionally equivalent to the conduct regarded as delict d in L^*c). Putting it this way perhaps disguises the important fact that what was regarded as delict in L^*c has been returned to the status of conduct simpliciter, but it does reveal the primary normative effect of the derogation; namely, to rule out a certain mode of sanction pro-cedure on the part of the norm-organ.

25. Regelsberger, *Pandekten: Systematisches Handbuch der Rechtswis-senschaft* vol. I, part 7 (1893), p. 109, cited EJRP, 343.

Bibliography

I. WORKS BY KELSEN

The following are the principal sources by Kelsen consulted in the preparation of this study. The most extensive published bibliography of Kelsen's works is by R. Métall, *Hans Kelsen: Leben und Werk* (Vienna: Franze Deuticke, 1969). A bibliography of Kelsen's English-language publications appears in *California Law Review* 59 (May, 1971): 816-819. Extensive bibliographies, including translations into several languages, appear in both German editions of *Reine Rechtslehre* and the 1961 English edition of *General Theory of Law and State*.

Aufsätze zur Ideologiekritik. Neuwied am Rhein: Luchterhand, 1964.

"Derogation." In *Essays in Jurisprudence in Honor of Roscoe Pound*, edited by Ralph Newman. Indianapolis: Bobbs-Merrill, 1962.

Essays in Legal and Moral Philosophy, edited by Ota Weinberger and translated by Peter Heath. Dordrecht: Reidel, 1973.

"The Function of the Pure Theory of Law." In *Law: A Century of Progress, 1835-1935; Contributions in Celebration of the 100th Anniversary of the Founding of the School of Law of the New York University*. New York: New York University Press, 1937.

General Theory of Law and State, translated by Anders Wedberg. New York: Russell and Russell, 1961.

"Die Grundlage der Naturrechtslehre." *Österreichische Zeitschrift für öffentliches Recht*. 13 (1964): 1-37.

Hauptprobleme der Staatsrechtslehre. Tübingen: Mohr, 1923. Reprinted, Reinheim, 1960.

"Juristischer Formalismus und Reine Rechtslehre." *Juristische Wochenschrift*, 58 (1929): 1723–1726.

"Law and Logic." In *Philosophy and Christianity: Philosophical Essays Dedicated to Professor Dr. Hermann Dooyerwerd.* Amsterdam: North-Holland Publishing, 1965.

"Norm and Value." *California Law Review* 54 (October, 1966): 1624–1629.

"On the Pure Theory of Law." *Israel Law Review* 1 (1966): 1–7.

Die Philosophischen Grundlagen der Naterrechtslehre und des Rechtspositivismus. Berlin, Charlottenburg: Pan-verlag, R. Heise, 1928.

Principles of International Law. New York: Rinehart, 1952.

"Professor Stone and the Pure Theory of Law." *Stanford Law Review* 17 (July, 1965): 1128–1157.

Pure Theory of Law. Translated by Max Knight. 2d ed. Berkeley: University of California Press, 1967.

"The Pure Theory of Law." Translated by Charles H. Wilson. *Law Quarterly Review* 50 (1934): 474–490.

"The Pure Theory of Law and Analytical Jurisprudence." *Harvard Law Review* 55 (1941): 44–70.

"Recht und Logik." Part I. *Forum* 12 (October, 1965): 421–425. Part II. *Forum* 12 (November, 1965): 495–500.

"Recht, Rechtswissenschaft und Logik." *Archiv für Rechts- und Sozialphilosophie* X52 (1966): 545–552.

Reine Rechtslehre. Leipzig: F. Deuticke, 1934. 2d ed., Vienna: F. Deuticke, 1960.

Society and Nature. Chicago: University of Chicago Press, 1943.

Vergeltung und Kausalität. The Hague: W. P. van Stockum, 1941.

What is Justice? Berkeley: University of California Press, 1960.

II. WORKS BY OTHERS

Allen, C. K. *Law in the Making.* 7th ed. Oxford: Clarendon Press, 1964.

Allen, Layman. "Logical Analysis of Positive Law." *Yale Law Journal* 61 (1957): 833–879.

Anderson, Alan Ross. "Formal Analysis of Normative Systems." In *Logic of Decision and Action,* edited by Nicholas Rescher. Pittsburgh: University of Pittsburgh Press, 1968.

_____. "Logic, Norms and Roles." In *Mathematical Methods in Small Group Processes*, edited by J. H. Criswell, et al. Stanford: Stanford University Press, 1962.

_____. "The Logic of Norms." *Logique et Analyse* 2 (1958): 84–96.

Austin, John. *Lectures on Jurisprudence*. London: J. Murray, 1869.

_____. *The Province of Jurisprudence Determined*. London: J. Murray, 1832.

Austin, John Langshaw. *How to Do Things with Words*, edited by J. O. Urmson. New York: Oxford University Press, 1965.

_____. *Philosophical Papers*, edited by J. O. Urmson and G. J. Warnock. Oxford: Clarendon Press, 1961. 2d. ed., 1970.

Bergmann, Gustav and Zerby, L. "The Formalism in Kelsen's Pure Theory of Law." *Ethics* 55 (1945): 110–130.

Boasson, C. "The Use of Logic in Legal Reasoning." *Mededelingen der Koninklijke Nederlande Akademie van Wetenschappen* 29, no.3 (1966).

Bondy, Otto. "Logical and Epistemological Problems in Legal Philosophy." *Australasian Journal of Philosophy* 29 (August, 1951): 81–97.

Carnap, Rudolf. *The Logical Structure of the World*, translated by Rolf A. George. Berkeley: University of California Press, 1967.

Clark, R. S. "Hans Kelsen's Pure Theory of Law." *Journal of Legal Education* 22 (1969): 170–196.

de Bustamante y Montoro, A. S. "Kelsenism." In *Interpretations of Modern Legal Philosophies: Essays in Honor of Roscoe Pound*, edited by Paul Sayre. New York: Oxford University Press, 1947.

del Vecchio, Giorgio. *The Formal Bases of Law*. New York: Macmillan, 1921.

_____. *Justice*. Edinburgh: University Press, 1952.

Dias, R. W. M. *Jurisprudence*. 2d ed. London: Butterworths, 1964.

Ebenstein, William. *The Pure Theory of Law*. Madison: University of Wisconsin Press, 1945.

_____. "The Pure Theory of Law: Demythologizing Legal Thought." *California Law Review* 59 no.9 (May, 1971): 617–652.

Engel, Salo, and Métall, Rudolf A., eds. *Law, State, and International Legal Order: Essays in Honor of Hans Kelsen*. Knoxville: University of Tennessee Press, 1964.

Engisch, Karl. *Einführung in das Juristische Denken.* Stuttgart: W. Kohlhammer, 1956.

――――. "Der rechtsfreie Raum." *Zeitschrift für die gesamte Staatswissenschaft* 108 (1958).

Fränkel, Karl J. *Recht und Gerechtigkeit bei Hans Kelsen.* Doctoral dissertation, law school Cologne, 1965.

Friedmann, Wolfgang. "Legal Philosophy and Judicial Lawmaking." In *Essays on Jurisprudence from the Columbia Law Review.* New York: Columbia University Press, 1963.

――――. *Legal Theory.* 5th ed. New York: Columbia University Press, 1967.

Fuller, Lon. *Anatomy of the Law.* New York: Frederick A. Praeger, 1968.

――――. *The Law in Quest of Itself.* Boston: Beacon Press, 1940.

Golding, M. P. "Kelsen and the Concept of 'Legal System'." *Archiv für Rechts- und Sozialphilosophie* 47 (1961): 354–386.

――――. *Philosophy of Law.* Englewood Cliffs: Prentice-Hall, 1975.

Guest, A. G. "Logic in the Law." In *Oxford Essays in Jurisprudence: A Collaborative Work,* edited by A. G. Guest. Oxford: Oxford University Press, 1961.

Hägerström, Axel. *Inquiries into the Nature of Law and Morals,* translated by C. D. Broad. (Acta Societas Litterarum Humaniorum Regiae Upsaliensis: *Kungl. Humanistiska Vetenskapssamfundet i Uppsala,* vol. 40). Uppsala, 1953.

Hall, Jerome. *General Principles of Criminal Law.* 2d ed. Indianapolis: Bobbs-Merrill, 1960.

――――. "Nulla Poena sine Lege." *Yale Law Journal* 47 (1938): 145–193.

――――. *Studies in Jurisprudence and Criminal Theory.* New York: Oceana, 1958.

Hart, H. L. A. *The Concept of Law.* Oxford: Oxford University Press, 1961.

――――. "Kelsen Visited." *U.C.L.A. Law Review* 10 (1963): 709–728.

――――. "Self-Referring Laws." In *Festskrift tillägnad professor juris doktor Karl Olivecrona.* Stockholm: Norstedt, 1964.

Hohfeld, Wesley Newcomb. *Fundamental Legal Conceptions as Applied in Judicial Reasoning.* New Haven: Yale University Press, 1919.

Horovitz, Joseph. "Ulrich Klug's Legal Logic: A Critical Account." *Étude de Logique juridique*, edited by Chaim Perelman. Brussels: Emile Bruylant, 1966.

Hughes, Graham. "Validity and the Basic Norm." *California Law Review* 59 (May, 1971): 695-714.

Jensen, O. C. *The Nature of Legal Argument.* Oxford: Blackwell, 1957.

Jöckel, Wilhelm. *Hans Kelsens Rechtstheoretische Methode.* Tübingen: Mohr (Paul Siebeck), 1930.

Kalinowski, Jerzy. *Introduction à la Logique juridique.* Paris: Librairie générale de droit et de jurisprudence, 1965.

Kaufmann, Felix. *Logik und Rechtswissenschaft: Grundriss Eines Systems der Reinen Rechtslehre.* Tübingen: Mohr, 1922.

Klug, Ulrich. *Juristische Logik.* Berlin: Springer, 1951.

Kunz, J. L. "Die definitive Formulierung der Reinen Rechtslehre." *Österreichische Zeitschrift der öffentliches Recht* 11 (1961).

Lauterpacht, Hersch. "Kelsen's Pure Science of Law." In *Modern Theories of Law.* London: Oxford University Press, 1933.

Martin, Richard M. "Leges sine Logica Vanae." In *Law and Philosophy*, edited by S. Hook. New York: New York University Press, 1964.

Mautner, Thomas. "Flaws in Laws." *Philosophical Review* 82 (January, 1973): 83-98.

Moore, Ronald. "The Deontic Status of Legal Norms." *Ethics* 83 (January, 1973): 151-158.

_____. "Kelsen's Puzzling Descriptive Ought." *U.C.L.A. Law Review* 20 (July, 1973): 1269-1288.

_____. "Legal Permission." *Archiv für Rechts- und Sozialphilosophie* 59 (1973): 327-346.

Naess, Arne. "Do We Know That Basic Norms Cannot Be True or False?" *Theoria* 25 (1959).

_____. "We Still Do Know That Norms Cannot Be True or False." *Theoria* 28 (1962): 205-209.

Oesterberg, Dag. "We Know That Basic Norms Cannot Be True or False." *Theoria* 28 (1962): 200-204.

Olivecrona, Karl. "The Imperative Element in the Law." *Rutgers Law Review* 18 (1964).

_____. *Law as Fact.* Copenhagen: E. Munksgaard, 1939.

———. "Legal Language and Reality." In *Essays in Jurisprudence in Honor of Roscoe Pound*, edited by Ralph A. Newman. Indianapolis: Bobbs-Merrill, 1962.

Oppenheim, F. E. "Outline of a Logical Analysis of Law." *Philosophy of Science* 11 (1944): 142–160.

Packer, Herbert L. *The Limits of the Criminal Sanction*. Stanford: Stanford University Press, 1968.

Paradies, F. *Recht und Logik*. Typescript in possession of Columbia Law Library, 1945.

Parker, Reginald. "The Pure Theory of Law." *Vanderbilt Law Review* 14 (1960): 211–218.

Paton, George W. *A Textbook of Jurisprudence*. Oxford: Oxford University Press, 1951.

Perelman, Chaim, ed. *Étude de Logique juridique*. Brussels: Emile Bruylant, 1966.

Prévault, Jacques. "La Doctrine juridique de Kelsen." *Annales de L'université de Lyon* 27 (1965): 1–67.

Radin, Max. *Law as Logic and Experience*. New Haven: Yale University Press, 1940.

Raz, Joseph. *The Concept of a Legal System*. Oxford: Oxford University Press, 1970.

Recaséns-Siches, Louis. "The Logic of the Reasonable as Differentiated from the Logic of the Rational (Human Reason in the Making and the Interpretation of the Law)." In *Essays in Jurisprudence in Honor of Roscoe Pound*, edited by Ralph A. Newman. Indianapolis: Bobbs-Merrill, 1962.

Rescher, Nicholas. *The Logic of Commands*. London: Routledge and Kegan Paul, 1966.

Ross, Alf. *Directives and Norms*. New York: Humanities Press, 1968.

———. *On Law and Justice*. Berkeley: University of California Press, 1959.

Salmond, J. *Jurisprudence*. 11th ed., edited by Glanville Williams. London: Sweet and Maxwell, 1957.

Sander, Fritz. *Kelsens Rechtslehre*. Tübingen: Mohr, 1923.

Sayre, Paul, ed. *Interpretations of Modern Legal Philosophers: Essays in Honor of Roscoe Pound*. New York: Oxford University Press, 1947.

Schaller, P. Leodegar M. *Der Rechtsformalismus Kelsens und die thomistische Rechtsphilosophie.* Doctoral dissertation, 1949, University of Freiburg, Switzerland.

Shuman, Samuel I. *Legal Positivism.* Detroit: Wayne State Univerity Press, 1963.

Silving, Helen. "Analytical Limits of the Pure Theory of Law." *Iowa Law Review* 28 (1942).

_____. "Law and Fact in the Light of the Pure Theory of Law." In *Interpretations of Modern Legal Philosophers: Essays in Honor of Roscoe Pound,* edited by Paul Sayre. New York: Oxford University Press, 1947.

Stone, Julius. *Human Law and Human Justice.* Stanford: Stanford University Press, 1965.

_____. *Legal System and Lawyers' Reasonings.* Stanford: Stanford University Press, 1964.

_____. " 'Non Liquet' and the Function of Law in the International Community." *British Year Book of International Law* 35 (1959): 124–161.

_____. *The Province and Function of Law.* Sydney: Associated General Publishers, 1946.

Summers, Robert S. "Logic in the Law." *Mind* 72 (1963): 254–258.

_____., ed. *More Essays in Legal Philosophy.* Oxford: Basil Blackwell, 1971.

Tammelo, Ilmar. Book Review. *Journal of Legal Education* 13 (1960–1961): 550–552.

_____. Book Review. *Journal of Legal Education* 15 (1963): 351–357.

_____. "Legal Formalism and Formalistic Devices of Juristic Thinking." In *Law and Philosophy,* edited by S. Hook. New York: New York University Press, 1964.

_____. *Outlines of Modern Legal Logic.* Wiesbaden: Fritz Steiner Verlag, 1969.

_____. "Sketch for a Symbolic Juristic Logic." *Journal of Legal Education* 8 (1955): 277–306.

Vernengo, Roberto J. "About Some Formation Rules for Legal Languages." In *Law, State and International Legal Order: Essays in Honor of Hans Kelsen,* edited by Salo Engel. Knoxville: University of Tennessee Press, 1964.

Voegelin, Erich. "Kelsen's Pure Theory of Law." *Political Science Quarterly* 42 (1927): 268–276.

von Ihering, Rudolf. *Law as a Means to an End*, translated by Isaac Husik. New York: Macmillan, 1924.

Vonlanthen, Albert. *Zu Hans Kelsens Anschauung über die Rechtsnorm.* Berlin: Duncker und Humblot, 1965.

von Mises, Richard. *Positivism.* Cambridge: Harvard University Press, 1951.

Von Wright, Georg Henrik. "Deontic Logic." *Mind* n.s. 60 (1951): 1–15.

————. "An Essay in Deontic Logic and the General Theory of Action." In *Acta Philosophica Fennica* 21. Amsterdam: North-Holland Publishing, 1968.

————. *Norm and Action.* London: Routledge and Kegan Paul, 1963.

Wedberg, Anders. "Some Problems in the Logical Analysis of Legal Science." *Theoria* 17 (1951): 246–275.

Williams, Glanville. "The Controversy Concerning the Word Law." In *Philosophy, Politics and Society.* 1st series. Edited by Peter Laslett. Oxford: Basil Blackwell, 1967.

Wittgenstein, Ludwig. *Tractatus Logico-Philosophicus*, translated by D. F. Pears and B. F. McGuinness. London: Routledge and Kegan Paul, 1961.

Wollheim, Richard. "The Nature of Law." *Political Studies* 2 (1954): 128–141.

Wroblewski, Jerzy. "Normativity of Legal Science." *Étude de Logique juridique*, edited by Chaim Perelman. Brussels: Emile Bruylant, 1966.

Index

ƻ *Production Notes*

The text of this book has been designed by Roger J. Eggers and typeset on the Unified Composing System by the design & production staff of The University Press of Hawaii.

The text and display typeface is California.

Offset presswork and binding is the work of Vail-Ballou Press. Text paper is Glatfelter P & S Offset, basis 55.